THE BOY WHO WOULD BE SHAKESPEARE

THE BOY WHO WOULD BE
SHAKESPEARE

A Tale of
Forgery and Folly

DOUG STEWART

x

DA CAPO PRESS
A Member of the Perseus Books Group

Designed by Pauline Brown
Set in 11 point Arno Pro by The Perseus Books Group

Cataloging-in-Publication data for this book is available from
the Library of Congress.

First Da Capo Press edition 2010
ISBN: 978-0-306-81831-8

Published by Da Capo Press
A Member of the Perseus Books Group
www.dacapopress.com

Da Capo Press books are available at special discounts for bulk purchases in the U.S. by corporations, institutions, and other organizations. For more information, please contact the Special Markets Department at the Perseus Books Group, 2300 Chestnut Street, Suite 200, Philadelphia, PA 19103, or call (800) 810-4145, ext. 5000, or e-mail special.markets@perseusbooks.com.

10 9 8 7 6 5 4 3 2 1

For Coco

CONTENTS

CHAPTER ONE

SHAKESPEARE LIVES!

I N THE WINTER of 1795, a poorly educated nineteen-year-old clerk named William-Henry Ireland stood petrified in his family's London study as two men in powdered wigs interrogated him. The visiting dignitaries, Samuel Parr and Joseph Warton, were among England's most esteemed men of letters. They had hurried to the Ireland home to inspect a tattered piece of paper the boy claimed to have found while rummaging in an old trunk.

"I confess I had never before felt so much terror," the young man wrote several years later, "and would almost have bartered my life to have evaded the meeting." He had no idea that the document he'd presented to his father after dinner one night, and the others that followed in succeeding days and weeks, would soon make him and his father the talk of London. He certainly never dreamed he was about to cause an uproar in the English literary world.

William-Henry Ireland was unaccustomed to attention. He was a quiet, unassuming boy who passed his time as an unpaid apprentice to a lawyer friend of the family. His father, Samuel, was a pompous, social-climbing writer, engraver, and collector of antiquities. To call on the Irelands at their comfortable home on the edge of London's theater district was to step inside Samuel Ireland's peculiar cabinet of curiosities. Here and there were paintings by Hogarth and Van Dyck, rare sixteenth-century books, a piece of a mummy's shroud, a Tahitian carpet made of bark, and a leather jacket worn by Puritan ruler Oliver Cromwell.

Samuel's latest and most remarkable acquisition, however, was the sheet of paper his son had ceremoniously handed him a month earlier. Worn at the edges and heavily creased, the paper was inscribed with florid handwriting in faded ink. Dated two centuries earlier, the document was an avowal of religious faith. On it, the writer declared himself "most solemnly" a Protestant. At the bottom was a signature with embellished capitals: "Wm Shakspeare."

It was an astonishing discovery. William Shakespeare, who had died in relative obscurity in 1616, had lately risen in popular esteem to become England's matchless literary genius. Will of Stratford was now a secular god: the immortal Bard! Yet aside from a few signatures, nothing written in Shakespeare's hand—not a letter, not so much as a couplet—had ever been found. If the yellowed note William-Henry Ireland had discovered was genuine, it was the literary equivalent of the Crown Jewels.

Samuel Ireland was ecstatic to have laid his hands on so precious an artifact. For years, the collector had lusted after Shakespeare memorabilia. He had often said, his son recalled, "that he would willingly give half his library to become possessed even of his signature alone." Providence had evidently delivered.

Huddled in the lamp-lit study, the Irelands' two learned visitors questioned the boy closely. In particular, they were curious about the trunk where he had found the note.

William-Henry's replies were polite but vague. He said the trunk was at the estate of a wealthy and reclusive acquaintance, where he had been sifting through old records. The gentleman, professing no interest in arcane manuscripts, had told him to help himself to any old papers he found. William-Henry couldn't be more specific than that, he explained to his inquisitors; the mysterious gentleman had demanded that his name be kept secret.

The boy tried to keep his voice calm and his gaze steady as he spoke. To the two scholars frowning at him, his story must have sounded like poppycock. As a schoolboy, William-Henry had endured more than a few canings for stumbling over a recitation. He was worried in particular about Dr. Parr, a squat, irascible man with bristling eyebrows who was known as a boxing enthusiast. At Harrow, where he had taught for many years, Parr had viewed himself as benevolent because he never flogged a pupil twice in a single lesson. Old Dr. Warton was a more benign presence, but he was an intimidating figure all the same. A renowned literary critic and a poet, Warton was said to have been one of the few men able to hold his own in arguments with the late Samuel Johnson, one of eighteenth-century England's most disputatious intellectuals.

But Warton and Parr were literary men at heart, not prosecuting attorneys. They seemed to accept William-Henry's story. In fact, like many in the English literary world, the pair had been waiting impatiently for just such a find—especially one proving that William Shakespeare was a steadfast Protestant like good Queen Bess, not a traitorous papist as rumors had alleged.

Now, as the two scholars bent over the table in the Irelands' study, examining the sheet of faded script like entomologists, William-Henry struggled to maintain an air of nonchalance. His father, by contrast, was confident, almost smug. Indeed, Samuel Ireland was perhaps more credulous than a collector ought to be. Seated in his accustomed place in his book-filled lair as he awaited his guests' verdict, he took comfort in knowing that the carved oak chair he occupied was the very one in which young Will Shakespeare had held Anne Hathaway on his lap—or so he'd been told by the Stratford man who'd sold him the piece two years earlier.

Dr. Warton at last set down the document and addressed his host with the gravity of a pilgrim before a sacred relic. "Sir, we have very fine passages in our church service, and our litany abounds with beauties, but here, sir, here is a man who has distanced us all!" *Here is a man.* To Samuel Ireland and his two guests, the Bard was suddenly a living presence in the room, having somehow materialized in Georgian London as eloquent as ever.

Standing quietly in a corner, William-Henry, too, was overwhelmed with a sense of miraculous possibility, but he wasn't thinking about William Shakespeare. Excusing himself, the boy withdrew to a small back dining room. A moment before, he had been almost too frightened to move. Now he was dizzy with elation.

"I reclined myself against the window frame, still ruminating on the words I had heard," he wrote in his 1805 memoirs, "fired with the idea of possessing genius to which I had never aspired."

Until that moment, William-Henry Ireland had never seriously considered that his ability as a writer might bring him success in life. He had certainly never imagined sharing a pedestal with Shakespeare. Now, unexpectedly, a world of possibilities had opened up—possibilities beyond the reach of any honest writer. What had started as a ploy, born of frustration, to win the respect of his chilly, Shakespeare-worshipping father, promised much more. The boy realized it was in his power not only to earn renown for himself and his father but also to reshape the reputation of England's greatest writer. And someday, perhaps, he might dazzle the world as an author in his own right.

In a sustained burst of manic energy in the months to follow, William-Henry Ireland would produce a torrent of Shakespearean fabrications: letters, deeds, poetry, drawings, and, most daringly of all, an original full-length play longer than almost any of Shakespeare's known works. A parade of notables—dukes, earls, a bishop, the poet laureate—would pay visits to the Irelands' home during 1795 as though to a holy shrine. The Ireland forgeries were hastily done and forensically implausible, but most of the people who inspected them were blind to their flaws. The newly discovered play, declared Francis Webb, secretary of the College of Heralds, was quite obviously the work of William Shakespeare. "It either comes from his pen," he wrote, "or from Heaven."

The improbable story of the Bard's teenage double—the most audacious literary forger in history—would never have unfolded had Shakespeare not recently become a god, for what is a god without holy relics? In Shakespeare's case, unfortunately, there were almost no tangible traces left from his time on earth. His life and the things that inspired him were largely a mystery. This was intolerable to his late-eighteenth-century worshippers. The news that Shakespeare's manuscripts had finally been discovered was easier to accept than the disheartening reality that none of them ever had and likely never would. People ached to see firsthand the poetry that had flowed so magically from the Bard's quill. Because the Ireland forgeries seemed to bring England's greatest literary hero within reach at last, his admirers let themselves be fooled.

As a result, much of England in 1795 would fail to notice that a naïve and reckless nineteen-year-old was impersonating the nation's greatest writer. This unremarkable teenager's first attempt at playwriting would be hailed as Shakespeare's lost masterpiece, and on April 2, 1796, the most celebrated actors of the day would recite his lines before a packed house at London's prestigious Theatre Royal at Drury Lane. William-Henry Ireland's name would be forever linked to that of William Shakespeare.

WHEN HIS EARLY forgeries transfixed much of London's intelligentsia, William-Henry Ireland was as astonished as anyone. He hadn't quite realized how desperately Englishmen yearned to see and hold a page inscribed in Shakespeare's hand. He had begun producing forgeries with the goal of pleasing just one person, his father. In this the boy succeeded spectacularly.

"It is impossible for me to express the pleasure you have given me," the collector had told his son in December 1794. That evening, William-Henry had presented his father with the first document signed with Shakespeare's scrawl at the bottom. He was thrilled to hear his father's words, even if they conveyed a collector's gratitude more than a father's affection.

In his nineteen years, William-Henry had almost never heard words of praise from his father. The boy was a watchful, solitary lad with unruly dark hair and a thin frame. He made little impression on the people he met. He seemed consigned to the shadow of his voluble, extroverted father, whom he referred to as Mr. Ireland. Even in the best of times, Samuel Ireland was an overbearing presence in his son's life.

Nearly forty years after his forgeries, William-Henry could vividly recall a family excursion on the Thames when he was a boy. As the boat had sailed slowly upstream past Alexander Pope's villa at Twickenham, Samuel had held forth on the late poet's glittering reputation—though he would have been hard-pressed to recite any of his verses. The collector styled himself an intellectual, despite a lack of education. Perhaps to compensate, he favored formal turns of phrase in his writing as well as his conversation. Patting his son's head, he had remarked, "I fear you will never shine such a star in the hemisphere of literary fame." It was unlikely anyone's child would grow up to rival Alexander Pope, of course, but for a parent to make such an off-hand comment to a child showed a tactlessness verging on cruelty.

Along with his father, William-Henry lived with his older sisters, Anna Maria and Jane, and the family housekeeper, a Mrs. Freeman. There was no Mrs. Ireland, and no one spoke of her; Samuel had presumably become a widower when the children were young. An older son, Samuel Jr., had died in early childhood. Samuel Sr. had taken to calling his surviving son Sam, as though it were Samuel Jr. who had survived and William-Henry who had vanished. It was not unheard of at the time for parents to do this, but it seemed to underscore the obvious fact that William-Henry was a disappointment to his father.

Indeed, in the latter's eyes, the boy was lazy and dull-witted, if not a hopeless dunce. Samuel on occasion hinted that William-Henry was not his natural offspring, suggesting that he would one day reveal a shocking secret. He never did, but William-Henry understandably came to have doubts about his parentage.

Samuel's one true love was Shakespeare. "Four days, at least, out of seven," William-Henry wrote forty years later, "the beauties of our divine dramatist became his theme of conversation after dinner; while in the evening, still further to impress the subject upon the minds of myself and sisters, certain plays were selected, and a part allotted to each, in order that we might read aloud."

Reading aloud was a well-practiced skill in Georgian England, one that was important enough to be taught in school. The Irelands read Shakespeare aloud so often that the Bard was almost a member of the household. Appreciative of the sound of his own voice, Samuel would reserve the starring role for himself. Shakespeare's already archaic language was thus a familiar part of William-Henry's childhood. He may not have learned any of the major roles by heart, but the general sound and syntax of Elizabethan verse was etched in his mind.

Often Samuel would hold forth by himself, reading from a play of his choice, usually a tragedy or a history, "dwelling with enthusiasm on such passages as most peculiarly struck his fancy," William-Henry wrote. After his recitation, Samuel would expound at length on the Bard's unsurpassed genius. "At such periods, there was no divine attribute which Shakspeare did not possess, in Mr. Ireland's estimation: in short, the Bard of Avon was a god among men."

When Samuel spoke of Shakespeare, the boy would listen without saying a word. Samuel may well have thought he was too dense to appreciate great literature, but William-Henry was paying rapt attention to his father's extravagant praises of the poet. Soon enough, he adopted them as his own.

ON THE SURFACE, the Ireland household was the picture of bourgeois respectability and contentment. The family lived in a stately brick townhouse on Norfolk Street, a fashionable residential lane that ran a few hundred feet from the banks of the Thames to the Strand, the busy, unpaved commercial spine of what was then London's West End. Samuel Ireland, a short, balding man with an air of self-importance, had achieved a modest renown as the author and illustrator of a series of popular travel books. He cultivated the image of a well-read, well-traveled gentleman, a prosperous widower in his early sixties who collected art and hobnobbed with the city's artistic and theatrical elite.

The man was not quite what he seemed. He had always been vague about his exact age and background. One uncle had apparently been a bricklayer, though Samuel never said as much. Having a common laborer in one's family tree was not something one bruited about in polite society. He was happier to let drop the fact that an ancestor, one William Ireland, haberdasher, was the occupant of an old London gatehouse that William Shakespeare had bought for himself—as an investment, not a dwelling—in 1613. Samuel knew all about the property because a friend and neighbor, Albany Wallis, had discovered the mortgage deed recording the purchase. The alley where the old house once stood, just beyond Blackfriars Bridge, was still known as Ireland Yard. Samuel had no actual proof he was descended from this William Ireland. He told his children there was a thirty-year gap in the genealogy. Even if he couldn't prove this William Ireland was a relation, even if there was no evidence that the haberdasher and England's great poet had known each other, still it pleased him to think about Shakespeare crossing paths with an Ireland, however briefly, in the golden age of the English Renaissance.

Samuel was a self-made man. In his own mind, he didn't need a pedigree to style himself a man of taste and refinement. He believed he came naturally by his ability to judge the value of things. In his youth, he had imagined a career as an architect, perhaps designing harmonious, symmetrical country houses in the neoclassical style. His schooling, unfortunately, had been limited. Samuel lacked well-born relations, influential friends, or rich patrons, so he knew that entrée into genteel society wouldn't be easy.

In 1760, when he was in his late twenties, England's newly formed Society of Arts held its first art exhibition—perhaps the first ever public art exhibition in England—and awarded Samuel a medal for one of his meticulous architectural watercolors. Imagining now that great things were to come, he drew a gilt-embellished coat of arms based on the armorial bearings associated with his family name: a dove perched on a knight's steel helmet. He carefully inscribed a motto underneath, quoting Horace: NEMO SINE VITIIS ("No one is without faults"). Samuel might have been alluding to his own fallibility. More likely, he was thinking of other people.

Whether through faults of his own or as a victim of circumstance, Samuel within a few years had given up his dream of being an architect. By the late 1760s, now in his mid-forties, he was struggling to eke out a living as a Spitalfields weaver. Spitalfields, a congested quarter of northeast London, was a center of the European silk-weaving industry. While a handful of

Spitalfields's master weavers were respectable enough to fraternize with telescope makers and pump builders in England's prestigious Mathematical Society, the vast majority of weavers, including newcomers like Samuel Ireland, were mired in the most proletarian of eighteenth-century London occupations. Tens of thousands of poorly compensated silk weavers, many of them Irish immigrants, crowded into tenement rooms in Spitalfields with their looms and their families, competing with one another and with cheap imports from across the Channel. Throughout the 1760s, weavers periodically left their looms to march on Westminster by the thousands, beating drums and demanding a ban on imported silk or shorter official periods of mourning (since the longer people wore black, the more the silk industry suffered).

Ireland's business failed, which was just as well. He was, after all, an ambitious man of taste living in a time of growing prosperity. He found his calling with the engraving boom then gripping England. Sparked by an influx of skilled Dutch engravers, London's print sellers by the mid-1700s were flourishing. They offered England's growing middle class a way to dress up their drawing-room walls with reproductions of the latest paintings: romantic scenes from literature, historical tableaux, and portraits of royalty in particular. Also popular, though not necessarily for display in polite company, were the barbed, sometimes lewd social satires of William Hogarth and of later caricaturists like James Gillray and Thomas Rowlandson. The throngs of pedestrians who rushed along the Strand and Fleet Street were often impeded by knots of people clustered in front of print sellers' shop windows, where dozens of the latest caricatures would be posted inside the panes, or by street vendors who displayed their wares in upturned umbrellas.

Samuel had never been formally trained in painting or illustration, but he had a keen eye, was sensitive to what people would pay for, and knew the importance of perseverance. Having learned on his own how to draw and use watercolors, he now taught himself the exacting craft of copperplate engraving. He concentrated on finely detailed landscape prints that catered to the vogue for the "picturesque": romantic vistas with old buildings in the middle distance, sometimes in ruins, the scene framed by luxuriant, asymmetrical foliage and perhaps a few dramatic clouds. Any human beings who wandered into the scene he kept at a safe distance, the better to disguise his clumsiness at figure drawing. He embarked on a series of plates based on paintings by two of his favorite artists: Hogarth, a painter known for his Rabelaisian caricatures, and Samuel's own friend John Mortimer, a painter of Anglo-Saxon historical scenes. He liked to think that his prints did justice to the originals, but later plates in the series that his daughters engraved were noticeably more lifelike than their father's.

By the early 1780s, Samuel was doing a brisk trade as a dealer in fine prints. As he grew more prosperous, he began acquiring art—paintings as well as prints—and rare books, along with the odd historical curio. Samuel considered himself a man of the arts: a writer, an artist, and a connoisseur. He downplayed the idea that he was someone who bought and sold things to make a living, like a shopkeeper, although it was true. If he could buy a well-preserved Chaucer in Old English black-letter type, though he owned a better copy, he was not against snapping it up and selling it at a profit.

As for the prints he handled, not everything was picturesque. Indeed, engravers and print sellers in London had a distinctly shadowy reputation. Even in the sanctity of St. Paul's Cathedral, worshippers were accosted by hawkers with obscene prints to sell. Samuel didn't traffic in ordinary pornography, but he was unruffled by some of Hogarth's earthier works. One of his favorite Hogarth prints, which he engraved and later published in one of his books, depicted the Virgin Mary feeding baby Jesus into a grinding mill; at the other end, a priest collected the holy wafers that emerged and offered them to kneeling communicants.

"The wit of it may, perhaps, at first glance, appear offensive to scrupulous observers," he wrote, but the picture illustrates one of "the many absurdities practiced in the church of Rome." Hostility to Catholicism was widespread in England—anti-Catholic rioting had convulsed London in 1780 and left hundreds dead—but Samuel gleefully flaunted what more circumspect people might share in private. His treading of the line of propriety, and occasionally crossing it, marked him as someone who, when given the opportunity, always chose to draw attention to himself. For Samuel Ireland, no fate was worse than anonymity.

BY 1780, SAMUEL WAS living in an elegant house at 9 Arundel Street, just off the Strand. In his late forties, he now had three young children and a live-in housekeeper. The housekeeper, Mrs. Freeman, was a witty, intelligent woman who "kept house" in the sense that she managed the household and served as Samuel's secretary. As the family's fortunes improved, she directed the household servants. Samuel sometimes introduced her as the children's aunt. Referring to oneself as Mrs. was a common way for older single women, actresses in particular, to avoid raising eyebrows about unchaperoned living or working arrangements.

Mrs. Freeman was as cultured as her employer, if not more so. Like Samuel, she had literary ambitions. Both had tried their hands at writing plays—a common obsession in the late 1700s—but London's theaters didn't encourage either of them. Mrs. Freeman contented herself with directing the children and their friends in lighthearted fare she wrote as after-dinner entertainments. She was more successful at poetry. In 1771, she published a short book, *The Doctor Dissected*, by "a Lady," that mocked in verse a popular cure for gout. The doctor in question, William Cadogan, had recommended regular foot washing and a one-meal-a-day diet:

> *Good spice he condemns, and what's very queer*
> *He prohibits all liquors, excepting small beer:*
> *Objects to their quality, hints that, sans useing 'em,*
> *We may live, if we please, to the age of Methusalem.*

Mrs. Freeman was not, in fact, the children's aunt. Her real name was Anna Maria Coppinger, née de Burgh. She may or may not ever have been married; it was later rumored that she was separated but never divorced from Mr. Coppinger, whoever he was. By the late 1770s, in any case, she was Samuel Ireland's mistress and the likely mother of all three children. There was no record that the Ireland children were ever baptized, so they were probably illegitimate. Nor was there a record of Samuel Ireland ever being married—to Mrs. Freeman or anyone else.

Perhaps one or both of the daughters knew or suspected that Mrs. Freeman was their mother, but William-Henry as a boy did not. Surely, when he was old enough to wonder, he had asked each of the two adults in the house who his mother had been and what had happened to her. Samuel and Mrs. Freeman would have had no trouble deflecting his questions. Mothers commonly died in childbirth in the eighteenth century; many more died of disease in an age when germs were unknown and medicine meant bleeding with leeches. Households were often composed of surviving members of an extended family along with, in wealthier homes, their loyal retainers.

Mrs. Freeman was an excellent impostor. Her maternal feelings, if she had any, were well concealed. Several friends of the family recalled her as disagreeable. On occasion she could be malicious. Several times, for no good reason, she took William-Henry aside and told him that Samuel didn't think he was the boy's father. It was easy for William-Henry to believe that this was a woman who was paid to look after him and his sisters. Perhaps Mrs. Freeman kept up the pretense to avoid the stigma of being what society deemed a fallen woman. Or it might have been Samuel who insisted she do so for the sake of his own social standing. Perhaps she maintained her deception to shield the children from the shameful truth: They were all bastards. The ruse may also have been her way of dodging the emotional entanglement of motherhood. Whatever her reasons, her masquerade was made easier by her natural aloofness. Mrs. Freeman was not an affectionate person—not toward her children and not toward her mate.

Samuel, for his part, was as emotionally stunted as she was, but he didn't have the excuse of needing to pretend the children weren't his. To William-Henry, his father doled out praise as though it were in short supply. He seemed incapable of honest affection. The boy learned to avoid provoking his father's temper—by contradicting him, for example. He often saw his father flare up at Mrs. Freeman for trivial matters. In the best of times,

Samuel treated the woman in a brusque, peremptory manner—quite as if she were a domestic servant, in fact.

There was little to make William-Henry wonder about the pair's relationship. He had certainly never seen Mrs. Freeman display any tenderness toward the man of the house. William-Henry had never heard her call his father anything other than Mr. Ireland. For his part, Samuel always addressed the housekeeper as Mrs. Freeman. To be sure, married couples in England at the time often called each other by their last names, within earshot of others at least. And British memoirs of the nineteenth century are filled with childhood memories of physically and emotionally remote parents who would summon their children by ringing for the nursery maid. Still, no child hurt by a parent's distance took comfort in knowing that others felt the same.

The Ireland household had another, more scandalous secret. Mrs. Freeman in her younger days had been the mistress of the notorious John Montagu, Fourth Earl of Sandwich. Lord Sandwich, a powerful figure in the House of Lords and in the Admiralty, was the Casanova of eighteenth-century England, a compulsive ladies' man whose seductions were made easier by his reputation for sexual adventuring. His philandering didn't hurt his career, even after he and his well-born friends were reputed to have consorted with prostitutes dressed as nuns at their private men's club. Only when Sandwich showed himself to be a hypocrite—rising in the House of Lords in 1753 to denounce a fellow member for printing a lewd poem for his friends (including Sandwich)—did his reputation begin to sour. His behavior earned him the popular nickname "Jemmy Twitcher," after the hero's betrayer in *The Beggar's Opera*.

When and for how long Mrs. Freeman had been the earl's paramour is unknown. Their dalliance occurred long before William-Henry's birth and most likely well before either Anna Maria or Jane was born. Mrs. Freeman was said to have had a fortune of £12,000 (about £700,000 or more than $1 million today). If so, some of this might have been a parting gift from the earl. Sandwich's perennial money problems could be taken as evidence either for or against his being her benefactor.

Mrs. Freeman's aristocratic liaison was a well-kept secret—presumably the children knew nothing about it—but even a rumor of an illicit affair could have made a woman unsuitable for marriage in polite society. Her racy past may have estranged her from her own family as well: A wealthy brother in London wanted nothing to do with her. Given the situation, a life as Mrs. Freeman, the unmarried lady of the house in a decorous Georgian household, may have been her best option. And if any of the children were hers but not his—as her older daughter and namesake, Anna Maria, may have been—the living arrangement would have been especially attractive.

If cohabitation with Samuel Ireland was a pseudomarriage of convenience for Anna Maria de Burgh Coppinger, aka Mrs. Freeman, the arrangement may have appealed, in an odd way, to Samuel's acquisitive lust. From the start, he may have regarded this former mistress of a famous earl not as a romantic partner but as the trophy of his collection of historical curiosities. Even if there was little ardor between the two, Ireland must have been pleased at having bedded the woman who had once been the rakish Fourth Earl of Sandwich's lover. Ireland, moreover, was ever mindful of financial opportunities; Mrs. Freeman's income was likely a factor in the pair's settling down together.

The Irelands, with their secrets and subterfuges, their evasions and reinventions, were not so terribly out of the ordinary. The art of deception was a widely practiced social skill in Georgian London. Gentlemen took mistresses, and ladies took lovers. The royal family set the tone. In 1795, when the Prince of Wales, King George III's dissolute son and eventual heir as King George IV, wed Caroline of Brunswick, he neglected to tell his bride that he was already married, the earlier wedding having taken place in 1785 without royal approval. In public, people harped on good manners and good breeding and on piety, industry, and virtue. But Londoners in the 1790s were no more pious, hardworking, or virtuous than people in other cities and in other eras. Rioting was a popular sport. Hangings outside Newgate Prison were so well-attended that London's lord mayor might as well have declared a public holiday.

The Irelands were more genteel than many of their contemporaries. Still, theirs was not a storybook English family. The parents' living arrangement was based on pretense. They not only presented a false front to the outside world but also deceived their children. As a young boy, William-Henry may not have suspected anything was amiss, but over time he surely sensed that the two adults in his life were highly selective in how they told the truth.

CHAPTER TWO

A BOY WITHOUT PROMISE

W ILLIAM-HENRY, LIKE his parents, bridled at accepting the identity that life had handed him. A bookish, moody child, he spent his free time pretending he was someone other than an ordinary English schoolboy. In his bedroom, when not reading about knights and damsels, he constructed elaborate model theaters using pasteboard. It was inevitable that he was drawn to the theater, a milieu founded on illusion. The stage appealed to his need to escape the dull here and now.

The whole Ireland family was theater-mad. The Ireland home was a ten-minute walk from the Drury Lane Theatre; its rival theatre royal, Covent Garden, was not much farther beyond. The Irelands' circle of friends drew mostly from the world of theater and music. Notable among these were their neighbors Thomas Linley and his family. Linley, a musician and composer, directed Drury Lane's musical productions and was part owner of the theater. Jane Linley, a daughter, and Jane Ireland were best friends. Another Linley daughter, Eliza, a ravishing singer whom society portraitist Thomas Gainsborough had immortalized in full-length paintings three times, was married to Richard Brinsley Sheridan, the most famous playwright in London. Sheridan was Drury Lane's manager and, like Thomas Linley, a part owner of the theater.

The Irelands' friendship with the Linleys provided them free access to Drury Lane, both the hall and backstage. Samuel and his son took full advantage of the privilege. William-Henry savored the thrill of standing in the wings and watching the latest productions. Comedies, tragedies, musical farces—he took them all in. A few dozen feet from his hiding place, illuminated by hundreds of candles, the regal John Philip Kemble, his lovely sister, Mrs. Siddons, and other giants of the English stage transformed themselves nightly into gallant heroes and dying monarchs.

In his fascination with the stage, William-Henry was typical of his time. The theater was the central amusement of eighteenth-century English life. At dinner parties and in coffeehouses, Londoners critiqued the previous night's productions from prologue to epilogue and debated how well the players had acquitted themselves in their roles. The theater was one place where shopkeepers, schoolboys, and peers of the realm rubbed shoulders. If King George III's subjects knew him to have a sense of humor, it was because they'd seen him guffawing in the velvet-upholstered royal box at Drury Lane during Colley Cibber's *She Would and She Would Not*.

Only a generation or two before, the profession of acting was deemed just slightly above that of prostitution. "I will, by no means, pay for whores, and their never failing consequences, surgeons; nor will I, upon any account, keep singers, dancers, actresses and *id genus omne*," wrote the Fourth Earl of Chesterfield in 1750 to his wayward teenage son Philip, then traveling in France. Lord Chesterfield had kept his own French mistress, as it happened— she was Philip's mother—but at least the woman hadn't been an actress.

The public standing of actors and actresses rose in mid-century with the career of David Garrick, a charismatic Shakespearean actor and impresario who became a popular celebrity and consorted with royalty. At Garrick's death in 1779, Sheridan orchestrated his spectacular funeral and burial at Westminster Abbey. Later, the Royal Academy exhibited George Carter's enormous *Apotheosis of Garrick*, depicting a pair of angels bearing the actor off to Parnassus, where the Bard and the muses await him in the mist.

By the 1790s, London's most popular players were idolized like royalty. It seemed only apt that the king's third son, William, Duke of Clarence, chose as his mistress the much-admired star at Drury Lane, Dorothea Jordan. Mrs. Jordan lived openly with the duke for twenty years and left him ten children. In some quarters, no doubt, their unmarried arrangement did nothing to improve the moral reputation of actors and acting.

William-Henry, like many younger people, did not have mixed feelings about the theater world. He found it thrilling. Although his recollections of early childhood were sketchy, he would vividly recall the first time he had a small speaking role in a play. It was a January evening in 1784, and he was eight years old. The event was a private staging of Allan Ramsay's popular musical drama *The Gentle Shepherd*, at Sheridan's opulent Bruton Street mansion in Mayfair. After-dinner performances at the estates of English's social elite would often consist of a costume drama, in much the way a dinner at the home of a less exalted host might be followed by a drawing-room recital for violin and pianoforte.

The cast of eleven, though young, was illustrious. The lead role of Sir William Worthy was played by a fledgling artist of nineteen, Richard Westall, who painted a watercolor of the cast at a dress rehearsal. Westall would be elected to the Royal Academy of Arts just ten years later and would end his career in the 1830s as Queen Victoria's art tutor.

The rehearsal took place at the Irelands' old house on Arundel Street with the Linley sisters stage-managing. In the painting William-Henry's teenage sister Jane is a bent-over witch in black. She accosts her older sister, Anna Maria, and Jane Linley, the alarmed pair dressed in plumed hats and other finery. Looking on are twelve-year-old William Linley holding a shepherd's crook; Sheridan's eight-year-old son, Thomas, eavesdropping in the background; and three brothers named Carr—two of whom, a writer and a musician, would eventually be knighted. At the far right of the watercolor sits little William-Henry Ireland, his brown hair curling past his shoulders, one arm holding a small bagpipe. It's doubtful the lad could play the bagpipes well, but the musical Linleys and Carrs on hand would have made sure that he could produce at least an acceptable drone.

Twenty years later, in his published *Confessions*, William-Henry recalled the glorious evening of their Bruton Street performance: "My character, though of a trivial nature, did not diminish the zest I felt on that occasion." His excitement came in part from discovering that the assembled guests for Sheridan's private theatrical included "a large part of nobility."

Much later—nearly fifty years after the fact—William-Henry was still reliving the applause and complimentary words of Sheridan's guests. He wrote in the margins of a book in the 1830s, as if to convince himself: "I was particularly noticed by the then celebrated Duchess of Devonshire and by the no less renowned C. J. Fox." The duchess, then twenty-six, was already famous for her beauty, her marriage—satirized by her host seven years earlier in *The School for Scandal*—and her outspoken political views. As for Charles James Fox, he was then the flamboyant leader of the Whig opposition in Parliament; until being removed by the king a few weeks earlier, he had been England's foreign minister.

It's possible that what imprinted the evening so sharply in William-Henry's memory wasn't the experience of performing so much as the experience of being praised by important people. During a childhood and youth in which he would continually disappoint the adults around him, he would grow into someone whom no amount of applause would ever satisfy.

BY HIS OWN admission, William-Henry was a dismal student. Though his family sent him off to a string of well-regarded schools that catered to the prominent and the well-to-do, he rarely studied and paid little attention in class. One of his few enthusiasms was getting into mischief with other students when his schoolmasters weren't looking. In an age when corporal punishment was a common teaching tool, William-Henry reported being "castigated" regularly.

At Great Ealing School, a huge boarding school in the countryside west of London, he found little of interest besides the school's lavishly staged musical dramas. He had a reputation, he later recalled, as a "blockhead." At thirteen he was sent home for the holidays with a note to his father from the headmaster, the Reverend Richard Shury, whom William-Henry recalled as "a very learned and a very strict master." The letter, according to William-Henry's recollections, stated that the boy was "so stupid as to be a disgrace to the school" and that allowing him to return after the vacation "was no better than robbing Mr. Ireland of his money."

But William-Henry was not at all stupid. He simply found schoolwork stifling. Why should he conjugate Latin or do sums? He had no intention of being a Latin teacher or a bookkeeper. His parents and his teachers failed to understand this. To them, the boy seemed unable or unwilling to do what other children did without trouble or complaint.

His last English school was in a small academy in Soho Square. Samuel chose the school so that his son would live at home, under his own supervision. During the day, however, the thirteen-year-old and his school chums were much on their own in the city. "I acquired the knowledge of every boyish folly much sooner than I should have done at a country academy," William-Henry wrote a few years later in an unpublished memoir. The walk each day between the Strand and Soho Square with his neighborhood mates was a long, crooked trek that passed through several of London's more unsavory neighborhoods—"not a circumstance beneficial to the health or instruction of youth," he remembered, especially after sundown.

On the walk home, he and his friends negotiated the crime-ridden Seven Dials neighborhood, then passed through the Covent Garden area. In the morning, the square alongside the theatre royal was a bustling marketplace; after dusk, the streets in the vicinity were London's most notorious red-light district—a scene lovingly recorded by Hogarth in the 1730s. At seedy bookstalls, if no one was looking, the boys could thumb through the latest edition of *Harris's Book of Covent-Garden Ladies*, which listed women for hire by name, address, age, price, and sexual specialty. Closer to home were cheap, noisy music halls and patent theaters on and off the Strand, which drew lads like William-Henry and his friends with acrobats, tumblers, singers, and short melodramas. The latter included mutilated works of Shakespeare in which only the love scenes and swordplay were intact.

William-Henry lasted at Soho Academy only one year, but his experience at the school was not a complete waste. As at Ealing, the highlight of each school year, for students and parents alike, was an elaborate stage production. Soho Academy prided itself on its quasi-professional Shakespearean dramas, which were presented along with a farce just before the Christmas vacation. Attending the school's performances was a major social event in Soho. The Shakespearean production in William-Henry's year was *King Lear*, in which he won a small part.

He and his fellow students—several of whom would go on to become playwrights and actors—devoted more attention to their months of rehearsing than to their lessons. *Lear* would be Soho Academy's last play. The school's puritanical young headmaster, the Reverend William Barrow, had inherited the tradition reluctantly. "Dramatick performances at school are not required to give the rising generation that assurance of which they already possess too much," Barrow later explained after banishing the practice. To young William-Henry, who thought little of his teachers and less of his studies, the knowledge that he and his friends' histrionics were barely tolerated by the Reverend Barrow must have made them all the more enjoyable.

His father concluded that the boy was a hopeless student. He knew William-Henry wasn't as thick-headed as his schoolmasters thought. The boy read voraciously without prompting, after all. He decided William-Henry would benefit from a change of scene. It was the summer of 1789. The Bastille in Paris had just been liberated by democratic partisans. In England, Whigs like Samuel Ireland were thrilled that France was poised to embrace parliamentary rule. France was reborn! He decided to place his son in a French school. Maybe the boy would never master algebra or geography or composition. Marooned in a French school for a few years, however, he would at least learn to speak French.

SAMUEL WAS ALREADY planning his own trip across the English Channel, but for quite a different reason. Given the curiosity in England about goings-on in France and the Continent, he had decided to write a book. It would be lavishly illustrated with aquatint etchings done from drawings he would make as he traveled. Instead of selling individual landscape prints for a few shillings, he could sell a book for several guineas. In so doing, he would have a chance to share his own carefully considered observations and opinions, which were abundant. He was also aware that a book illustrated with his hand-tinted landscapes and portraits would, if successful, boost the value of any print graced with his tidy signature.

Samuel knew there was a market for what he had in mind, because illustrated books about travelers' sojourns in the British Isles—travel guides for tourists, essentially—had recently become popular. The man who started the trend was an energetic vicar from Salisbury named William Gilpin. Seven years earlier, Gilpin had published *Observations on the River Wye and Several Parts of South Wales*, with engravings by the author. Gilpin's idea of sightseeing was highly selective. If there were no old ruins to be seen, he was apt to move quickly on to the next spot. Dramatic clouds, however, could earn a long, earnest paragraph.

Gilpin's much-admired books, with their carefully composed landscape views, helped popularize the notion of the picturesque. They also inspired a boom in excursions to the scenic corners of Britain and the Continent. Tourists of the picturesque were typically well-heeled travelers carrying volumes of paper for composing poems or sketching landscapes themselves.

In the fall of 1789, soon after leaving his son with a private tutor in Amiens, a small city north of Paris, Samuel set out on a tour through northern France and the low countries. The result, *A Picturesque Tour Through Holland, Brabant, and Part of France*, appeared in London the following year. His landscapes were more inert and mechanical than Gilpin's romantic vistas, but they served their purpose.

The tone of Samuel's writing was, like the man, cocksure, condescending, and xenophobic, although he could be amusing. Of Amsterdam's canals, he wrote: "The stench arising from them, in summer is insufferably offensive: and hence that immoderate use of tobacco with which [the Dutch] eternally fumigate themselves, in the hope of purifying the air." He missed by one night a Dutch-language performance of *Hamlet*, which locals considered much finer than the English original. Samuel was indignant. "Judge what improvement the elegant and sublime passages of our immortal bard can derive from the guttural rumbling of the Dutch language!" he wrote. Indeed, the production may not have been a particularly tasteful version of Shakespeare's play: Samuel was told that when the Dutch Hamlet saw his father's ghost, a hidden spring lifted his wig.

The book was an immediate success in England: The first printing sold out in days. It was timely, certainly, with the Continent so much in the news, and the illustrations were mostly quite pleasant. But sales were also spurred by Samuel's irreverent tone and subject matter. In particular, the book included a visit to a Dutch brothel. It was common enough for young Englishmen on the grand tour of France and Italy, when not inspecting Renaissance art or Classical ruins, to wander into a brothel. But to publish an account of one's visit—this was not something a gentleman did.

Samuel's actual description of the brothel in *A Picturesque Tour* is, in itself, inoffensive. "The number of those houses is incredible. A chandelier is lighted up in the middle of the room, at the farther end of which are placed a sleepy fidler and harper, who play, if necessary, till morning: you pay a florin at entrance, and see all that is necessary through immense clouds of tobacco smoak." This was as far as he ventured. "Our stay was but short, the ugliness and impudence of the women soon causing us to make a precipitate retreat." He habitually referred to himself in the plural; he was apparently alone.

Samuel was aware that Gilpin and other such writers did not include brothel visits in their definition of the picturesque. Still, he knew there were readers who would enjoy such scandalous information. Within a year, he had earned enough money from the book to move from Arundel Street to a larger house on even more fashionable Norfolk Street, a block away.

Characteristically, he dedicated his first book not to a wealthy aristocrat, as was the custom, but to a corpulent, hard-drinking antiquarian and militiaman named Francis Grose. Captain Grose was notorious for having recently published a book of English slang, *A Classical Dictionary of the Vulgar*

Tongue. The book was not one to be caught reading in polite company. Grose informed his readers that a *fire ship* was "a wench who has the venereal disease," a *duck f-ck-r* was "the man who has the care of the poultry on board a ship of war," and *riding St. George* described the action of a woman "uppermost in the amorous congress." More than a few people were outraged that such a book had been allowed to be printed; others read it cover to cover, no doubt chuckling over choice phrases. Samuel Ireland, obviously, was among the latter.

Behind his façade of comfortable gentility, Samuel was a man who enjoyed violating taboos. His transgressions were minor, but they marked him as someone with his own ideas about correct behavior. In a few years, his status as something less than a proper gentleman would come into play when his character and truthfulness became a matter of public dispute.

WILLIAM-HENRY SPENT a year learning French in Amiens. For a change, he applied himself. By the spring of 1790, the fourteen-year-old was comfortable enough speaking French to have begun forgetting his English. His father next placed him in a distinguished academy in the nearby town of Eu, on the English Channel. The College d'Eu had been attended by scions of the Second Estate for generations. A student named Louis-Philippe, two years older than William-Henry, was a member of the embattled Bourbon dynasty; years later, with Robespierre and Napoleon gone and the French monarchy reinstated, he would be crowned King Louis-Philippe, the last monarch of France.

The school was attached to a convent, and the boys lived within the high walls of a seminary next door. Despite the revolutionary fervor then gripping much of France, the school was an oasis of calm. Here William-Henry spent several uneventful years, which he would remember as the best years of his life. He wasn't judged as he was in England. As a foreigner, his particular differences—his lassitude, his introversion—didn't stand out and attract comment or rebuke as readily as they had in England. The physical and social isolation that might have made another young Englishman feel stranded instead made William-Henry feel at home. He was most comfortable when alone with his thoughts. When his father finally arrived in Normandy to take him home to England, "I was pained beyond description," William-Henry later wrote.

Louis XVI would soon be guillotined, and war was about to break out between England and France, but William-Henry was unperturbed by these looming events. He would rather have remained cloistered in coastal Normandy, like a monk or an orphan, than return to the noisy maelstrom of London. Perhaps, too, he was unhappy at the prospect of living once again under the gaze and authority of his disapproving father.

BACK IN ENGLAND, further schooling was out of the question. Samuel announced that it was time for his son to learn a profession. The boy was nearing seventeen. His father decided he should be groomed for the law.

Lawyers were not held in high esteem in Georgian England. The exception was barristers, or trial lawyers, who were considered part of the gentry, like physicians and surgeons, according to a popular handbook for visitors, *The Picture of London for 1803*. The great mass of lesser attorneys, according to the guidebook, was generally equivalent in status to apothecaries and "the better sort of shop-keepers, with the exception of some (and unfortunately not a few) of the class of attornies who may well be placed on a level with the *vilest officers of the law*, or even with the *worst offenders against the law*."

Becoming a lawyer in England at the end of the eighteenth century was not difficult. There were no law schools and no qualifying examinations. Formal admittance to the profession required only a willingness to swear an oath denouncing the pope. Young men learned the profession, such as it was, by working as legal apprentices, starting in their late teens.

Samuel arranged for a lawyer friend, William Bingley, to take on his son as an apprentice early in 1793. Bingley was a conveyancer, an attorney who specialized in real estate transactions. His chambers were a set of small, cramped rooms at New Inn just across the Strand from Norfolk Street, not much more than a five minutes' walk from the Irelands' home.

New Inn was a campuslike set of three long, featureless brick buildings from the time of William and Mary—each having three stories with a dormered fourth—that formed three sides of a square. In the center was an expanse of gardens laid out with walkways and neat rows of shade trees. Facing New Inn from the other side of the courtyard was Clement's Inn. Like London's other inns of court, these were originally residences for young men planning a career in the law. Now the inns were little more than convenient dormitories and offices for anyone who worked in the courts or nearby, whether lawyers or not.

William-Henry's labors on behalf of Mr. Bingley were easy enough. He sorted through old documents, ran errands, made transcripts, and performed other clerical tasks that required neither skill nor speed. In the office were countless old deeds and conveyances on parchment dating from the time of King Henry VIII and earlier, bound or tied into bundles and gathering dust on shelves and in disused corners, their wax seals brittle and discolored.

A generation later, fifteen-year-old Charles Dickens worked as a solicitor's clerk on nearby Chancery Lane, a lawyer-infested precinct just beyond where the Strand became Fleet Street. In *Bleak House*, Dickens would borrow from his experience there to describe a fictional lawyer's office in one of the smaller inns of court: "A smell as of unwholesome sheep, blending with the smell of must and dust, is referable to the nightly (and often daily) consumption of mutton fat in candles, and to the fretting of parchment forms and skins in greasy drawers."

William-Henry found he had imbibed his father's taste for the things of the past. It was part of what made working for Bingley endurable as he sifted through the piles of moldering documents to retrieve some ancient record or another.

LIKE OTHERS AT the dawn of the Romantic era, William-Henry felt a sense of nostalgia for Old England, especially a medieval England that was largely imaginary. For years he had lost himself in old volumes of Chaucer and Malory, traveling back to the days of chivalry and courtly love. The Europe of Lancelot, Roland, and William the Conqueror seemed nobler and more heroic than his own humdrum world.

He collected pieces of old armor and decorated his bedroom with them. If a suit of armor was missing a piece, he, like Don Quixote, fashioned the missing part using pasteboard. He would remember his room as "a regular armory." At night, he sometimes sat up in bed, startled by moonlight glinting from a helmet or breastplate, and he would fantasize about an England he was born too late to know.

"Various old romances and tales of knights-errant excited my attention to such a degree that I have often sighed to be the inmate of some gloomy castle," he wrote. "Sometimes I have wished that by the distant chime of a bell I had found the hospitable porch of some old monastery." Following a humble meal shared with the monks and a peaceful night's sleep, "I might afterwards, . . . with the abbots blessing the ensuing morn, have hied me in pursuit of fresh adventures."

Truth be told, William-Henry was never one to pursue physical adventure. The kinds of adventures he prized had to do with words and jests, not lances. As a child, he had pictured himself becoming an actor, but he had soon realized he was too shy for a life on the stage. Now, like so many young men and women in Georgian London, he fancied himself becoming a writer—a playwright perhaps, or a poet.

William-Henry did indeed have natural fluency with a pen. If his schoolmasters had failed to notice or encourage his intellect, that was their shortcoming, not his. To amuse himself, the boy would imitate in verse the antiquated language of bygone poets he admired, Chaucer being a particular favorite.

Sometimes he indulged in more slavish imitation. Copying word for word the language of an admired writer was a popular method for students in the eighteenth century to learn penmanship and composition—"making extracts," it was called. William-Henry had detested the rote busywork of the classroom; on his own, however, he enjoyed copying out scenes from Shakespeare's plays. Transcribing the Bard's texts, like reading them aloud with his family, helped him absorb the language of the dramas.

As a copyist, the boy strived for authenticity. From sixteenth-century deeds and other old documents, he was familiar with the script that educated men in the Elizabethan era had been taught to use. It was a calligraphic style of penmanship known as the secretary hand. William-Henry relished copying Shakespeare elegantly. It was a revelation to write something that immediately had the look of antiquity. The boy was especially pleased to think that no one alive had seen these passages in Shakespeare's hand. There was nothing against which to compare his efforts. Who could say they weren't the very image of the original?

CHAPTER THREE

THE COLLECTOR OF CURIOSITIES

WILLIAM-HENRY'S LIFE might have passed in obscurity had it not been for his father's obsession with collecting antiquities. Samuel Ireland had always preferred the old to the new. He was the kind of collector the writer John Earle had in mind when he described an antiquary in 1628: "Hee is one that hath that unnaturall disease to bee enamour'd of old age, and wrinckles, and loves all things (as Dutchmen doe Cheese) the better for being mouldy and worm-eaten."

Samuel took a father's pride in his timeworn valuables, which he displayed in his study in glass-fronted mahogany cases eight feet tall. The glass doors and drawers were kept locked, but William-Henry knew where the keys were. He would sometimes borrow one or another old tome—a Shakespeare First Folio perhaps, bulky as a large family Bible, or an older, pocket-sized sextodecimo of *Love's Labour's Lost*—take it to his bedroom, and inspect it at his leisure.

Samuel Ireland's interests extended well beyond old books and papers. He was an early adherent of the cult of celebrity: He paid particular attention to the fame, or notoriety, of an object's past owner. The ambiance of

8 Norfolk Street had more than a touch of the macabre, death by decapitation being a notable theme. There were a red velvet purse that King Henry VIII had given poor Ann Boleyn; a pair of gloves that the doomed Mary, Queen of Scots, had given her cousin, Queen Elizabeth; a scrap of a cloak worn by Charles I some time before his own death on the block; and a gold ring containing hair from the ill-fated head of Louis XVI.

William-Henry could see that his father was immensely gratified by the historical minutiae he had amassed, but the boy could be disconcerted by his father's acquisitive lust. Many times he had watched in silence as the collector had shepherded some distinguished visitor through his mélange, boasting about this or that moldy trifle. He wondered how his father could be so sure that this snippet of hair really came from the coffin of King Edward IV, or that the cracked pink shoe had really belonged to Lady Lovelace. And wasn't there something faintly undignified about extracting a fruit knife from a locked case and asking a visitor to reflect on its illustrious past—and, by implication, on the achievement of Samuel Ireland in becoming its sole possessor? A fruit knife once owned by the essayist Joseph Addison was still just a fruit knife.

Samuel Ireland never had any such doubts about his treasures and their importance. He was not a man easily abashed. For all his eccentricities, he was in some ways typical of his time. In Europe in the late eighteenth century, there was a new fascination with antiquity for its own sake: for judging things, whether buildings or poems, not on their aesthetics so much as their age and pedigree. For antiquarians, acquiring and displaying rare objects—old books, classical statuary, antique armor—was a way of showing a proper reverence for the glories of the past. Among gentlemen of means eager to show off their worldliness, in fact, collecting had become a fashionable mania.

An added incentive for some antiquarians, and surely for Samuel Ireland, was that building an impressive cabinet of curiosities was one of the few ways for a commoner to gain entrée to the upper reaches of polite society and even to mix with royalty. King George III was a collector. So was his wife, Queen Charlotte. Their eldest son, the Prince of Wales, collected paintings with a zeal that was said to border on gluttony. The prince collected other things as well. At his death in 1830, as King George IV, his closets and wardrobes were found to contain a vast hoard that included three hundred whips and an appalling quantity of women's hair, some of it still powdered and pomaded.

Over the course of the eighteenth century, however, collecting was increasingly seen not just as a hobby for aristocrats but as the symbolic accumulation of experience and knowledge. Periodicals like the *Gentleman's Magazine*, which emphasized antiquarian subjects, reached beyond an elite of insiders to the well-read public. The personal collection of many a Georgian gentleman might include works by Ovid in Gothic black-letter type, a shelf or two of seashells, a war club that had found its way to England aboard an East Indiaman, and a stone chip the collector had chiseled from the Colosseum during his grand tour. As with some of Samuel Ireland's prized objects, questions of authenticity could arise. In 1751, the collection of the venerable Royal Society on Crane Court just off the Strand included a bone from a mermaid's head.

That same year, King George II, an avid collector of rare books and manuscripts, had authorized the founding of the Society of Antiquaries. This was a club for England's most distinguished collectors of historical artifacts. At a time when professional historians didn't exist, when reliable works of history were unknown—Edward Gibbon finished his groundbreaking *History of the Decline and Fall of the Roman Empire* only in 1788—serious-minded amateurs dominated the study of antiquity. Scholarship was still a gentlemanly pursuit.

Samuel Ireland was serious-minded but not always gentlemanly. Antiquarian collectors liked to copy inscriptions from the stones in rural churchyards, examine old metal pots dug up by farmers, and argue with one another over whether a grassy mound had been a Roman battlement. Ireland, while researching one of his travel books, was once guided to a reputed burial site at an old battlefield in Northamptonshire. Noticing slight depressions here and there, Ireland called for shovels. Here was no armchair antiquary. Let others trace the carvings on gravestones—he would dig up the graves.

Ireland's brashness could be irritating. At a time when one didn't approach gentlemen one didn't know without a proper introduction, let alone call on them at home, Ireland was known to do both. He was a name-dropper and a self-promoter. In 1789, friends put his name up for membership in the Society of Antiquaries. The group met Thursday evenings in a grand curio-filled hall at Somerset House, a palatial new building just up the Strand from the Irelands' home.

With Ireland's name up for consideration, the antiquaries took a vote and turned him down. "No" votes were unusual at a time when the society was adding new members rapidly. For Ireland, the verdict was a shock and a humiliation. His friends tried again; the club rejected him once more. Ireland was blackballed. There was just something about the man that didn't sit well with the status-conscious men of London society.

Although the heart of Samuel Ireland's collection was rare books and papers, he was not especially well-read. As with other book collectors, what mattered to Ireland was an ancient volume's age, rarity, and appearance. "People are in love with good binding rather than good reading," observed a disgusted onlooker at a 1726 London book auction. Ireland responded viscerally to the sight and smell of old paper and bindings, the way a connoisseur of old masters would to crackled varnish and worn gilt frames.

Not everyone admired what was ancient, of course. Samuel Pepys recorded in his diary in 1665 that a London friend, John Evelyn, showed him some autograph letters he had acquired, including letters written by both Queen Elizabeth and Mary, Queen of Scots. Pepys was impressed by the letters' lineage, "but, Lord! how poorly, methinks, they wrote in those days and in what plain uncut paper."

By Samuel Ireland's day, old books with uncut pages—a condition guaranteeing that they were both unread and unreadable—were much prized. The late eighteenth century was a heyday for literary collectors in England. Many distinguished old families were living in straitened circumstances, while London's nouveaux riches, like Samuel Ireland, hungered for things with a patina of age. He was a familiar face at estate sales and book and manuscript auctions held in London's coffeehouses and fading mansions during the 1780s and 1790s. Unlike more fastidious collectors, he had no aversion to scouting for treasures in musty old bookshops and at print sellers in some of London's shabbier neighborhoods.

Elizabethan papers—missals, sermons, and other printed items—could still be bought for pocket change. A 1609 first edition of Shakespeare's *Sonnets*, printed during his lifetime, cost four or five shillings in the 1760s. As late as 1777, a Shakespeare First Folio could be had for five pounds. Prices for old Shakespeare editions were rising rapidly, however. At an auction in 1790, the Duke of Roxburgh was admired for his sangfroid as he kept upping his bid for a First Folio in excellent condition, finally winning it for thirty-five pounds. Within a few years, it would be remembered as a steal.*

Printed editions of Shakespeare were all very well—Samuel Ireland owned them in all ages and formats. But even First Folios were mass-produced artifacts; hundreds of them existed. What Ireland craved was something unique: something written in the Bard's own hand.

In the summer of 1793, William-Henry's father was preparing to visit Warwickshire and the villages of the Upper Avon, the subject of his fourth history-cum-travel book. He had already made brief forays to the region on his own, sketching and gathering tales. Samuel Ireland didn't travel light, what with his notebooks and artist's materials. Having his son along this time would make his expedition less arduous. Bingley, Samuel's old friend, agreed to grant his new apprentice a leave.

Samuel planned for a stay of a week or two in Stratford-upon-Avon. Even if this placid region of central England had lacked the picturesque views he sought, he later explained, "the honour it derives from having produced our immortal Shakspeare" would alone have justified his book's publication. What's more, Samuel had an ulterior motive for the trip: In Stratford, if anywhere, lay overlooked papers and relics from the Bard's life.

---

* In 2006, Sotheby's in London sold a First Folio for £2.8 million or more than $5 million.

Like other collectors, Samuel was perplexed that no one had yet found where Shakespeare's manuscripts were hidden. The oldest known examples of his poetry and plays were printed texts. As for his original longhand drafts—written with such ease, according to his friends John Heminge and Henry Condell, that he rarely left blots on the paper—none had turned up. Strange but true, there was no hard, ink-on-paper evidence that the greatest writer in the history of English literature could write a complete sentence. No one doubted that Shakespeare was literate, of course, but it was frustrating that no documents had been found to prove it. That Englishmen of an earlier era might have discarded Shakespeare's handwritten poetry and play scripts as insignificant was too shameful to consider.

In the 1820s, theater critic James Boaden looked back at the mood in the 1790s among would-be collectors of Shakespeareana: "It was a subject of infinite surprise," he wrote, that even though Shakespeare's patrons included two monarchs and a number of earls, "not a single letter can be found subscribed with his name." It was as if some malign power had gathered up all his papers and destroyed them. Much more probable, in the view of Shakespeare's admirers at the time, including Boaden, was "that the task of collection had by some affectionate hand been duly made; and that, perhaps, in our time a rich assemblage of Shakspeare papers would start forth from some ancient repository, to solve all our doubts, and add to our reverence and our enjoyment."

Now that so many people knew their value, it was reasonable to expect that Shakespeare's papers would soon be located. Scholars awaited their retrieval impatiently. Samuel Ireland was one of many people vying to be the first to uncover the hidden archive, wherever it was. The papers' discovery would shed new light on England's matchless Bard and bring him within an intimate distance of his eager worshippers at last. The papers would turn up any day now, they were sure. It seemed only a matter of time.

WILLIAM-HENRY didn't share his father's utter fixation with Shakespeare—few people were as obsessive on the matter as Samuel Ireland. Still, the boy looked forward to seeing for himself the birthplace of the man he acknowledged as "our dramatic lord."

Stratford, a small market town, had grown little since Shakespeare's day. The well-to-do lived in half-timbered manors, many more people in spartan cottages. Until the 1700s, the Warwickshire village had barely been aware of its native son. Traditionally a Puritan town, Stratford had long lacked a theater and frowned on traveling acting troupes. In fact, Shakespeare's old stage company, the King's Men, had paid a visit just six years after Shakespeare's death, hoping to earn some money by performing at the town hall. The town fathers weren't interested. An entry in the borough chamberlain's books reads: "To the King's Players for not playing in the Hall, 6/1-." During the 1600s, admirers of Shakespeare had inquired about him in Stratford from time to time. After a few such queries, a local vicar, John Ward, made a note to himself in his diary: "Remember to peruse Shakespeare's plays, and bee versed in them, that I may not bee ignorant in that matter."

Although a full-scale tourist trade had yet to develop by the time the Irelands visited Stratford in the 1790s, the occasional literary pilgrim was now a familiar sight. A typical visitor of the day was Oxford student James Plumptre, who had made an overnight visit in 1790. Plumptre, a nineteen-year-old theater enthusiast and would-be playwright, wrote in his diary that he woke up early "to quaff the inspiring waters of the soft-flowing Avon." Later, he stopped at the rundown house that was now accepted as Shakespeare's birthplace. The house belonged to Thomas Hart, a butcher descended from Shakespeare's sister Joan. The only person home when Plumptre visited was an old woman.

"In the inner Room, on one side of the fireplace," he wrote in his diary, "is a chair fixed into the wall, where our bard used to sit. Here I sat myself down, and found an enthusiastic ardor spread itself all over my frame which prompted me to take out a knife to cut off a sacred relic." The old woman, "who had watched me narrowly," immediately scolded the lad and confiscated the piece.

At the time of the Irelands' visit three years later, the old oak chair had vanished from its corner of the birthplace; a Polish antiquarian, Princess Izabella Czartoryska, had bought it a few months after Plumptre's visit for the handsome sum of twenty guineas. Despite the chair's absence in 1793, Samuel added it to his illustration of the cottage's interior, just as he liked to add sailboats and swans to his picturesque river scenes. When art and truth clashed, Samuel, as a man of taste, preferred art.

The Irelands' guide during their visit was Stratford's unofficial authority on Shakespeare, a burly wheelwright and failed poet named John Jordan. Despite a lack of literary distinction, Jordan was known locally as "the Stratford Poet." A quieter and more sober-minded Shakespeare authority in Stratford at the time, Robert Wheler, described his garrulous townsman as "one of those humble geniuses to whom a little learning, if not a dangerous thing, proved almost useless." For a small consideration, Jordan happily squired the pair around town.

As they toured the village, Jordan and the Irelands were a conspicuous sight: Jordan rangy and convivial, making introductions, pointing out sights, and telling well-practiced stories; Samuel short, doughy, and intense, striding importantly alongside his guide, querying locals, and nosing about the old buildings; his son following silently in their wake, a sketchpad and drawing materials under his arms.

One of the first places Jordan took the Irelands was the shop of an old watchmaker and wood-carver named Thomas Sharp. Nearly forty years before, Sharp had had the foresight to buy the wood of an old mulberry tree that had been growing next to Shakespeare's last Stratford residence, known as New Place. According to village lore, the Bard had planted the tree himself.

By the 1750s, out-of-town visitors had taken to carving their initials in the hallowed mulberry's trunk and breaking off branches as souvenirs. This had infuriated Francis Gastrell, the cranky retired vicar who'd bought New Place in 1753. Gastrell hadn't regarded Shakespeare as his idol, nor had he viewed New Place as a shrine. He had the mulberry pulled down; then he left town. Later, resenting his taxes as an absentee landlord, Gastrell had the house pulled down, too. His peevish actions ensured that local historians would keep his name alive as Stratford's most vilified former resident.

Sharp was soon carving ornate souvenirs from the salvaged wood: match boxes, tea chests, tobacco stoppers, ink stands, and other odds and ends. When the Irelands poked their heads into his shop—lo and behold!—the remains of Shakespeare's tree were still piled up in abundance, ready to be carved. Samuel was impressed.

William-Henry was somewhat less credulous. He knew the story of Shakespeare's mulberry tree, and he accepted the idea that the tree was sacred, but he knew it wasn't enchanted. While in the shop, he later wrote, he tallied the busts, stoppers, and other souvenirs "all carved from the wood, which (like pieces of the *real cross* in catholic countries) have so multiplied that I much fear a dozen full-grown mulberry trees would scarcely suffice to produce the innumerable mementoes." William-Henry kept his thoughts to himself; his father saw nothing amiss about the wares on display. He bought an ornate mulberry goblet. In London, he would have it trimmed in silver.

William-Henry may not have been awed by memorabilia, but he found himself deeply moved nonetheless to tread the ground that Shakespeare had walked. He felt somehow in Shakespeare's presence. When he stepped inside the modest church where the poet's bones lay buried, he wrote, "It would be impossible for me to describe the thrill which then took possession of my soul."

As they explored Stratford and its environs, Samuel kept up a more or less constant chatter, asking questions or, just as often, making pronouncements: about the architectural character of the area, the most pleasing views of the river Avon, the nature of English life in the time of Elizabeth, and especially the Bard and his incomparable genius. At dawn, his first words had to do with Shakespeare. Before bed each night, he would raise a glass to his undying memory. During this time, William-Henry wrote, "I am fully convinced, not one hour was spent but in the favourite pursuit; while the conversations at our dinners and suppers were still of Shakspeare, the immortal and divine Shakspeare."

Jordan regaled the Irelands with stories about the poet's early days, many of which he had published around 1780 as *Original Collections on Shakspeare and Stratford-on-Avon*. In it, Jordan drew on local legends and a dash of literary license to portray young Will of Stratford as a rascal and a libertine, the leader of a pack of boisterous, ale-swilling scofflaws for whom deer poaching was a favorite activity. Samuel Ireland would duly incorporate some of this information into his own book.

Ironically, the Irelands' future nemesis, the eminent Shakespeare scholar Edmond Malone, was himself duped by the genial wheelwright. Malone, who met Jordan in Stratford a few months before the Irelands did, had been corresponding with him for many years and had read with interest his book of Bardic lore. Though Malone was a born skeptic, Jordan succeeded in selling him an unpublished poem that Shakespeare had supposedly written while living in Stratford. Malone had included the poem in his magisterial ten-volume edition of Shakespeare's complete works, published in 1790. The poem was actually one of Jordan's own compositions. It was one of the very few the wheelwright ever managed to have published.

William-Henry later described Jordan as a "civil inoffensive creature" and "a very honest fellow." He evidently didn't think the old man was a fabulist. He was impressed by his industry, noting that Jordan "had made frequent visits to the neighbouring villages and ancient houses, endeavouring if possible to glean any new anecdote or traditionary tale" about Shakespeare's life. It was common for even serious antiquarians to collect old stories and ballads and treat them as historic documents.

Robert Wheler, Jordan's antiquarian townsman, had his doubts about the man's honesty, however. In 1814, several years after Jordan's death, Wheler recalled an unsettling experience. Jordan, he wrote, "shewed me a publication, of which I unfortunately forget the title, printed in the period of Shakspeare, upon the fly leaf of which he had introduced our bard's name, which he imitated from a facsimile of his signature, that it might be supposed to have once belonged to the poet." Jordan was proud enough of his forgery to boast about it to his fellow villager; he was no doubt more discreet with out-of-town visitors. If he tried to impress the Irelands with his precious autographed book, neither of them wrote about it—but within two years, William-Henry would be engaged in exactly the same ruse. Conceivably, he was shown Jordan's handiwork and spotted it for a fake right away.

Thanks to Jordan's tale-telling, Samuel's forthcoming book would include a narrative about the time that Shakespeare, who "addicted himself to ale as lustily as Falstaff to his sack," passed out by the side of a country road after a drinking bout. Breaking new ground, Samuel would include a detailed rendering of the old crab-apple tree under which Shakespeare and his band of merrymakers had collapsed. "Surely the tree that has spread its shade over him, and sheltered him from the dews of the night, has a claim on our attention," Samuel wrote. Not long afterward, Shakespeare's crab-apple tree would suffer the same fate as his mulberry, and apple-wood carvings would begin flooding the souvenir market.

Samuel was far more interested in old papers, of course, than stories and keepsakes. From some of Stratford's older citizens, he learned that a trove of old papers from New Place, Shakespeare's last residence, had been carted off some time before the house had been demolished. The papers were said to have been moved to a place on the outskirts of town called Clopton House.

Once home to Hugh Clopton, London's lord mayor in the reign of Henry VII, Clopton House was a rambling manor with seven chimneys and at least as many gables. The estate owner was now a wealthy but coarse-mannered miser named Williams. To avoid a tax on lighted rooms, he kept most of the windows tightly shuttered. As a result, much of the ancient building was in darkness when the Irelands visited. Barely visible in the dim and empty rooms were a few worn furnishings as old as the house. The mansion had the air of having been abandoned in the fifteenth century. In the gloomy parlor, Samuel asked his elderly host if there were any old papers about from the time of William Shakespeare.

"By God I wish you had arrived a little sooner!" the man burst out, according to William-Henry's account. "Why, it isn't a fortnight since I destroyed several baskets-full of letters and papers in order to clear a small chamber for some young partridges." The four-story house was a labyrinth of rooms, with space aplenty for partridge breeding. "As to Shakspeare—why, there were many bundles with his name wrote upon them. Why, it was in this very fireplace I made a roaring bonfire of them."

Samuel had grown increasingly agitated as Williams spoke, according to his son, who took in the scene a good deal more calmly. Samuel now jumped to his feet. "My God! Sir, you are not aware of the loss which the world has sustained. Would to heaven I had arrived sooner!"

Williams cued his wife, who had been waiting in the next room. Did she remember bringing down several baskets of old papers from the partridge room, he asked, some with Shakespeare's name on them?

"Yes, my dear, I do remember it perfectly well, and if you will call to mind my words, I told you not to burn the papers, as they might be of consequence."

Samuel was devastated. Borrowing a lantern, he rushed off to inspect the partridge room himself but found only partridges. With his host, he searched the rest of the house by lantern light, especially the attic with its many odd-shaped chambers, among them a tiny chapel. Centuries-old bric-a-brac littered some of the rooms, but there were no old manuscripts.

From the detritus strewn about a cramped attic loft that had once been a roost for cocks, Williams extracted an ancient drawing on lambskin showing Elizabeth of York, the wife of Henry VII, lying in state. He told his guest to keep it, explaining: "Being on vellum, it would not do to light a fire." Samuel was appalled at the man's callousness.

It never occurred to the horrified collector that he was being toyed with. He never suspected that Williams and his wife might have performed their skit for other relic-seeking visitors, just as he never considered that kindly old John Jordan might have had a stake in local souvenir sales.

Chroniclers of the Irelands' misadventures have usually assumed that William-Henry, too, believed the Williamses' up-in-flames story. Given the young man's opéra-bouffe presentation of the incident, however, it's likely he knew his father was being played for a fool. William-Henry, quiet and watchful in his father's presence, was never as dull-witted as many of his acquaintances thought. Nor was he as naïve as his father in matters of truth and deception.

Samuel didn't leave Stratford empty-handed. Besides the wooden goblet, he bought a small purse of glass beads that Shakespeare was said to have given his future wife, Anne Hathaway, and a toothpick case of the requisite mulberry wood. Later, at the cottage in Shottery where Anne had grown up, Samuel was delighted to purchase the oak chair—or perhaps one just like it—in which the poet had wooed his beloved.

Back home on Norfolk Street, enthroned in his new armchair, Samuel night after night would lament his failure to procure any of Shakespeare's papers. "Frequently," William-Henry recalled in 1832, "my father would declare that to possess a single vestige of the poet's handwriting would be esteemed a gem beyond all price." Hadn't their own neighbor, Albany Wallis, uncovered in 1768 the gatehouse mortgage deed marked with Shakespeare's crabbed scrawl? Donated to David Garrick, the oversized document, its body professionally inscribed and festooned with four wax seals, had been one of the actor's most treasured possessions.

William-Henry would listen silently to his father's keening. He didn't particularly believe his promise of awarding half his valuables—or sometimes all of them—to whoever brought him a scrap of paper with the Bard's signature. But he was certain that nothing he could do would ever delight his father more than to present him with just such a scrap. So, as his father fretted week after week about the missing autographs, the boy listened, saying little, "swallowing with avidity the honied poison."

THERE WERE GOOD reasons that Shakespeare's papers seemed to have vanished, even if Samuel Ireland was mostly unaware of them. Paper in Elizabethan England, first of all, was scarce and expensive. Most of it was handmade in France. Paper was too valuable to be used just once and then discarded, or to be filed away forever. Ordinarily, when a piece of writing no longer needed to be read—for example, after a play script was set into type—the paper would be reused: to package a bit of pepper or tobacco, perhaps, or to stiffen a book binding. Antiquarians dreaded to think so, but the first draft of *Hamlet* could have ended up inside the cover of someone's King James Bible.*

Audiences who enjoyed plays at the Globe and other stages often neither knew nor cared who had written them. Half the time, Shakespeare's name never appeared on the title pages of his plays that were published during his lifetime. He had little control over what was printed and how it appeared. He didn't own the words. He was just the writer.

Furthermore, the things he was writing were passing entertainments, diversions for London's stage-happy public. Even in print, his plays—any plays—were considered something less than literature. Ben Jonson, on publishing a collection of his plays in 1616, was ridiculed for labeling his crowd-pleasing ephemera "works." When Thomas Bodley set up the Bodleian Library at Oxford University in Shakespeare's time, he refused to include play texts at all. He viewed them as rubbish for lowbrows. A handwritten draft of a play? Not interested.

As for letters and diaries, these were mostly the indulgences of aristocrats. Commoners who worked for a living, like Shakespeare, rarely dabbled in such things. Only in the eighteenth century would letter writing and diary keeping explode in popularity, making Georgian England a golden age of gossip, opinion, and self-chronicling.

Shakespeare did produce manuscripts, of course, but even at the peak of his career as a successful playwright with a string of hits, saving such hard-to-read preliminary documents for posterity wouldn't have occurred to anyone. The idea of venerating an object because it had been owned or touched by a famous person wouldn't catch on for two more centuries. For now, only saints and monarchs rated such treatment.

Had Samuel Ireland and other eighteenth-century admirers of the Bard understood all this, they wouldn't have wondered that his original writings had disappeared. Instead, they would have wondered when Shakespeare's

---

* In 1992, the binding of a four-hundred-year-old edition of Homer's *Odyssey* was found to contain two handwritten pages of dialogue from an unidentified Elizabethan play. The scene bears more than a passing resemblance to a tavern scene early in *Henry IV, Part I*.

papers suddenly began to turn up in London at the end of 1794, one amazing document after another.

There was a more fundamental reason that Shakespeare's manuscripts were unlikely to have survived him. The cold reality, which to Samuel Ireland and other eighteenth-century admirers was inconceivable, was that during his lifetime William Shakespeare was never idolized. He was a sharp-elbowed businessman in the not very reputable world of London public theater—just one theatrical name among many at work during the reigns of Queen Elizabeth and James I. No one was even quite sure of the spelling of his name. Was it Shakspere, Shaxspere, Shagspere, or maybe Shaxberd? For all his success as a writer, he was never knighted or otherwise honored. Those who knew him never thought of him as a genius; they would have laughed—or recoiled—to hear him described as immortal.

The few details known of his life were distinctly unimpressive. He was born in Stratford early in the reign of Queen Elizabeth I to an illiterate glove maker—or was he a butcher?—and his wife. Young Will's education ended with grammar school. As an adult, he was known in his hometown as a grain merchant and landlord, not a poet. By the time he died at age fifty-two, several years after retiring to Stratford, his plays were already out of fashion. He was buried there in an anonymous grave, his passing unnoticed and unmourned in London.

Small wonder that doubts began to arise in the eighteenth century as to who the author of his three dozen plays and 154 sonnets really was. Alternate candidates put forth ranged from Francis Bacon and later Edward de Vere, the Seventeenth Earl of Oxford, to Queen Elizabeth herself. To the Bard's eighteenth-century admirers, the uncertainty about his appearance was particularly troubling. The First Folio portrait wasn't engraved until 1623, seven years after Shakespeare's death. The anatomically awkward rendering was the work of a none-too-talented Dutch artist named Martin Droeshout. The portrait's subject looked distant and slightly uncomfortable, as though he'd rather not be posing at all.

Eighteenth-century England preferred a more manly, self-assured poet. For a large relief on the façade of John Boydell's Shakspeare Gallery, a London museum that opened in 1786 to display scenes from the plays, sculptor Thomas Banks gave the Bard the musculature and languorous pose of a Greek god. With virtually no information to work from, other than a bald head, artists portraying Shakespeare, like those portraying Jesus, were free to comply with the public's expectations. Shakespeare was becoming the man people wanted him to be.

CHAPTER FOUR

THE GILDED SNARE

W ILLIAM-HENRY, who had turned eighteen the summer he visited Stratford with his father in 1793, fell back into the dull routine of working for Bingley. New Inn was pleasant enough. It offered a tranquil, airy refuge from the dense metropolis on all sides. Like a medieval city wall, its long brick buildings showed their backs to the crooked alleys and tightly packed wooden houses of the surrounding neighborhood. "It is so secluded that one might well live in London all one's life and never know of it," London writer Emily Constance Cook commented a century after William-Henry's apprenticeship, shortly before New Inn was torn down.

A single arched gateway on the south edge opened onto narrow Wych Street, its once-grand residences now given over to shabby taverns, tobacco shops, and eating houses offering four-penny dinners. Visible from the gate, the wedding-cake steeple of St. Clement Danes, whose chimes at midnight the roistering Falstaff and Swallow heard, poked above the steeply pitched roofs across the street.

William-Henry's work for Bingley occupied him from nine to three each day. His employer was rarely around, which was no surprise. The boy was an articled clerk, which meant his father had signed him over to work for Bingley for five years without pay. In lieu of a salary, William-Henry would supposedly be learning from Bingley the arcana of property transfers. To make the arrangement worth Bingley's while, Samuel would have paid the conveyancer a fee of several hundred pounds for his trouble. After the fee was paid, Bingley had little incentive to see that the boy learned the ins and outs of conveyancing. Why would he want to groom a competitor? No wonder William-Henry saw little of Bingley at New Inn.

Articled clerks were numerous enough in London to constitute their own social class. They had a reputation as pretentious idlers. It was true that, as a rule, they were intelligent young men who didn't have enough to do. In William-Henry's case, the small amount of paperwork that was expected of him he completed quickly. In his abundant free time, he began frequenting the old bookstalls and curiosity shops of the neighborhood. Each day on his way to and from work, he would cross Holywell Street, a narrow road running between St. Clement Danes and St. Mary le Strand that was lined with dilapidated Elizabethan houses. Under their worn overhangs were shops selling ancient books of every size and description. On a whim, if the price was right, he would pick up some old booklet or engraving that intrigued him. It would then enter the embryonic cabinet of curiosities he was assembling in his room.

Despite his academic failings, William-Henry had the traits of a good antiquarian: patience, tenacity, and an eye for detail—none of which he had ever exhibited in the classroom. "Nothing gave me so much gratification," he later wrote, "as exciting Mr. Ireland's astonishment" when he would return home with "some rare pamphlet which chance or research had thrown my way." One of his father's collector friends was equally impressed, especially when the boy found a rare tract the collector had asked him to search for. William-Henry had never lacked for self-confidence, even if others thought him lucky to be a clerk—and an unpaid one at that. Now, he imagined, people would begin to see they had underestimated him. This dunce, this callow apprentice, had uncovered things that seasoned scholars and antiquaries had not.

At first, naïvely, William-Henry imagined that if he was diligent, he might soon turn up something with Shakespeare's signature that he could bestow on his father. He began his search in his own workplace. It seemed a logical starting place: Bingley's chambers were overflowing with old records, bound and unbound, many of them from Shakespeare's lifetime. Finding no Shakespeare autographs there, he widened his treasure hunt to the shops of neighborhood vendors of old books and papers. Many of these premises looked promising, with their documents stuffed into bins or stacked in disorderly piles. How likely was it that a snooty member of the Society of Antiquaries had burrowed through these flyblown stacks, looking for a faded signature?

In his spare time over the next few weeks, William-Henry immersed himself in old books and papers, but nowhere could he find what he was after. He was frustrated—almost as frustrated as his father had been in Stratford—but only for a time. He was an industrious lad, in his own way. And once he embarked on a task, he wasn't prone to giving up.

When William-Henry began work at New Inn, there were two other men in Bingley's employ: a young office boy and an emaciated older man who worked as a messenger. The office boy soon left, and the emaciated man died. Most days, William-Henry was completely alone at chambers. Sometimes he had the welcome sensation of being cloistered once again behind the seminary walls at Eu, alone with his thoughts. He began to contemplate ways to solve the problem of the missing signature. He had plenty of time, plenty of old paper, and no one watching him.

EXACTLY WHEN THE idea of turning to forgery first took root in William-Henry's mind is unknown. It may have been the evening his father unlocked one of his bookcases after dinner and pulled down a small autographed book entitled *Love and Madness: A Story Too True, in a Series of Letters Between Parties Whose Names Would Perhaps Be Mentioned Were They Less Known and Lamented.* Putting aside for once his cherished Shakespeare, Samuel announced to the family that he had chosen this to read aloud. Its author, he explained to the children, was an old friend, a parson named Herbert Croft. Mrs. Freeman seemed familiar with the book already. Perhaps it was too familiar, for she did not appear to enjoy the readings. Indeed, the book was an odd choice for evening entertainment in the Ireland home.

Love and Madness explored a sensational crime of passion that had occurred on April 7, 1779. A young army officer turned cleric, James Hackman, had waited outside the Covent Garden Theatre for his former lover, a singer named Martha Ray, to emerge. The woman, as it happened, was the current mistress of the Fourth Earl of Sandwich and the mother of his children. As she climbed into the earl's carriage, her jealous suitor stepped forward and shot her in the head. Hackman was tried at the Old Bailey, London's criminal court, and hanged at the gallows at Tyburn west of town twelve days later.

Croft's account, purporting to be a series of letters between the lovers, appeared the following year. Love and Madness was an immediate best seller and went through seven editions. That Samuel would see fit to read this tale aloud in the presence of Mrs. Freeman, an earlier claimant to his lordship's affection, suggests either gross insensitivity to his partner's feelings or a sadistic streak.

The lover's triangle was not the part of Love and Madness that drew William-Henry's interest, in any case. Croft's tale took an odd detour of more than a hundred pages to discuss a young poet, Thomas Chatterton. Based in large part on Chatterton's private letters, this part of the book had nothing whatsoever to do with Hackman, Ray, or Sandwich. Croft had been researching a book on Chatterton when the Covent Garden murder took place, and he decided to fold the two stories together. Love and Madness for the first time laid out details of the young poet's pitifully brief life.

Chatterton had been born to a poor, newly widowed mother in Bristol in 1753. He was an able poet at an early age. Later, he would write verse in his own version of Chaucer's English, sometimes in a pseudoantique hand on scraps of old parchment that he dyed or rubbed with dirt. From the age of fourteen, when his schooling ended, Chatterton worked from eight in the morning to eight at night in a tiresome job—as an articled clerk to a lawyer, in fact. Alone at his workplace, he was idle most of each day, so he was free to write poetry. When acquaintances asked about the manuscripts, he said he had found them in an old trunk in Bristol's imposing St. Mary Redcliffe Church, next door to the Chattertons' home, and that they had been written by an obscure fifteenth-century monk, Thomas Rowley.

Those who read the Rowley poems praised them, although a few people suspected forgery, notably the aristocratic writer Sir Horace Walpole. When Chatterton first sent him sample poems, Walpole offered to see that they were published. After Chatterton revealed in a follow-up letter that he was just a working-class youth, Walpole changed his mind, citing qualms about authenticity.

Chatterton, furious, resolved to succeed as a writer under his own name. Ambitious and more than a little arrogant, he had broken his legal indenture and fled to London to pursue the writer's life. He was unable to earn more than a pittance as a writer, however. Stooping to manual labor was unthinkable. In 1770, alone in his garret room, bitter and despondent, wasting away from disease and starvation, Chatterton drank arsenic and died. He was seventeen years old.

The young poet's pathetic end made him England's archetypal romantic hero: the suicidal starving artist, a real-life version of Goethe's sorrowful young Werther. When his Rowley verses in archaic English were published a few years after his death, a lively public debate ensued over whether a boy of fifteen could have written them. One literary scholar, Jacob Bryant, wrote that he "could as soon believe the moon was made of green cheese" as believe a teenager was their author. Later, the Romantic poets Coleridge, Wordsworth, Byron, and Keats would all champion Chatterton as a brilliant artist spurned by a vicious literary establishment. Walpole, rather unfairly, was made the villain of the story.

As for the accusations of forgery, Croft in *Love and Madness* was outraged. How could critics praise someone's poetry yet denounce its author merely for pretending he hadn't written it? Croft called Chatterton "our Bristol Shakespear" and declared: "For Chatterton's sake the English language should add another word to its dictionary; and should not suffer the same term"—forgery—"to signify a crime for which a man suffers the most ignoble punishment, and the deception of ascribing a false antiquity of two or three centuries to compositions for which the author's name deserves to live forever." To Croft and many others, the boy was guilty of no more than backdating work that he had written under a pseudonym.

On his own, William-Henry read and reread every detail of Croft's account of the late Bristol poet. "The fate of Chatterton so strongly interested me that I used frequently to envy his fate," he wrote in 1805. In an unpublished note, he was more direct about the reason for his envy: "I would gladly die as he did to achieve such fame."

The young Londoner felt an intense kinship with Chatterton, the neglected genius whose poems would be hailed as masterpieces of English literature. Both had been raised without a loving father; both had been regarded as simpletons at school; both had been trapped in dreary jobs as lawyer's clerks. Most importantly, both were young poets enchanted by the language of Chaucer and the romance of Old England. Like Chatterton, William-Henry wondered if he had been born several centuries too late. He adopted the young suicide as his personal hero and role model.

William-Henry's lifelong disdain for the English literary establishment began with his disgust over Chatterton's vile treatment. With some bitterness, he recognized that he himself stood little chance of winning acclaim as an author. Talent had little to do with it. In England's pantheon of famous writers, a majority had always been men of gentle birth. Few of them ever had to work for a living. Shakespeare, as a commoner who wrote for money, was an anomaly.

The pattern persisted in Georgian England. The most esteemed writers, especially the poets, were still men from the upper reaches of society. If a writer wasn't independently wealthy, he or she needed a patron who was. Middle-class writers seeking to live by the pen alone had little choice but to labor as Grub Street scribes: fast-working hacks who churned out essays, opinion, satire, political comment, gossip, and whatever else London's scrum of newspapers had room to publish. It was a hard way to make a living. Even well-published writers were sometimes paid in free newspapers.

A few talented writers—notably Jane Austen, a few months younger than William-Henry—turned to writing novels, usually under pseudonyms. William-Henry had been transfixed by Horace Walpole's macabre *The Castle of Otranto*, the forerunner of the gothic novel, originally published in 1764. As the son of a prime minister and a man in line to become the Earl of Orford, Sir Horace evidently didn't think a person of his breeding should be writing popular novels. In his book's original preface, he explained that what followed was translated from an Italian black-letter account published in Naples in 1529. Only when the novel proved popular did Walpole concede in the second edition that he was its author. How this was different from what Chatterton had done was hard to say, but Walpole escaped censure at the time for his little deception. Some readers, no doubt, were pleased to learn the book's real author was so distinguished.

Most writers didn't have Walpole's advantages. Charles Lamb, another would-be writer exactly William-Henry's age, was an unpaid clerk at East India House at the same time that William-Henry was articled to Bingley. A close friend of Wordsworth and Coleridge, Lamb saw himself as a poet, essayist, and critic. He eventually won attention for his 1807 children's book *Tales from Shakespeare*, written with his sister Mary. Still, Lamb was never able to support himself as an author. To survive, he spent his entire career filling in account ledgers at East India House. Lamb accepted his plight with admirable grace. In his thirtieth year on the job, he wrote a friend that he had, at least, spared himself "the miseries of subsisting by authorship" and had never sunk to being a "slave to booksellers."

William-Henry, too, was intent on being published, but he was less willing to endure the status quo. He refused to accept his youth and anonymity as handicaps. Hadn't many of the most important public figures of the day burst into prominence as young men? Charles James Fox had become England's most powerful Whig politician at twenty-five, while William Pitt the younger had become prime minister when he was twenty-four. Richard Brinsley Sheridan wrote *The Rivals* at twenty-three. Just as William-Henry had never accepted his schoolmasters' superiority, so he was unlikely to accept the peremptory judgments of London's literary arbiters. If the establishment was biased in favor of the titled and the privileged, then he would have to tip the scales in his own favor.

WILLIAM-HENRY'S FIRST forgery had nothing to do with Shakespeare. Nor was it an attempt to cast his own writing in a more favorable light, as with Chatterton. It was more a harmless trick than a polished deception. If it hadn't worked, his career in forgery would likely have ended there. He would have served out his indenture and become a conveyancer with his own clerks, a prosperous man who collected rare first editions and paid to have his little books of poetry published in editions of fifty.

In the summer of 1794, a thin book caught his eye in one of the out-of-the-way curiosity shops off the Strand that he liked to prowl. It was a two-hundred-year-old prayer book decorated with woodcuts and bound in vellum, but it wasn't in particularly good condition or of any historical note. The author had prefaced it with a dedication to his reigning sovereign, Queen Elizabeth, which was a common enough gesture. In tribute to the queen, the writer had arranged for the royal Tudor coat of arms to be stamped on the cover in gold.

William-Henry had bought the prayer book mainly because it was old and he liked the way it looked, but leafing through it a few months later, he began daydreaming. What if the author had presented this book—this very book—to England's legendary Virgin Queen? The idea appealed to him. There was no way to know if the prayer book had ever graced a shelf in one of the queen's palaces, but he preferred to think that it had. He resolved to remove the uncertainty.

The next day, Bingley's office was deserted as usual. "I weakened some common ink with water," he recalled in his 1805 confession, "and on a piece of old paper wrote a dedicatory epistle, as if from the author to Elizabeth, requesting her gracious acceptance and countenance of this work." The boy's habit of copying out old texts in the secretary hand proved useful.

Without hesitation, he mimicked the script and the language of an obsequious Elizabethan minister.

William-Henry intended to impress his father by claiming he had found the letter slipped under the book's vellum cover, which had come loose, but he had second thoughts about his handiwork. Samuel Ireland was a man known as a connoisseur of old documents, even if he was not the expert he pretended to be. The boy decided he'd better show the letter to an impartial judge first.

From Bingley's chambers, he hurried across New Inn's courtyard to a narrow alley leading off from it called New Inn Passage. The covered walkway tunneled through the western side of the inn to the grimy alleys of Clare Market beyond, a dense quarter packed with slaughterhouses and butcher shops. William-Henry opened a door midway down the dark passageway and entered the bookbinding shop of Thomas Laurie. The shop specialized in sewing old legal documents into huge volumes complete with calfskin bindings and marbled endpapers. Like other clerks at New Inn, William-Henry had often dropped off sheaves of records there to be bound.

He handed Laurie the presentation letter. "I unequivocally told him, with a smile, that I had just executed it," he recalled. William-Henry explained that the person he was hoping to fool was his father, the collector. What did Laurie think his chances were? The bookbinder said the letter certainly looked old enough to him. One of Laurie's two young helpers was quicker to see fault. The ink looked watered-down, the lad said, not old and faded.

"He immediately mixed together in a phial three different liquids used in marbling," William-Henry wrote. The young man shook the vial until the inks frothed and darkened, then, dipping a quill, signed his name. The signature was quite faint. "However, on holding it for a few seconds before the fire, the ink gradually assumed a very dark brown appearance." William-Henry paid the young man a shilling for his trouble and left with the vial of ink.

Back at his office, William-Henry rewrote his letter using the new ink, then held it over a candle to brown the script. Satisfied, he brought it home and slipped it inside the prayer book's cover. That evening he showed his father the prayer book and extracted the curious letter he'd found tucked inside it. Samuel was suitably impressed, if less than astonished. Yes, the collector allowed, the letter appeared to be authentic.

The verdict meant more to the boy than to the father. "It was the first thing of the kind I ever attempted," William-Henry recalled. In a few months' time, he would be so practiced at forgery that he would worry this first clumsy attempt might not survive general scrutiny. Tricking his father hadn't been hard; tricking more astute observers was another matter. The boy retrieved the prayer book, which he had given his father, removed the letter, and burned it.

William-Henry tried one more test of his skill with old handwriting. In a curio shop, he bought an old terra cotta bust of Oliver Cromwell, the Lord Protector of the 1650s after the fall of Charles I. It had been sculpted, the shopkeeper had told him, by an obscure young artist who had died young. William-Henry had thought the statue "spirited." Now he tried an experiment. At New Inn, using his special blend of ink, he inscribed a note signed by John Bradshaw, the judge who had condemned Charles to death (and whose body would be exhumed during the Restoration so that his head, along with Cromwell's, could be stuck on a pike over Westminster Hall). Bradshaw's supposed note, which William-Henry glued to the back of the bust, stated that Cromwell had given it to him as a gift. It was an unlikely scenario—Cromwell and Bradshaw had detested each other—but William-Henry didn't know this.

The boy carried the statue home to show his father, who once again was impressed by this rare discovery. In the ensuing days, Samuel invited several of his art-minded friends to come see the bust for themselves. They agreed the head was a superb work of art. They decided, in fact, that it must have been molded by none other than Abraham Simon, a prominent sculptor of the day. They even compared Justice Bradshaw's signature to that on the king's 1649 death warrant and confirmed that they were from the same hand.

Though William-Henry kept his thoughts to himself, he was stunned. In part, he found the response to his little joke amusing, but his amusement was tempered by indignation. He knew his father and his father's friends wouldn't have given the bust a second look had they known the artist was a young man of no reputation. The boy learned an unexpected lesson, too: Once people decide they know what they're seeing, they use new information to reinforce what they already know. All the forger does is suggest a plausible story. The forger's victims see to it that the story comes true.

THAT FALL, IN 1794, William-Henry had noticed something unusual while thumbing through one of his father's few books of recent vintage. Edmond Malone's 1790 edition of Shakespeare's complete works contained a facsimile of the most recently unearthed signature of William Shakespeare. It was part of a reproduction of the gatehouse deed that Albany Wallis had found in 1768.

William-Henry was by nature a risk taker. Still, he wasn't ready to pass off his own language as Shakespeare's. First of all, he was doubtful his father would mistake his faux-antique script for the playwright's handwriting. As for William-Henry's literary ability: For all his dreams of being a writer, he had written at most a handful of poems.

Having under his roof a facsimile of Shakespeare's signature suddenly put within reach his goal of giving his father something—anything—of Shakespeare's. He would forge a new deed, with different names. He would take the book containing the Bard's signature to Bingley's office, where he would practice tracing it until he could write it with his eyes shut. Then, using blank parchment from an old rent roll, he would write a new deed, copying the script and legal verbiage of this and other deeds. At the bottom, he would affix the priceless scribble, "Wm Shakspeare."

First, however, he needed to lay some groundwork. He couldn't keep up the pretense that he was happening upon rare treasures by mad luck. So, in late November, a month or two after "discovering" his Cromwell bust, he told his father about a wealthy young gentleman he had just met while dining at a friend's house. The gentleman, whom he didn't identify, asked the boy if he would consider doing some legal chores for him. Samuel was sufficiently pleased to mention in his diary that night that his son had made the acquaintance of a person "of very considerable property."

Ten days later, in early December, William-Henry announced great news. The gentleman had invited him to his London home. (He had another in the country.) There, having learned of William-Henry's fascination with historical curiosities, he had directed the young clerk to an enormous oak trunk. Inside were bundles of old documents that the man had inherited but never examined. The gentleman had no interest in such things; the boy was free to keep any that he fancied. Almost immediately, William-Henry told his father, he had come across an old deed signed by the Bard of Avon himself.

The deed recorded a transaction between two parties: Shakespeare and his friend and fellow actor John Heminge, on the one hand, and a Michael Fraser and his wife, on the other. Both Shakespeare and Fraser had signed it. William-Henry had rushed over to his host to show him the deed, which the gentleman was astonished to see. But "having promised me everything I should find worthy my notice," William-Henry told his father, "he would not be worse than his word, and desiring only that I would make him a fair transcript in my own handwriting, he told me the deed was at my service."

Samuel, too, was astounded by the discovery. But where was the deed? He couldn't be satisfied until he had inspected it. Regretfully, William-Henry needed more time to write out a copy for his patron. His gentleman friend had left for the country and wouldn't return to London for a week or two. Somehow the collector would have to contain his impatience till then.

William-Henry actually needed the time to begin teaching himself the details of forgery. He knew how two-hundred-year-old deeds were constructed—Bingley's office had plenty of them, expanses of leathery parchment covered in neat script. Threaded through slits near the bottom of an Elizabethan deed were narrow loops of parchment, one per signature. The ends of each folded strip were held together with a blob of wax. Before hardening, the wax would be stamped with the signer's distinctive seal. The arrangement was intended to deter forgery.

It almost deterred William-Henry. When he heated up wax seals from old deeds to transfer them to his forged parchment, the red wax crumbled instead of turning sticky. He managed to attach the old seals to his parchment using new wax, but the colors didn't match. Giving up on finesse, he rubbed the bright-red new wax with soot. Like copying portions of the famous gatehouse deed verbatim, this was a shortcut that lay ready to be exposed by someone with a keen eye and a skeptical temperament. Fortunately, his father had neither.

After dinner on the evening on December 16, 1794, the Ireland family was gathered in the drawing room when William-Henry walked in, flushed and nervous. He pulled the newly forged deed from inside his coat and gave it to his father, saying more loudly than he intended, almost as if in defiance: "There, sir! What do you think of that?"

Samuel unfolded the forgery and examined it in silence for several minutes, paying special attention to the seals. In addition to Shakespeare's signature, William-Henry had scrawled a sloppy-looking signature for Fraser with his left hand, to give it a different character. At last, Samuel refolded the parchment. "I certainly believe it to be a genuine deed of the time," he said, a bit more calmly than William-Henry had hoped. This was William Shakespeare's signature, after all—the gem that Samuel had said he'd sacrifice half his collection to attain. Instead, the collector said, "There are the keys of my bookcase. Go and take from it whatsoever you please. I shall refuse you nothing."

William-Henry had imagined a more dramatic scene. To his father's offer, he politely demurred. Samuel arose and fetched from a bookcase a copy of William Stokes's *The Vaulting Master*, a rare seventeenth-century riding manual worth ten or twelve guineas. This he presented to his son with great formality.

Another lesson William-Henry was learning was that gullible people feel more sure of themselves when they have company—the emperor's-new-clothes effect. A few days later, Samuel showed the deed to a friend,

Sir Frederick Eden, an expert on old seals. Eden not only pronounced the deed authentic but also identified the image stamped in the seal directly below Shakespeare's signature. The indistinct T-shaped outline in the wax (an image William-Henry hadn't even noticed) was a contraption called a quintain, Eden explained. A medieval device, a quintain was a swiveling horizontal bar mounted on a post at which a young horseman would aim his lance when learning to joust.

As to why the Bard had chosen this gadget as his personal insignia—why, of course, it was an object at which a rider would "shake" his "spear." The two men were exhilarated by their discovery. They had just advanced the cause of Shakespeare scholarship. As for the Bard's signature, how could it be anything but authentic, sealed as it was with his own distinctive emblem?

IN A SENSE, William-Henry's forgeries were a natural outgrowth of his times. For most of the 180 years since Shakespeare's death, the rare discovery of a document or other object from the poet's life was of interest mainly to Shakespearean scholars, not to the public and the press. Only in recent years had a virulent Cult of Shakespeare swept the British Isles like a contagion. Only now were collectors—Samuel Ireland was just one of many—hungering for authentic Shakespeare relics.

Restoration dramatists of the late seventeenth century had dismissed the dead playwright as a provincial has-been who had pitched his bawdy, bloody dramas to the coarser tastes of his era. Attending *Romeo and Juliet* in March 1661 (possibly with his eyes closed), Pepys deemed the play "the worst that ever I heard in my life." He updated his judgment a few months later after seeing *A Midsummer Night's Dream*, "which I have never seen before, nor shall ever again, for it is the most insipid ridiculous play that ever I saw in my life."

The late Will of Stratford had his theatrical supporters during the seventeenth century, but even they felt the playwright would benefit from drastic rewriting. In 1669, poet laureate John Dryden, ostensibly an admirer, short-ened *Troilus and Cressida* by excising what he called "that heap of Rubbish, under which so many excellent Thoughts lay wholly bury'd." An unnamed critic early in the following century scolded Shakespeare "for ignoring the ancients, for violating decorum by resorting to tragicomedy and supernatural characters, and for using puns and blank verse." Passages like the grave dig-gers' scene in *Hamlet* were regarded as tasteless and inappropriate in a serious tragedy.

Shakespeare won new attention during the eighteenth century as writers like Alexander Pope, in 1725, and Samuel Johnson, in 1765, published fresh editions of his plays. To Johnson, Shakespeare was entirely mortal. "Shake-speare never has six lines together without a fault," he told his future bio-grapher James Boswell in 1769. "Perhaps you may find seven, but this does not refute my general assertion." Nonetheless, condescending attacks on Shakespeare by critics like Voltaire were, to Johnson, "the petty cavils of petty minds." By the second half of the eighteenth century, Shakespeare's plays—many of them adulterated, to be sure—had become a staple of play-houses across England. From 1776 to 1800, the three tragedies staged most often at Drury Lane and Covent Garden were *Hamlet, Macbeth,* and *Romeo and Juliet.*

More than anyone else, it was the Irish-born actor David Garrick who launched a full-blown Cult of Shakespeare. Garrick made his spectacular London debut in 1741 as Richard III at the Theatre in Goodman's Fields. Garrick's style of acting, in contrast to the traditional approach of standing with chest out and declaiming one's lines like an orator, was almost shame-lessly naturalistic. Here was a man who cried on cue and looked as if he meant it. To theater audiences, Garrick was electrifying. Alexander Pope, dazzled at his debut, returned for a second night and then a third. "That young man never had his equal," Pope wrote, "and never will have a rival."

As manager and star of the Drury Lane Theatre, Garrick went on to stage at least ten plays by Shakespeare each season. He added to the reper-tory works like *The Taming of the Shrew* and *Antony and Cleopatra* that had been gathering dust for most of the past century. Garrick the actor, as

Hamlet, Richard III, and Henry V and in a dozen other roles, created riveting, poignant, flesh-and-blood characters from Shakespeare's texts, which he freely rewrote as needed. Similarly, Garrick's heavyset fellow actor Charles Macklin was a revelation to London audiences as an angry, tormented Shylock; until then, actors had played him as a buffoon.

Garrick and Macklin rescued Shakespeare from his own unadmired epoch. "It seemed as if a whole century had been stepped over in the passage of a single scene," wrote playwright Richard Cumberland after attending a performance early in Garrick's career. "Old things were done away, and a new order at once brought forward, bright and luminous, and clearly destined to dispel the barbarisms of a tasteless age."

Garrick, unlike his one-time schoolteacher Samuel Johnson, had no qualms whatsoever about singing Shakespeare's praises. To Garrick, the Bard was nothing less than "the God of our Idolatry." If Shakespeare made Garrick a star, Garrick turned Shakespeare into a deity.

It was Garrick who changed Stratford-upon-Avon into a cultural mecca. In 1769, he mounted an elaborate jubilee in the village in honor of the Bard's two hundredth birthday—though he was actually five years too late. The *Gentleman's Magazine* provided advance publicity for the event, including the first published image of the now decrepit house on Henley Street where Shakespeare was supposedly born: "The humble shed, in which the immortal bard first drew that breath which gladdened all the isle, is still existing; and all who have a heart to feel, and a mind to admire the truth of nature and splendour of genius, will rush thither to behold it, as a pilgrim would to the shrine of some loved saint; will deem it holy ground, and dwell with sweet though pensive rapture on the natal habitation of the poet."

The Great Shakespeare Jubilee, held in September, exuded as much pomp as an English coronation. Thirty cannon were rolled into place for an opening-day salvo. Parades, speeches, dancing, and fireworks followed. Crowding an amphitheater built for the occasion were dukes and duchesses, viscounts and countesses, as well as hordes of the Bard's untitled admirers. Toasts were raised to the Sweet Swan of Avon. Songs were sung in honor of the mulberry tree.

Not all of Stratford's citizens understood what was happening. Many of them had never heard of Shakespeare. Of those who had, some suspected the gala was a satanic rite intended to resurrect the poet from the dead.

Despite all the genuflecting to Shakespeare, Garrick neglected to have any of the Bard's work read or performed during the jubilee. Seated on the amphitheater's stage, Garrick instead recited a lengthy ode of his own composition. The audience joined in the chorus:

> *Let rapture sweep the trembling strings*
> *And Fame, expanding all her wings,*
> *With all her trumpet-tongues proclaim*
> *The lov'd, rever'd, immortal name!*
> SHAKSPEAR! SHAKSPEAR! SHAKSPEAR!

Some of those in attendance were taken aback by the festival's undisguised commercial side: There was a large assortment of Shakespeare-themed knickknacks for sale—many of them made of mulberry wood.

Souvenir vendors may have profited, but the extravagance of the jubilee cost Garrick dearly. He quickly made up his losses and then some, however, when he mounted a musical pageant called *Jubilee* at the Drury Lane Theatre that fall. Actors appeared in the guise of Stratford villagers and Shakespearean characters. Seated next to a bust of Shakespeare that he'd commissioned, Garrick recited his ode to that "blest genius of the isle" nightly. The production drew sellout crowds for forty consecutive nights.

Shakespeare was reborn, not as a playwright this time but as a god. Even if Garrick's delirious idolatry was extreme, the idea took hold that Shakespeare was incomparably greater than any writer who ever lived and greater than any present or future writer could ever aspire to be. His legions of new admirers—"Bardolaters" George Bernard Shaw would call them in 1901—sang his praises in ways that had little to do with textual analysis. "O Shakespeare," called out an enraptured cleric, Martin Sherlock, to his deified idol in 1786. "Enchanting, astonishing, sublime, graceful, thy variety is inexhaustible. Always original, always new, thou art the only prodigy which

Nature has produced. Homer was the first of men, but thou art more than man."

Shakespeare was far more famous now than he had ever been. He was widely and rather unthinkingly acclaimed as the quasidivine embodiment of the nation's unique genius—a symbol of Englishness beyond criticism and without rival. Every English schoolchild and citizen knew his plays and their characters as intimately as they knew the Bible. "Everything nowadays has to do with Shakespeare," the poet George Hardinge observed in 1800. "The difficulty is to find out what has not to do with him."

The most besotted members of the Cult of Shakespeare, like Samuel Ireland, weren't content to read his poetry and see his plays. They lusted for cult objects. The most precious of these were objects Shakespeare had used, touched, or owned in Stratford or London. David Garrick since mid-century had collected Shakespearean artifacts of questionable provenance, including a gray leather glove, a blue and yellow saltshaker, and a signet ring with the initials W. S. Much later, in 1810, another signet ring with the initials W. S. turned up in a field in Stratford. The second ring's discovery prompted the painter Benjamin Robert Haydon, who apparently knew nothing of the earlier ring, to near apoplexy. He wrote to his friend and fellow Shakespeare cultist, the poet John Keats: "I shall certainly go mad! In a field at Stratford upon Avon, in a field that belonged to Shakespeare, they have found a gold ring and seal, with the initial W. S. and a true lover's knot between. If this is not Shakespeare who is it?—a true lover's knot! . . . As sure as that you breathe, & that he was the first of Beings, the Seal belonged to him—O Lord!"

Perhaps the ring was Shakespeare's, but there was no evidence for it beyond the initials. Of course, this didn't stop merchants in Stratford from mass-producing it for tourists.

"LORD, WHAT FOOLS these mortals be!" William-Henry's thoughts mirrored those of Shakespeare's Puck as he began to see how readily people would convince themselves that a forgery, however questionable, had come from the Bard.

He had never intended to be a second Shakespeare. For much of the past year, he had nurtured one overriding ambition, to get his hands on the Bard's autograph. Now Shakespeare's ink-on-parchment signature was to be on display at Norfolk Street as the centerpiece of his father's collection. Samuel Ireland would, at last, feel a sense of fulfillment, as well as gratitude. He owned something that England's greatest collectors had coveted for decades, and he had his long-overlooked son to thank for it.

That William-Henry should seek to win his father's approval by making him the target of a hoax suggests how tortured their relationship was. On the surface, the boy treated his father respectfully, as any future gentleman must. But he was aware that the man was too easily impressed by titles and power, too eager to ingratiate himself with those who could help him, and too ready to reach conclusions without evidence. In Stratford, William-Henry had been a silent witness to his father's foolishness. Yet in his father's eyes it was William-Henry who was the simpleton, the half-educated drudge who lacked his father's intellect and sophistication.

In his original confession in late 1796, the boy dismissed his turn to forgery as a whimsical practical joke that "might occasion a little mirth and shew how far credulity would go in the search for antiquities." In hindsight, he was obviously trying to downplay the seriousness of what he'd done. Who, exactly, would have found mirth in his doctored manuscripts? Not his father, certainly, nor any of his father's friends, nor many of Shakespeare's admirers.

Though people at times mistook William-Henry's boredom and taciturn manner for obtuseness, he never doubted his own intelligence. He was accustomed to being underestimated. Still, he resented being judged by those who were too closed-minded and status-conscious to see his intellectual promise—foremost among them, his father.

Even as he had sought to ingratiate himself with the collector by helping him in his search for Shakespeareana, a part of the boy relished the idea of taking advantage of his greed. By fooling his father with a well-made facsimile of a Shakespeare heirloom, William-Henry would now be doubly rewarded: His father would be forever grateful to him, and the boy would have the satisfaction of proving to himself that he, William-Henry, was the superior connoisseur. And the simple truth was: The boy always loved a good prank, even if the mirth it aroused was mostly his.

So he hoped, but he misjudged the situation. Yes, his father expressed gratitude—if a bit stiffly, as though accepting the Shakespeare deed was only his due. But Samuel's obsession with Shakespeare was only whetted, not eased. Word of the deed spread quickly, and small groups of his father's friends and fellow collectors would convene in the drawing room in the evenings to discuss it.

"Several persons told me," William-Henry wrote two years later, "that wherever it was found, there must undoubtedly be all the manuscripts of Shakspeare so long and vainly sought for." Visitors invariably pressed him for the name of the mysterious gentleman. "It was then for the first time I began to discover the unpleasant predicament in which I had involved myself." To conceal one well-meaning deception, he would have to concoct new ones.

He improvised new details about how he had come to meet the gentleman and dig through his trunk. As to why the man, whom he referred to as Mr. H., insisted on anonymity, William-Henry told visitors "that the gentleman, being possessed of a large fortune, . . . did not think fit to subject himself to the impertinent questionings of every individual who conceived himself licensed to demand an explanation."

This rather brusque put-down would never do for his father, who was becoming insistent on the subject. Samuel had to know: Who *was* this gentleman, and what else might be hidden in his oaken trunk? What letters, manuscripts, diaries, and notes from the hand of Shakespeare had some caretaker in the days of King James put aside for posterity, eventually to find their way to the gentleman's London townhouse? To Samuel, a mere signature already seemed trivial. Where were all the outpourings of the Bard's sublime genius?

"I was sometimes supplicated; at others, commanded to resume my search among my supposed friend's papers," William-Henry recalled many years later, in 1832, "and not unfrequently taunted as being an absolute idiot for suffering such a brilliant opportunity to escape me."

The boy pleaded with his father for patience. The gentleman's trunk was not his to be ransacked. He urged his father to give him time to investigate what other valuable papers Mr. H. might have inherited. As for identifying the man, William-Henry said that as a condition of taking the deed he had sworn never to disclose his gentleman friend's name to anyone. He tried to explain to his father how deeply the gentleman dreaded the prospect of Shakespeare cultists laying siege to his homes, eager for more priceless artifacts. Surely his father could understand.

The boy was becoming a well-practiced liar, as one deception led to another. He had to concentrate in order to keep his stories straight. Yet he didn't see himself as a swindler. Indeed, like Chatterton, William-Henry saw nothing harmful or immoral in what he was doing. He had fulfilled his father's dream, had he not? From now on, however, enhancing his father's collection—and getting credit for it—began to recede as a motive for his fakery. He was an undistinguished clerk who had taken pen in hand and produced a document judged to be priceless. For the first time in his life, he felt powerful and important. "Thus urged, partly by the world, and my own vanity, I determined on attempting something further."

His next forgery was a departure. Instead of closely mimicking old documents, he was ready to give the world the Bard's own language, fluent and impassioned. The two-page profession of faith, the yellowed document that the worthy Doctors Warton and Parr were to bless as indisputably Shakespeare's, was William-Henry's attempt to fill a troubling gap in the writer's biography. For years, critics had mused that England's national poet might have been a closet Catholic. To the English establishment, the idea was nearly as odious as suggesting that he was a bloody-minded French spy, or even an atheist. One reason for suspicion was the ghost's soliloquy in *Hamlet*:

> *I am thy father's spirit,*
> *Doom'd for a certain term to walk the night,*
> *And for the day confined to fast in fires,*

Till the foul crimes done in my days of nature
Are burnt and purged away.

Good Protestants dismissed the concept of purgatory as a popish fairy tale. A more recent hint of apostasy had appeared in Edmond Malone's 1790 Shakespeare opus. A document found above a rafter in the birthplace at Stratford and purporting to be the last will and testament of John Shakespeare, the poet's father, suggested the family was secretly Catholic.* Like many of Shakespeare's English admirers, William-Henry was fiercely anti-Catholic, considering the religion a witch's brew of "superstition and bigotry." He refused to believe that Shakespeare was anything but a good Protestant. He resolved to use his personal proclamation in the Bard's own hand to settle the matter.

The young forger sat down at New Inn with facsimiles of Shakespeare's signatures before him as a guide, his vial of special ink, and two half-sheets of seventeenth-century paper free of any watermarks (from his father's friends he had learned the danger of anachronistic watermarks). Then, without a first draft, he wrote almost without pause a pious, self-abasing declaration. In it, he had the Bard admit: "O omnipotente and greate God I am full offe Synne I doe notte thynke myselfe worthye offe thye grace." In a closing plea to the Almighty, he invoked a striking religious metaphor: "O cheryshe usse like the sweete Chickenne thatte under the coverte offe herre spreadynge Wings Receyves herre lyttle Broode ande hoverynge overre themme keepes themme harmlesse ande in safetye— Wm Shakspeare."

The script was the boy's own version of the secretary hand. To be safe, he repeated the ten lowercase letters in Shakespeare's signature as frequently as he could. "I was also particular in introducing as many capital *doubleyous* and *esses* as possible," he recalled. Later, after the hoax was exposed, critics would mock the boy's habit of affixing *e*'s to almost every word (as his hero Chatterton had done), as well as his habit of avoiding nearly all punctuation.

---

* Malone later renounced its authenticity. The document, which vanished, may well have been another of old John Jordan's forgeries.

When his father and others saw the manuscript—William-Henry presented it to his father on Christmas Eve 1794—details like spelling, punctuation, and poultry metaphors were far from their minds. They were already believers in the sacred trunk. Now the fluid, quasi-Elizabethan script filling the pages made a stunning impression on all who beheld it. William-Henry, as usual, had prepared his father, telling him in advance of his startling discovery of the avowal of faith among the other papers at Mr. H.'s townhouse. Embellishing the story, he reported being so moved and heartened by the Bard's words that he had memorized them. In fact, he told his father, he had begun reciting them each evening as a prayer before bed.

The boy was gaining confidence in his subterfuge. He spent less time worrying that he might at any moment be exposed as a forger. Overriding any possible quibbles about his latest document's bona fides, he knew, was the general urge to believe it to be authentic—to confirm finally that, yes, the Bard was a God-fearing son of Protestant England, as he had to be. After Warton and Parr's benediction, the possibilities opening up to William-Henry seemed limitless. He had reached a point of no return, and with his father's deluded encouragement, he raced past it. With each new forgery, he was becoming further entangled in "the gilded snare which afterwards proved to me the source of indescribable pain and unhappiness."

CHAPTER FIVE

A GENTLEMAN SHAKESPEARE

J ANUARY 1795 WAS the most bitterly cold month in London in more than a century. Day after day, the air was frigid outdoors and in, even with a fire burning, while afternoon temperatures never rose above freezing. Obituaries claimed twice their usual space in London's newspapers, as the ill and the frail succumbed in large numbers to the cold.

Undaunted by the chill of Bingley's empty chambers at New Inn, William-Henry was now working obsessively from morning often until well into the night, interrupting his labors only to heap more coal onto the grate so that his fingers and his precious ink wouldn't freeze. In the space of little more than a month, the law clerk concocted a profusion of antique documents, from thank-you notes and IOUs to original verse, nearly all of them graced with William Shakespeare's autograph. It was as if the boy had vowed to outdo in pen and ink the output of Stratford's industrious mulberry carvers. Later, when the papers were under attack as forgeries, their defenders' chief retort was that not even a group of conspirators could have forged so many documents in so brief a time.

As with the profession of faith, William-Henry was guided in what he chose to forge by his preferred image of the Bard. In the papers and parchments he created at New Inn, he fleshed out the amiable fellow of John Jordan's tall tales, a character whom Shakespeare's imaginative first biographer, Nicholas Rowe, had described in 1709 as "a good-natur'd man, of great sweetness in his manners, and a most agreeable companion." Perhaps so, but Shakespeare had sued a Stratford neighbor over, among other things, a debt of two shillings, and a London acquaintance, fearful of being murdered, had once urged that the playwright and several of his companions be locked up. This was not the Shakespeare Englishmen in the 1790s wanted to hear about.

Showing his idol to be a gentleman of courtesy and correctness, William-Henry produced a promissory note from the young playwright in 1589 stating that he would pay his "good and Worthye Freynd" John Heminge five pounds and five shillings for some unmentioned errand. He then forged a receipt signed by Heminge acknowledging payment of the sum precisely thirty days later. Not only was Shakespeare conscientious about repaying his debts; he was also as punctual as a bank clerk. The peculiar idea that two close friends would exchange financial papers over a payment of five guineas struck no one at the time as odd.

The source of Shakespeare's wealth, or at least his material comfort, had long been something of a mystery. It was rumored that in 1594, when Shakespeare was a fledgling playwright of thirty, he received a lavish gift of a thousand pounds (more than $200,000 today) from handsome young Henry Wriothesley, Third Earl of Southampton. The writer had just dedicated his epic poem *Venus and Adonis* to Southampton, who had come into his inheritance that year. William-Henry decided the poet should leave the world no doubt that he was humbly grateful for his patron's largess—especially as the nineteen-year-old earl had just lost five times that sum in a lawsuit brought by Queen Elizabeth's chief minister, Lord Burleigh, for backing out of a marriage to his daughter.

Forging a letter of thanks from Shakespeare freed William-Henry from the straitjacket of legal and religious prose. He could let the man express his feelings, even if they were entirely obsequious, more like the sentiments of a late-eighteenth-century fop than those of a great Renaissance wordsmith. To explain how the letter had remained in Shakespeare's possession, the boy wrote along the top as an afterthought, "Copye of mye Letter toe hys grace offe Southampton." "Mye Lorde," William-Henry began, as usual dispensing with punctuation and sprinkling terminal *e*'s throughout:

> Doe notte esteeme me a sluggarde nor tardye for thus havynge delayed to answerre or rather toe thank you for youre greate Bountye I doe assure you my graciouse ande good Lorde that thryce I have essayed toe wryte and thryce mye efforts have benne fruitlesse I knowe notte what toe saye Prose Verse alle all is naughte gratitude is all I have toe utter and that is tooe greate and tooe sublyme a feeling for poore mortalls toe expresse O my Lord itte is a Budde which Bllossommes Bllooms butte never dyes itte cherishes sweete Nature ande lulls the calme Breaste toe softe softe repose Butte mye goode Lorde forgive thys mye departure fromme mye Subjectte which was toe retturne thankes and thankes I Doe retturne O excuse mee mye Lorde more at presente I cannotte

> Yours devotedlye and withe due respecte
> Wm Shakspeare

Shakespeare was too discreet to name the specific figure for which he was thanking his patron. And William-Henry was too cautious to commit himself to a number that might someday be contradicted by new evidence.

The boy produced a reply from Southampton—a "Deare William" note that was rather too chummy for an earl addressing a commoner, but no matter—thanking the poet for his thank-you. Shakespeare and his circle were turning out to be more courteous than anyone imagined. "Why dearest Freynd talke soe muche offe gratitude," the earl asked. "Mye offerre was double the Somme butte you woulde accepte butte the halfe." Such an admirable gentleman this Shakespeare. Offered a fee, he protests it's twice what he's worth.

William-Henry scribbled Southampton's note using his left hand in a barely literate scrawl, as he had in impersonating both Fraser and Heminge earlier. He assumed, wrongly, that no examples of the earl's handwriting existed. In fact, Southampton's hand was as tidy and compact as an engraver's, but the Irelands and their circle were not yet aware of this. Still, several people expressed surprise that a cultured young man like the earl had such atrocious handwriting.

The drawing room at Norfolk Street most evenings was now taking on the air of an antiquarian men's club. Men in powdered wigs took turns inspecting the latest literary discoveries with the self-conscious reverence of Egyptologists entering a pharaoh's tomb. The two letters exchanged between the playwright and his noble patron, visitors decided, "were deemed highly curious and valuable," William-Henry wrote, "and the style of Shakspeare's was applauded beyond measure." The Bard, so adept at hiding his personality behind his published lines, was here at last revealing his private thoughts on paper. Once again, the happiness people felt in deciding that the papers were authentic outweighed whatever satisfaction they could have taken in concluding they were not. William-Henry gave Shakespeare a decidedly Georgian cast—he was affable, gracious, and socially correct—because he liked his idol better that way, but he was learning that others did, too. This was making his success as a forger easier than he expected.

One of William-Henry's ingenious labor-saving ideas was to reverse-engineer some of Shakespeare's works. He could simply transcribe the printed text of a play into longhand and—voilà!—here was the masterwork's long-lost original. Rather imprudently, William-Henry had already told his father in late December that Mr. H. had in his possession an entire handwritten draft of one of Shakespeare's tragedies. The boy didn't specify which tragedy. He was already a clever enough forger to realize that if he was to deliver a play's original manuscript, he couldn't slavishly copy the wording he found in bound editions of the collected plays. These had all been compiled and edited well after the playwright's death. William-Henry didn't want to be tripped up by an anachronism—he needed an earlier printed text to copy. Unfortunately, these were extremely scarce, and he couldn't find one.

As luck would have it, Samuel in early January brought home a rare 1608 quarto of *King Lear* to add to his collection. It had been cheaply published as a popular booklet two years after *Lear* was first performed. Now, of course, the crudely printed play was an expensive collectible. William-Henry quietly borrowed the booklet and took it to work the next morning. A few weeks later, he presented his delighted father with an entire manuscript of *King Lear*. The boy had tinkered with the play's language as he copied it, omitting lines and adding a few short passages of his own here and there. It was an unusual way for a novice poet to make his first efforts public.

Encouraged by his success, William-Henry soon told his father he'd uncovered a first draft of *Hamlet*—he was announcing his discoveries almost as quickly as he could dream them up. He never had time to transcribe more than a fragment of *Hamlet* into longhand, but here too he revealed to posterity what Shakespeare had *really* written (starting with the title, which turned out to be *Hamblette*).

Like his contemporaries, William-Henry was a good deal more prudish than his idol. In forging his Shakespearean master documents, he made a point of leaving out "that ribaldry which is so frequently found in the compositions of our bard." Gone from *Lear*, for example, were the Fool's indecent prattling and Kent's scurrilous attack on Oswald. Later, scholars would exult at finally hearing Shakespeare's unadulterated poetry, no longer sullied by careless printers or incompetent editors. They suspected that actors of Shakespeare's day had improvised the plays' many crude jokes and lecherous exchanges and that these had been duly inserted into the theaters' prompt books—and from there into print.

In the eyes of those who inspected them, the boy later wrote, the manuscripts "proved beyond doubt that Shakspeare was a much more finished writer than had ever before been imagined." At heart, however, William-Henry was more interested in correcting Shakespeare's personal biography than his literary one. Few details about the playwright's life were as troubling as his neglect of his wife. He had married Anne Hathaway when he was eighteen; she was twenty-six and already pregnant with their first daughter. The arrangement suggested a shotgun wedding rather than a marriage of true minds. Abandoning her to Stratford, Will spent his entire theatrical career living a bachelor's life in London. His notoriously uncharitable will bequeathed his wife only his "second-best bed." Could this woman be the figure who inspired him to create such poignant romantic heroines as Juliet, Rosalind, and Imogen?

Yes, she could be, and she should be, William-Henry decided. To buttress his case, he composed a five-stanza love poem, ostensibly from the couple's wooing days. It began:

> Is there inne heavenne aught more rare
> Thanne thou sweete Nymphe of Avon fayre
> Is there onne Earthe a Manne more trewe
> Thanne Willy Shakspeare is toe you. . . .

> Though Age withe witherd hand doe stryke
> The forme moste fayre the face moste bryghte
> Still dothe she leave unnetouchedde ande trewe
> Thy Willys love ande freynshyppe too

> Though deathe with neverre faylynge blowe
> Dothe Manne ande babe alyke brynge lowe
> Yette doth he take naughte butte hys due
> And strykes notte Willys hearte still trewe

Accompanying the poetry was a love letter from Will to his "dearesste Anna" along with a luxuriant lock of brown hair. William-Henry tied the hair—a keepsake from an old girlfriend, actually—with a strip of antique woven silk to "give an imposing air of genuineness to the lock," he later explained. In the love letter, he had Shakespeare tell Anne how carefully he had bound up the lock as his special love token. "Neytherre the gyldedde bawble thatte envyronnes the heade of Majestye noe norre honourres moste weyghtye wulde give mee halfe the joye as didde thysse mye lyttle worke forre thee."

To Samuel and his fellow Bardolaters, these effusions were the most exciting revelation yet about England's cherished author. The letter was not much loftier than whatever note William-Henry's ex-girlfriend might have included with the lock in the first place, and the poetry was sentimental doggerel. But encountered under lamplight as hard-to-decipher script on sepia-colored paper, the documents seemed to be a window directly into Shakespeare's heart.

Samuel, more than anyone, was the perfect target for his son's hoax. His gullibility was an outgrowth of his abundant self-confidence. He was quick to make judgments, and once he made them, he held onto them. Ironically, his certitude could make him, in some situations, a hard man to fool. In the late 1780s, Londoners had flocked to the Sunday evening séances of a Dr. de Mainauduc, trained in Paris in the mystic art of animal magnetism by Dr. Mesmer himself. De Mainauduc was actually an Irishman, and he was no doctor, but society luminaries from Eliza Sheridan to the Duchess of Devonshire had quickly fallen into paralyzing trances at his West London home, to the horrified delight of onlookers. Ireland came one evening with friends and volunteered to be mesmerized. According to an eyewitness, painter Henry Angelo, de Mainauduc subjected the collector to a long rigamarole of gestures and incantations, "but in vain, for his patient, determined not to be conjured or seduced out of his reason, laughed his attempts to scorn."

Ireland's self-assurance, which verged on pigheadedness, was evident in the books he wrote. His favorite authorial expression was "we flatter ourselves." He flattered himself that he could tell good art from bad, decent architecture from dreary, pleasing landscapes from dull ones. He liked to second-guess the attributions of paintings and sculptures. Ireland was so sure of his critical acuity that he would not only attack a building's appearance but also disparage—in print—the person he guessed had built it.

Ireland boasted in some of his prefaces that he relied on no authorities but himself in writing his various books. Later, a few historians would interpret this as an admission that he, like his son, wrote fiction and called it true. The truth was simpler: Samuel Ireland trusted his own judgment far above anyone else's.

IN MID-FEBRUARY 1795, the first reporters arrived at 8 Norfolk Street to see the spectacular literary rarities that Samuel Ireland had on display. The young forger was relieved to find they typically showed as little discernment as his father and his friends had. The *Telegraph*'s reporter pronounced the papers genuine without even looking at them all. Taken together, evidently, the pages exuded Shakespeare's personal stamp. More sensitively, critic James Boaden, who edited a daily London newspaper called the *Oracle*, beheld the papers with a "tremor of purest delight." In the love letter and poem to Anne Hathaway, he detected "the utmost delicacy of passion and poetical spirit." Boaden would come to regret his enthusiasm.

Plenty of Londoners, of course, weren't caught up in the excitement. Many either reserved judgment on the papers or suspected a hoax. Early on, few of the skeptics made their doubts public. One was cleric and occasional playwright Sir Henry Bate Dudley, known as "the Fighting Parson of Grub Street." Bate Dudley in his younger days had been inordinately fond of dueling. Now, as the combative editor of London's *Morning Herald*, he indulged his belligerence by ridiculing public figures and anyone else who displeased him.

On February 17, just days after the first Shakespearean documents went on display at the Irelands' home, Sir Henry—who hadn't bothered to visit—published a mocking news item listing the papers from Mr. H.'s trunk that were on view, along with others that Ireland was promising to exhibit. "In the same chest are said to have been also found an antique MELANGE of *love letters!—professions of faith!—billets doux!—locks of Hair!—and family receipts!*—The only danger, respecting *faith in the discovery,* seems to be from the indiscretion of *finding too much!*" In a follow-up bulletin two days later, the *Herald* announced the discovery of Shakespeare's favorite recipe for a "goodlie plumbe pudinge."

Samuel was infuriated by these light-hearted taunts, which he considered slander. He sent a long letter complaining about the newspaper's "malevolent and injurious" insinuations and demanding a correction. He stopped just short of challenging the editor to a duel. Bate Dudley's one-sentence reply was a picture of baffled innocence: "Your letter to me is of so extraordinary a kind that you must allow me to decline giving you any further answer than acknowledging the receipt of it."

William-Henry, understandably, didn't share his father's indignation. The boy knew that Bate Dudley's witticisms were on the mark. This was new territory for him. His Shakespeare scheme was now being subjected to the glare of publicity, and he was worried that those outside his father's circle, like Bate Dudley, would find his sham obvious. But a part of him savored all the attention he was drawing. As with any author, he realized, he would have been foolish to expect all the public comment to be favorable.

In any case, the *Herald*'s tweak was based on hearsay. In an era when London had a dozen thriving daily newspapers that specialized in sensationalism, sarcasm, and crime—when outrage and denunciation were journalism's lifeblood (one journal called itself the *Tomahawk*)—this was mild stuff. Even Samuel, once he'd calmed down, had to see this was so. Newspapers had been lampooning respectable collectors of old books and manuscripts for most of the century. In the *Tatler* in 1710, Joseph Addison had called the stereotypical book-auction enthusiast a "learned idiot." If Sir Henry failed to appreciate the ineffable preciousness of an expense receipt written by William Shakespeare, the Irelands would take it in stride.

WILLIAM-HENRY WAS now plotting a host of new forgeries. His modus operandi was a mixture of impulsiveness and careful planning. When his early, experimental efforts began flowering into something like a career as Shakespeare's double, he took the precaution of stocking up on antique paper. He kept a large supply of it, along with his specially brewed ink, hidden under a locked window seat at Bingley's office. His best source of old paper was the bookshop of George Verey on St. Martin's Lane, just north of Charing Cross.

The shop was in Great May's Building, an indoor emporium of small shops and art dealers. The locale's reputation wasn't entirely wholesome. In *Taste*, a Samuel Foote comedy performed at Drury Lane in 1752, the building was the site of a fictional workshop where a forger named Scrape painted old masters. When William-Henry turned up at Verey's with the rather suspicious request that he wanted to extract the flyleaves from any disintegrating old books on hand that were roughly two hundred years old, Verey stated his price—five shillings—without arching an eyebrow. What the lad planned to do with all that blank Elizabethan paper wasn't Verey's business.

For a self-taught forger, William-Henry was, in many ways, unusually careful. His attention to detail went beyond procuring old paper on which to write with old-looking ink. To tie loose documents into bundles, as was the custom in storing old papers, he even went to the trouble of using old thread. The idea occurred to him one day when he was accompanying his father to the gallery of the House of Lords to watch King George give a speech. The walls of the rooms leading to the main hall, he noticed, were hung with tattered old tapestries. Hanging back until he was alone, he grabbed a dangling string from a tapestry and pulled until he had unraveled several yards, which he stuffed in his pocket. In the coming months, he snipped short lengths from this wad of antique string whenever tying up documents.

At other times, the boy could be surprisingly indiscreet about what he was up to. An irony of forgery is that its practitioners have to disavow their handiwork; Chatterton's admirers marveled not just that he wrote such beautiful poetry but also that he was content not to take credit for it. William-Henry liked to impress acquaintances by demonstrating his knack for Elizabethan handwriting. On occasion, he would dash off Shakespeare's signature as easily as if it were his own. Unlike Chatterton, William-Henry bridled at not being able to show off his cleverness.

At Bingley's chambers one day in February, not long after finishing *King Lear*, he spent several hours cooking up a note from Queen Elizabeth thanking "goode Masterre William" in 1588 for some "prettye Verses" he'd sent her and requesting of his company of actors a command performance at

Hampton Court, the sooner the better. William-Henry had just found an original autograph from the queen in his father's collection, and he based his script on the letters in her signature. That England's mighty sovereign would write out—without a scribe—a fawning letter to a young actor who had not even begun writing his own plays was certainly a breach of royal decorum, but the forger, like his public, preferred to imagine Will and his queen as dear friends.

Nearly the whole time he worked at the document, a cleaning woman was doing chores in the room. She was accustomed to seeing Bingley's young apprentice hunched over old pieces of foolscap or holding paper over a candle until it started to brown. This time, William-Henry called the woman over and handed her what he'd written. Would she guess that the manuscript was something very old, he asked her. Indeed so, she answered, "adding, with a laugh, that it was very odd I could do such unaccountable strange things."

When William-Henry had begun his indenture at New Inn, he had befriended a lively young fellow named Montague Talbot. He, too, was articled to a conveyancer, and he, too, was bored with his job. Talbot's one love was the theater—he intended to become an actor. He frequented the rowdy patent theaters in the neighborhood, where young apprentices like him could pay for the opportunity to perform before their friends in ragged one-act melodramas.

Talbot had become a regular evening visitor at Norfolk Street, where music and drama were centers of conversation and the company was apt to include the theatrical Linleys. Talbot would eye with bemusement the esoterica crowding Samuel Ireland's glass-fronted cases: the Roman rings, the 250-year-old shoes, the dessert plates painted by Raphael with signs of the zodiac. Like so many noncollectors, he viewed antiquaries as daft. He teased William-Henry about his own fondness for moldering books and antique armor, though he had to admire his friend's mastery of archaic penmanship.

Talbot was out of town when William-Henry began his forgeries in December 1794. Calling at Norfolk Street on his return to London that winter,

Talbot was startled to see that Samuel Ireland's collection now included personal papers of William Shakespeare. In the privacy of William-Henry's room, Talbot was gleeful. "Having seen me imitate old handwritings, he laughingly told me that he was well convinced the deed of Fraser and the other papers were my own fabricating," William-Henry later wrote. The young forger claimed innocence, but his good-humored guest ignored his protests. Talbot was not about to spoil things by sharing his suspicions with the boy's father. He seemed to think that forgery was an excellent prank.

William-Henry's friend had a disconcerting habit of dropping in unexpectedly at Bingley's chambers. It was only with "infinite difficulty" that William-Henry would have time to stuff in a drawer whatever manuscript he was working on whenever Talbot burst in. For the sake of vigilance, he always worked facing a ground-floor window that gave him a view of all comings and goings. One day, Talbot ducked down and crept past the window. "Thus unobserved he suddenly darted into the chambers," William-Henry recalled. Before the forger had a chance to hide the manuscript he was inscribing, Talbot seized his arm with one hand, snatched the paper with the other, "and by this stratagem became at once acquainted with the whole mystery." William-Henry, fearful of his father's rage if he learned all his treasured Shakespeare papers were fakes, pleaded with his friend to stay mum about what he'd seen.

Talbot soon abandoned the legal drudgery he detested and headed for Dublin, intent on making his name as an actor. Before he left, he urged William-Henry to keep him informed of every detail of his latest forgeries and their reception. The two worked out a secret code. Each kept an identical sheet of paper perforated with holes; when placed over a letter that appeared to be gibberish, the holes revealed the sender's real message. The boys' playful subterfuge was a far cry from Mary, Queen of Scots, smuggling elaborately encrypted letters in casks of ale while plotting Elizabeth's assassination in 1586. And Samuel Ireland was not the keen-eyed detective that Elizabeth's spymaster, Sir Francis Walsingham, had been. The boys took a degree of childish pleasure in the caper on which William-Henry had embarked. It was, on one level, a practical joke that had succeeded amazingly well.

Perhaps too well. Samuel Ireland was becoming extremely impatient. Here the great mother lode of Shakespeare's personal papers had at last been located, and the boy was refusing to tell his father where it was. Yes, he understood that this Mr. H. was nervous about publicity, but that was a trifling matter compared to what the discovery meant for England's literary heritage—and, of course, for his own private collection. Why, Samuel demanded, was the boy so slow in turning over new documents? Why did the collector have to wait several days for each new artifact to appear?

He pestered the boy continually for an introduction to the elusive Mr. H. and a chance to dig through the man's trunk himself. Samuel's badgering wasn't something his son had anticipated. By now, the boy was spending his every free moment scribbling on old flyleaves and parchment scraps at New Inn. Forging Shakespeare was hard enough; forging him under pressure was becoming a nightmare.

To appease and distract his father, William-Henry kept promising him new treasures that he'd sighted in Mr. H.'s archive. The gentleman had more than one trunk full of old papers, it seemed. Other rare Shakespearean material had surfaced at his country house, William-Henry told his father. Without thinking through the consequences, he stunned his father with news that he had come across not one but *two* First Folios with uncut leaves. And more: an early edition of Holinshed's *Chronicles*, the historical tales from which Shakespeare had cribbed so many of his plots—this one with marginalia in the playwright's own hand. Not to mention a full-length portrait of the Bard, painted from life.

Like hoaxes before and since, William-Henry noticed that the grander the claims he made, the more eagerly people believed him. Early on, he'd brashly announced to his father—before he'd produced the love poem to Anne Hathaway or even Queen Elizabeth's thank-you note—that he'd discovered an unknown play in Shakespeare's handwriting. The play had never been published or performed, he told his father in amazement. It was an opus new to English literature.

The boy was motivated by a toxic mix of desperation (anything to allay his father's impatience) and near-delusional self-confidence (everything he wrote was being greeted as authentic, so why think small?). He hadn't yet decided what the subject of the play should be, so he gave his father no details at first. His forgeries were starting to take on a life of their own. He was beginning to feel he'd found his life's calling.

FIRST, HOWEVER, THERE were details to attend to. For all his early success, William-Henry knew he was promising more than he could deliver. He understood from listening to his father's friends that the more voluminous and varied the papers were, the more believable they would be. One could imagine Shakespeare's benighted heirs stowing the whole mass in an attic and forgetting about it. William-Henry needed a way to keep up production "without much labor of the brain."

One tactic he devised was to use small slips of old paper for making timeworn miscellanea: playhouse receipts, expense notations, memoranda, and the like. Then he thought of a more ingenious way to placate his father and his fellow Bardolaters: he would "discover" books from Shakespeare's personal library. The great man must have been a voracious reader, people agreed, yet no one had ever come across a book with his signature or book plate.

Surreptitiously, William-Henry began buying vast quantities of old books at shops in and around Fleet Street and the Strand and carting them back to New Inn. In a short time, the floor in his office was piled with nearly one hundred musty volumes, among them sermons, a two-volume edition of Spenser's *Faerie Queen* from the 1590s, and John Foxe's ever-popular *Book of Martyrs* from 1563. When he began bringing them home to his father in twos and threes, Samuel was gratified to see that Shakespeare had taken care to sign the title page of every book. William-Henry had filled the margins with handwritten notes, especially alongside passages about Shakespeare's kings. In the margins of an account of the 1605 execution of Guy Fawkes, he had the sensitive playwright confess that he hadn't attended the hanging as he "lykedde notte toe beholde syghtes of thatte kynde." The boy never delivered the promised Holinshed's *Chronicles* to his father, but not because he didn't try. He couldn't find an edition with margins big enough to write in.

Despite the pressures he was under, William-Henry was settling into his role as Shakespeare's impersonator. His schemes were gulling people who should have known better. Francis Webb, the secretary of the College of Heralds—an organization known for its expertise in old documents—pronounced the marginalia in Shakespeare's newly unearthed library to be just the sort of jottings one would have expected of him. Peering at the worn pages of Shakespeare's books, Webb was entranced. In a pamphlet he published in 1796, he wrote that he could "see this immortal poet rise again to life, holding these sacred relics in one hand, and hear him say, *These were mine.*"

One of the visitors to Norfolk Street offered Samuel the lavish sum of sixty pounds for the autographed *Faerie Queen* alone. Ireland dismissed the suggestion out of hand. He was not so crass as to discuss the Shakespeare trove as a commodity to be traded away for bank notes. In any case, he knew from his son that young Mr. H. had refused an offer of two thousand pounds for the whole lot (nearly £100,000 or more than $150,000 today), having judged its real worth to be at least ten times as much. Fortunately, the high-minded Mr. H., a man of his word, was letting Samuel's nineteen-year-old son take whatever he wanted—and for nothing. If Samuel had thought about it, he would have realized that the generosity of Mr. H.'s arrangement was even stranger than the fecundity of his bottomless trunk.

William-Henry had given his father a semiplausible explanation of why he stood so prominently in the good gentleman's favor. The legal work that the young clerk had done for Mr. H. soon after meeting him had been un-expectedly fruitful. "During my research among the deeds of my friend," he told his father, "I discovered one which established his right to certain property that had long been an object of litigation." William-Henry had thereby saved his gentleman friend a considerable sum of money. Letting William-Henry keep whatever Shakespeare manuscripts he found seemed to Mr. H. like fair compensation.

Samuel accepted the story but continued to nag his son for an introduction. William-Henry reminded his father of Mr. H.'s insistence on complete anonymity. Samuel settled for giving his son a letter to pass along to his young benefactor. In it, the collector requested permission of Mr. H. to announce formally the papers' discovery and his own custody of them. Trying unsuccessfully to hide his unquenchable desire for more of everything, Samuel also asked when he could expect more documents, "not only papers but pictures drawings &c." And he reminded Mr. H. that he awaited the full-length oil portrait of the Bard. He could already picture it hanging over his drawing-room mantel.

Samuel was heartened by the swiftness of Mr. H.'s reply, even if it dodged most of his inquiries. Instead, in courteous language and graceful handwriting that the collector didn't recognize as his son's, the letter delivered a spirited defense of the character and abilities of young William-Henry. "It may appear strange," Mr. H. wrote, "that a young man like myself should have thus formed a friendship for one whom he has so little knowledge of but I do assure you Dear Sir without flattery that he is the young man after my own heart in whom I would confide and even consult on the nicest affair."

A lively correspondence would ensue in the following months between the collector and his son's imaginary friend. In succeeding letters, Mr. H. struck a more personal tone. The gentleman had heard that Samuel looked askance at his son's unpowdered and ever-lengthening hair. Mr. H. advised Samuel that his son's "flowing locks" were much in fashion. What's more, he protested, "You cannot be an enemy to the manner in which our Willy wore his hair." William-Henry was finding the fanciful Mr. H. a useful ally in confronting his overbearing father.

As Mr. H. didn't explicitly forbid Samuel from publicizing the papers' discovery, Samuel felt he was within his rights to do so. He was then, in early 1795, readying for publication his *Picturesque Views on the Upper, or Warwickshire Avon*, with its ruminations on Stratford and the town's most famous inhabitant. In the book's preface, he disclosed that since visiting Shakespeare's birthplace, he had acquired a unique literary treasure:

It is [the author's] intention, so soon as opportunity shall serve, to lay before the public a variety of authentic and important documents respecting the private and public life of this wonderful man: one of his most affecting and admired Tragedies [*King Lear*], written with his own hand, and differing in various particulars of much curiosity and interest from any edition of that work now extant; and at a future day to present a picture of that mind which no one has yet ever presumed to copy, an entire Drama! yet unknown to the world, in his own hand-writing.

Samuel at this point had never seen the manuscript of the unknown play, and he had no idea of its title or subject. He had it only on his teenage son's authority that Mr. H. possessed the treasured document and that he, Samuel Ireland, was to become its custodian. The collector could be as impulsive as his son. And he fiercely wanted to believe.

CHAPTER SIX

THE LOST MASTERPIECE

ILLIAM-HENRY HAD promised his father a new play by William Shakespeare. Now he had to write it.

Despite other demands on his time—answering visitors' questions at Norfolk Street about the papers' discovery, restocking trips to various dealers and shops, and the production of other, smaller forgeries to corroborate his earlier ones—the boy set to work at Bingley's deserted office at New Inn. Like Shakespeare two hundred years before, he kept close at hand a copy of Holinshed's *Chronicles*, borrowed from a mahogany case in his father's study. Having "with my usual impetuosity" told his father of the play's existence "before a single line was really executed," William-Henry later wrote, he had been "unceasingly tormented for the manuscript, which I brought forward in small portions as I found time to compose it."

He chose as his subject a fifth-century English warlord-turned-king named Vortigern and a young woman named Rowena with whom, according to legend, he fell in love. A print of Rowena giving wine to Vortigern had long hung prominently above the fireplace in the Irelands' study. Somehow this coincidence never troubled the boy's father.

The tale of Vortigern was a story worthy of Shakespeare, certainly. Had the Bard lived longer, he might well have adapted it from his own well-thumbed Holinshed. At the outset of William-Henry's new drama, old king Constantius decides, Learlike, to divide his kingdom, giving half to brave Vortigern. The crafty warlord, a distillation of Lord and Lady Macbeth, begins scheming immediately to increase his share. In an opening-scene soliloquy, the would-be king takes stock of his situation:*

> *Fortune, I thank thee!*
> *Now is the cup of my ambition full!*
> *And, by the rising tempest in my blood,*
> *I feel the fast approach of greatness, which,*
> *E'en like a peasant, stoops for my acceptance.*
> *Yet hold: O! conscience, how is't with thee?*
> *Why dost thou whisper? should I heed thee now,*
> *My fabric crumbles, and must fall to nought?*
> *Come, then, thou soft, thou double-fac'd deceit!*
> *Come, fawning flattery! silence-sealing murder!*
> *Attend me quick, and prompt me to the deed!*
> *What! jointly wear the crown? No! I will all!*

William-Henry's familiarity with Shakespeare's language was paying off. His play was choppy and sometimes confusing, the pace uneven, the poetry often trite, but some passages in *Vortigern and Rowena* were undeniably gripping. At a banquet in Act 4, the king's sons object when he invites comely Rowena to sit next to him in a seat that belongs to their mother, the queen. Vortigern explodes in rage:

> *Must I then humble,*
> *And stoop the neck to bear my children's yoke?*

---

* The original forgery has disappeared. What follows is from the version of the play that William-Henry published in 1832.

Begone, I say! lest that my present wrath
Make me forget the place by blood I hold,
And break the tie 'twixt father and his child.

It was a situation William-Henry knew all too well, a father berating his sons. At heart, however, the play was a pastiche of characters and scenes lifted from Shakespeare's repertoire. William-Henry borrowed liberally not only from *Lear* and *Macbeth* but also from *Richard III, Hamlet, Pericles, Julius Caesar, As You Like It*, and other plays. He stuffed his elaborate plot with betrayals, conspiracies, deceptions, murder, love, abandonment, and warfare.

Early on, William-Henry had realized he'd never be able to deliver the play fast enough to placate his father if he wrote every scene in Shakespeare's handwriting. Instead, he wrote the opening scenes on antique paper in his flowery secretary hand, but thereafter he wrote the pages in his own handwriting. He explained to his father that Mr. H. was hanging on to the original a bit longer so that he could have built for it an iron case to be covered in red velvet and studded with gold. In the meantime, the collector would have to be content with a transcription that his son was making from Shakespeare's pages. Grudgingly, Samuel accepted the arrangement.

William-Henry resented his father's impatience. After all, the young forger was composing his first drama almost as quickly and as fluently as Shakespeare had written his own—and without a draft. Even with constant interruptions, William-Henry was to complete the play in just six weeks. It seemed absurd that he could be expected to work more furiously than he was already doing. He wanted to proclaim his rare talent to his father and his literary friends: he was writing Shakespearean verse almost as fast as his pen could move.

Vortigern's conscience may have bothered him, but William-Henry's remained unclouded. He was proud to be carrying on the work that Shakespeare had begun. He seemed only dimly aware that he was imitating, not creating, like a pianist who could improvise in the style of Mozart but never played anything memorable. Unlike Chatterton, who pretended his poems had been written by an unknown, William-Henry had chosen to imitate England's most famous writer. What plaudits he was to win would always be posthumous praise for Shakespeare more than appreciation for William-Henry Ireland.

BY LATE FEBRUARY 1795, Samuel had on display in his drawing room the opening pages of *Vortigern and Rowena* in Shakespeare's handwriting, the complete manuscript of *King Lear*, the profession of faith, the love letter to Anne Hathaway, and assorted other documents. The Irelands' home was becoming a pilgrimage site for Shakespeare lovers of all kinds. The collector, ensconced like a monarch in his Shakespeare chair, liked to choose from among his prized documents, call for quiet, and read aloud a few choice passages. For the hushed visitors, hearing the Bard's unpublished words was at least as transfixing as Dr. de Mainauduc's ministrations had been.

Handling of the sacred relics was part of the worshipful ritual. The oversized deed on parchment with its dangling seals was passed gingerly from hand to hand. The lock of dark hair from the love-struck Will of eighteen was stroked with curious fingers. But it was the unfinished *Vortigern* manuscript that was the center of attention. Guests seldom inspected more than a few pages, but Samuel's full-throated readings from it were persuasive enough. To allay the puzzlement of visitors as to why Shakespeare had kept this magnum opus hidden from view, unpublished and unperformed, William-Henry forged a letter suggesting the playwright viewed it as his crowning achievement, so he deserved a higher fee for it than his printer was willing to pay.

The College of Heralds' Francis Webb, transported by his proximity to Shakespeare's letters and manuscripts, lost his ability to think critically. After a visit, he wrote a friend: "These papers bear not only the signature of his hand; but the stamp of his soul, and the traits of his genius. His mind is as manifest as his hand." The *Oracle*'s James Boaden was just as certain the papers came from Shakespeare's hand. "The conviction produced upon our mind," he grandly wrote, "is such as to make all skepticism ridiculous." Boaden labeled his rival editor at the *Morning Herald*, the unbelieving Henry Bate Dudley, an "ignoramus."

On the snowy afternoon of February 20, a carriage pulled up at Norfolk Street containing the eminent writer and man-about-town James Boswell. Years later, William-Henry would recall the occasion vividly. Seated in the Irelands' study, Boswell, now portly and double-chinned, held up the opening pages of *Vortigern* to the lamplight and squinted at the florid penmanship through his spectacles for long minutes. Several times he interrupted his excited inspection to call for hot brandy and water. Finally, the great man set down the manuscript, took off his spectacles, lowered his bulk unsteadily into a kneeling position, and kissed the topmost page. "I shall now die contented," he breathed, "since I have lived to see the present day." Boswell died three months later, presumably content.

In his calmer moments, William-Henry realized that the flattery he was hearing was misplaced. Of Francis Webb's delirious praise of his writing, he later wrote: "His enthusiastic regard for every thing relating to our immortal Shakspeare (which for once overcame his better judgement) has led him to pour forth praises . . . much above my humble deserts." The boy was to learn firsthand the hollowness of so many claims of literary expertise. It was a useful lesson for any ambitious young writer. Moreover, although the sweep and seriousness of his hoax had blossomed well beyond the bounds of a practical joke, he still took a prankster's satisfaction in watching it succeed.

William-Henry realized, too, that the steadier the flow of visitors to Norfolk Street, the more likely it was that doubters would begin to make their voices heard. He was particularly nervous about the impending visit of Joseph Ritson, a well-known scholar and critic. Ritson, who had spent much of his life collecting old ballads about Robin Hood, was an eccentric, cantankerous man. One of his eccentricities was his abrupt way of speaking. Originally named Richardson, he had changed the spelling to match his pronunciation.

In print, Ritson was pathologically ill-tempered and abusive. In 1782, he had attacked poet laureate Thomas Warton as a cheat and a liar. Samuel

Johnson and his fellow Shakespeare editor George Steevens were inexcusably ignorant; Bishop Thomas Percy, a befuddled fool. "Of the numerous individuals who came to inspect the manuscripts, no one excited my fear so much," William-Henry wrote. "The sharp physiognomy, the piercing eye, and the silent scrutiny of Mr. Ritson filled me with a dread I had never before experienced." While studying the papers, the critic said very little, but his questions to William-Henry about their source were sharp and to the point. The boy was sure that Ritson saw through the fraud immediately. "He was not to be hoodwinked," William-Henry wrote. Without a word of small talk, with no congratulations or any expression of surprise at the documents laid out before him, the visitor turned and left as abruptly as he'd arrived.

To the forger's relief, Ritson never made public his verdict on what he'd seen. In a letter to a collector friend in Edinburgh, however, Ritson made his thoughts clear: "The Shakspeare papers, of which you have heard so much, . . . are, I can assure you, a parcel of forgeries, studiously and ably calculated to deceive the public." He judged them to be the work of "some person of genius and talents"—not one of the Irelands, certainly—who "ought to have been better employed." Ritson marveled that the forger had gone to the trouble of procuring parchments and seals that were "indisputably ancient & authentic." He concluded the forger had laboriously erased the original writing on them.

Why Ritson never sounded the alarm publicly is a mystery. Perhaps, having attacked a bishop, a poet laureate, and two of eighteenth-century England's most distinguished Shakespeare editors, he viewed the Irelands as unworthy of his wrath. Or perhaps he enjoyed seeing so many self-professed literary experts making fools of themselves, and he didn't want to discourage them.

By the mid-1790s, in any case, Ritson's opinions didn't carry as much weight as they once had. Not long after his visit to the Irelands, he began slipping into dementia. He died several years later in a London insane asylum, where he'd been taken after barricading himself in his rooms at Gray's Inn and making a bonfire of his manuscript collection.

In late February, to combat rumors that the Shakespeare papers were fakes, a core group of believers took a united stand. Boswell composed an endorsement of the papers for everyone to sign. The pugnacious headmaster and critic Samuel Parr rejected Boswell's wording as too tepid. Parr hadn't even a fleeting doubt that the papers were Shakespeare's. In his view, "they were either written by Shakespeare or the Devil." Parr immediately drew up a more ringing declaration for everyone to sign. This Certificate of Belief, in William-Henry's recollection, stated that the undersigned "entertained no doubt whatsoever as to the validity of the Shaksperian production." (Parr left out the possibility that the devil was responsible.) Thereafter, whenever visitors to Norfolk Street finished admiring the yellowed documents, Samuel would guide them to the certificate on a small table nearby and ask if he could trouble them for their signatures.

In a short time, a who's who of English dignitaries had affixed their names to the testament: Warton, Parr, Boswell, and Webb, of course, as well as Samuel's old friend Herbert Croft, whose defense of Chatterton in *Love and Madness* had unwittingly helped inspire William-Henry's escapade. Innumerable scholars, poets, and clergymen signed the document. So, too, did several distinguished members of the Society of Antiquaries, the club that had scorned Samuel's attempt to join it six years earlier. Henry Pye lent the prestige of his office—he was England's reigning poet laureate—even if "the poetical Pye," as novelist and antiquarian Sir Walter Scott referred to him, was "eminently respectable in everything but his poetry." Of more importance to Samuel, a duke, an earl, and a baron all signed, as did the Garter king of arms, Sir Isaac Heard. Georgian England was preoccupied with social status; a gentleman with a title was a more impressive ally than a gentleman of learning. Samuel may well have fantasized about the day when he, too, would be elevated to the peerage.

Edmond Malone, then widely considered the foremost Shakespeare scholar in England, knew all about the Shakespeare papers at the Irelands' home. In London literary circles, Malone was a less vitriolic but far more influential critic than Joseph Ritson was. His publisher was on the Strand a few blocks east of Norfolk Street, and he often passed within sight of the

Irelands' front door. Yet Malone had no interest in stopping in to see the papers for himself. Even if he had, he was quite certain he would not have added his signature to Samuel Ireland's Certificate of Belief.

THAT WINTER, William-Henry made a careless mistake that almost led him to confess everything to his father. Years later, the incident would cast a shadow in turn on Samuel's innocence.

As part of his effort to fabricate a believable miscellany of old papers from Shakespeare's life, William-Henry one day dashed off a one-sentence receipt on a slip of old paper and signed it, as usual, with the playwright's name. On the receipt, the Bard acknowledged receiving fifty pounds from Queen Elizabeth's favorite, the Earl of Leicester, for a performance by Shakespeare's troupe at Kenilworth Castle, the earl's Warwickshire home. The receipt was dated 1590.

When William-Henry presented the document to his father that evening, the collector recognized at once that something was wrong. It was well-known, even if William-Henry had never learned it, that Leicester had died shortly after commanding the ground troops massed to repel the Spanish Armada in 1588. If the receipt was genuine, Shakespeare had procrastinated two years before writing it.

Samuel immediately called his son's attention to the discrepancy. Surely Shakespeare's company hadn't staged a play for the entertainment of a dead nobleman. William-Henry felt his muscles tighten. He forced himself to breathe normally. For one long moment, he thought his career as Shakespeare's alter ego was over. But to his surprise, his father was neither outraged nor confounded by the telltale date. Nor did he seem to connect his son with the document's flaw. Instead, he began tossing out rationalizations for it. Perhaps Shakespeare had forgotten to date it until later, or maybe it was a sloppily made copy. Whatever had happened, the two agreed the misdated receipt was a problem. The boy offered to burn it on the spot. Nonsense, his father replied. The receipt was too valuable to be destroyed. It was signed by Shakespeare, wasn't it? Instead, he let his son just tear off the corner with the offending date.

In his published *Confessions* in 1805, William-Henry never mentioned the details of this near-calamity. He wrote that he himself caught the error and tore off the date before showing the receipt to anyone. This account was obviously an attempt to protect his father from being labeled an accomplice, for in an unpublished account he admitted his father's role in altering the supposedly priceless document.

Later, it would be widely assumed that Samuel Ireland was in on the forgeries and perhaps had orchestrated them. It's clear from his diary and from private letters he wrote to his son before his death in 1800, however, that he never stopped believing the papers were authentic historical relics. He certainly never dreamed his son was delivering them as soon as the ink had dried. In Samuel's view, Mr. H. and his trunk were real, and his son was little more than Mr. H.'s errand boy. It was a perfectly believable scenario to him. Like everyone else in England at the time, Samuel had every reason to expect that Shakespeare's writings were lying uncatalogued and forgotten in someone's dusty country manor. In William-Henry's unpublished opinion, his father was "absolutely blind" to what he had been up to. If his father had been more observant—if he had been suspicious about the misdated receipt and asked the boy if he had forged it—"I could not have resisted but made a full disclosure."

As for why Samuel was willing to tamper with a Shakespearean relic, the most plausible explanation is that Samuel assumed that all of the papers were authentic historic documents but that perhaps, just perhaps, they weren't all from Shakespeare's hand. Someone early in the seventeenth century—a well-meaning heir or admirer—could have forged some of the documents, motivated by the tragic absence of the Bard's authentic papers or by guilt at not having preserved them. Samuel had no way of knowing. The collector wanted to believe that the Shakespeare papers were genuine. From what he could tell, they were.

But Samuel Ireland was not an unbiased observer. If contrary evidence surfaced, he suppressed it with as free a conscience as if he were shouting down the opinions of a rival collector. Whatever qualms he may have felt about the papers, his greed as a collector likely overwhelmed whatever natural skepticism he may have had. And he didn't have much: witness the wooing chair and the mulberry cup. With his son adding rare Shakespeare manuscripts to his collection week by week, Samuel may not have wanted to dwell too deeply on the source of his good fortune.

CARRIAGES WERE NOW pulling up at 8 Norfolk Street at all hours—at breakfast time, even on weekends. The curious and the skeptical debarked to see for themselves the miraculous Shakespeare papers. Some of the visitors were strangers who arrived without an introduction. The Ireland home was taking on the character of a public gallery, which neither Samuel nor the servants were entirely happy about. This was the home of an important private collector, not the manager of an amusement hall. In early March, he began limiting visiting hours to Monday, Wednesday, and Friday, noon to three PM.

Although Samuel never considered selling any of his son's discoveries, he had been thinking a great deal about other ways to cash in on the windfall. He decided his next book would be a portfolio of the Shakespeare papers in reproduction. Those who signed up in advance for a copy would be given tickets allowing them admission to view the manuscripts.

William-Henry objected vehemently to the idea of publishing the papers, claiming Mr. H. refused permission. Until now, they'd been hard-to-read curios. People eager to see them had no choice but to visit the Irelands' home, where they'd struggle to decipher the swooping handwriting as Samuel hovered nearby with a proprietary air.

Should the nineteen-year-old's writings now be set into type, they would be subject to clear-eyed scrutiny by paying customers. William-Henry understood the danger. For all the flattery his writings had inspired, what truly stirred those who saw them was the feeling of holding the ancient pages the Bard had inscribed. "I had an idea of hazarding every opprobrium and confessing the fact [of forgery], rather than witness the publications of the papers," he wrote.

In the back of his mind, he was aware of a graver danger than exposure and humiliation. In London's business world, forgery was a hanging offense. Convicted forgers over the past century had been sent to the gallows regularly. Several of the cases in recent decades had been public sensations. In 1775, a pair of fashionable West End gentlemen, identical twins named Robert and Daniel Perreau, were tried for forging bonds in order to cover gambling debts. In their defense, the twins tried to shift blame for their elaborate scheme onto Daniel's mistress. This unsportsmanlike stratagem ensured that a loud and unruly crowd attended the brothers' hanging at Tyburn.

Two years later, an even more respectable gentleman, William Dodd— a popular preacher, chaplain to the king, and author of *The Beauties of Shakespeare* no less—was hanged for the same crime. Dodd, another dandy with a gambling habit, had forged a £4,200 bond in the name of Philip Stanhope, the future Fourth Earl of Chesterfield, whose tutor he'd been. (This was the same Philip whose hedonistic pursuits in France had drawn a scolding from the Third Earl.) Prominent public figures urged the king to pardon the imprisoned cleric. Samuel Johnson wrote a contrite sermon in Dodd's name—a forgery, in effect—entitled "The Convict's Address to His Unhappy Brethren." When a skeptical friend questioned how Dodd could have written such an elegant essay, Johnson made his famous remark: "Depend upon it, sir, when a man knows he is to be hanged in a fortnight, it concentrates the mind wonderfully."

William-Henry, like any Londoner, was well aware of these notorious cases. Law clerk that he was, he had a smattering of legal knowledge, though it was sketchy. He told himself he wasn't a forger-for-profit like Dodd or the Perreau twins. No, he was a poet, like Chatterton—he was crafting works of beauty. In any case, up to now no money had changed hands, he reminded himself, so no fraud had occurred. Literary deception, in itself, wasn't a criminal offense. But having the forgeries appear in print, he later wrote, "would throw a degree of infamy on the business, as the receipt of money would stamp it a pecuniary transaction." Whether that would put him in the same league as Dodd and the Perreaus he very much doubted. Still, the idea of publishing his forgeries was making him uneasy, if not exactly conscience-stricken.

His father refused to be deterred. He kept badgering William-Henry about why Mr. H. objected to seeing the papers published. At one point, desperate to check his father's relentless pressure, the young forger asked him, "Suppose they should not be really manuscripts of Shakspeare's?" Even if England's greatest authors confessed they had conspired to produce them, Samuel replied, "I would not believe them."

Up until now, William-Henry had imagined that eventually, when the time was right, he would reveal to his father his astonishing achievement. He wasn't clear about how this would play out. The collector would be pained to learn that his precious Shakespeare papers were forgeries. On the other hand, he could only rejoice to learn that his own son was the eighteenth century's embodiment of Shakespeare. But now the boy was becoming aware of unforeseen obstacles to this happy ending. If his father would never believe that a team of illustrious writers had secretly written the papers, how would he ever be persuaded that his untalented, unremarkable son had composed them single-handedly?

William-Henry finally gave in to his father's pestering and said that Mr. H. grudgingly consented to the papers' publication. A few days later, on March 5, Samuel issued a prospectus for an expensive, subscription-only volume to be published at Christmastime. The book would be a large leather-bound folio edition, perfectly matched for display with folio collections of Shakespeare's works, for those subscribers who owned one.

Folios, whose pages were half the size of a full printed sheet, were increasingly rare. Four years earlier, when Boswell toyed with printing his *Life of Johnson* in folio, Malone talked him out of it: "You might as well throw it into the Thames, for a folio would not now be read."

The new Shakespeare folio would contain engraved facsimiles of all the papers except *Vortigern and Rowena*, which would be the centerpiece of a second volume. Samuel's prospectus promised "authentic and important documents of this wondrous man," including the full handwritten first draft of *King Lear*. The love note to Anne Hathaway he referred to teasingly, like a carnival barker, as "the expression and feeling of his very soul upon a subject the most momentous that can occupy the thoughts of mortal man." Along with the facsimiles, the book would provide transcripts of all the documents. The price was four guineas—about what a workingman earned in two months.

Malone's observation notwithstanding, more than one hundred people subscribed in short order. They included some of England's most important public figures. In addition to the loyal Believers who had signed the Certificate of Belief, these included Richard Brinsley Sheridan, Prime Minister William Pitt the younger, philosopher Edmund Burke, poet Robert Southey, the Duke of Leeds, the Earl of Charlemont, Viscount Torrington, the actress Dora Jordan, and old Shylock himself, Charles Macklin, now nearly a hundred years old.

THIS WAS VASTLY better treatment than any of Shakespeare's written works received in his lifetime. During his career as a London playwright, in fact, Shakespeare appeared not to care greatly whether his plays were printed and sold for popular consumption. The publication of plays was almost an afterthought. At a time when most people in England were barely literate, live performances were what mattered.

Nearly half of Shakespeare's plays never appeared in print until the First Folio was published in 1623, seven years after his death. The theater friends who compiled the texts sometimes had to scrounge for old prompt books—copies of play scripts made by a theater's scribe—and then piece scenes together. In many cases, passages could be reconstructed only by tracking down actors who had played a part years before and asking them to recite their lines from memory. Printers both before and after the playwright's death used their own judgment in interpreting the handwritten pages they had to work from, giving rise to multiple versions of the plays.

Hamlet variously bemoaned his "too, too solid flesh" and his "too, too sullied flesh."

Beyond that, there was the issue of editorial tampering in the ensuing two centuries. Not surprisingly, it was hard for people in England in 1795 to know what exactly Shakespeare had written. There were no authenticated manuscripts and no texts printed with the author's explicit approval. Small wonder that so many people who had come to the Irelands' home to judge for themselves if the papers were authentic were a trifle unsure of what they were looking for.

CHAPTER SEVEN

THE AGE OF FORGERY

ONE DAY EARLY in 1795, as William-Henry was racing to keep up with his father's demand for manuscripts, his vial of special ink ran dry. By this time, the discovery of the Shakespeare papers had been trumpeted by London's newspapers, and much of the public was acquainted with the story of how William-Henry Ireland, the collector's son, had found them in a trunk. Amid the clamor, the boy was apprehensive about venturing out to restock his forgery supplies. But in his own heedless way, he was a perfectionist. He wanted his ink to look two hundred years old, so he had no choice. He had soliloquies to write and battles to stage. And his father was waiting, impatiently.

From his chambers at New Inn, William-Henry walked briskly to the dim passageway nearby, where Thomas Laurie's bindery was hidden. When he'd stopped in a few months earlier to show off his first attempt at forgery—the minister's note to Queen Elizabeth—William-Henry had been cavalier about what he was up to. He'd laughed as he'd explained to Laurie and his two assistants that he wanted to see if he could fool his collector father. This time, he made no small talk, and he hoped none of the other New Inn law clerks he knew popped in while he was there.

The same young bindery man who had formulated his original vial of ink was in the shop. William-Henry told him, as casually as he could, that he'd like a new batch. Neither Laurie nor his helper made any comment about this curious yen for old-fashioned ink, "although the fame of the manuscripts was perfectly well known to them, and I was the person supposed to have discovered them." Without a word, the assistant brewed his mixture of ink, which he tinged with a bit of acid until it frothed. He charged the same fee as before, one shilling.

The three men in the shop seemed utterly unruffled that one of their young customers was a forger. Later, after skeptics had gone to great lengths to expose the manuscripts' flaws, William-Henry was amused to think that Laurie or his assistants could have instantly "blown apart the entire fabric of deception to the winds," had they cared to.

This was apparently not the first time the bindery man had mixed his special blend of new ink that looked old. Indeed, William-Henry was just one among many people in England who were then faking old manuscripts and documents for their own purposes. Few were as skillful and none as ambitious, or as reckless, as William-Henry Ireland. Their collective efforts, however, would cause historians to look back at the eighteenth century as the Age of Forgery.

IN A BROAD SENSE, forged writings had abounded in Britain for centuries. Faked or altered documents were an age-old means of enhancing a genealogy, redirecting an inheritance, or bestowing ecclesiastical favor. Shakespeare was familiar enough with forgery to use it as a convenient plot device, sometimes for comic purposes, sometimes for moral ones. In *Twelfth Night*, the dour steward, Malvolio, makes a fool of himself after a forged letter leads him to believe that Lady Olivia is infatuated with him and that she'd love him all the more if he wore long yellow stockings and smiled constantly. In a less innocent vein, Hamlet thwarts Claudius's secret order that he be executed during a trip to England by substituting a forged letter, sealed with his late father's signet ring, that condemns Rosencrantz and Guildenstern to death instead.

Printers in Shakespeare's day indulged in a casual sort of forgery: They put his name on the title page of plays he had no hand in writing. It wasn't illegal, and it wasn't quite forgery, but it was an underhanded way to boost sales. More than a century later, in 1747, novelist Henry Fielding complained of the same thing: Booksellers "have indeed behaved to me like the most infamous harlots, and have laid many a spurious as well as deformed production at my door." In these cases, he added sarcastically, "my good friends the critics have, in their profound discernment, discovered some resemblance of the parent."

With the explosion in printing and literacy in eighteenth-century England, literary forgery and other kinds of mass-produced artifice became widespread. The notion of authorship was still hazy. As in Shakespeare's time, authenticity was a slippery concept. ("What fools these mortals be!" weren't even Shakespeare's words. He stole them from the Roman philosopher Seneca the Younger.) Literary piracy, disguised authorship, unrestrained plagiarism—all were routine. Most people didn't care.

Among England's pioneering novelists, it was common to present a story as a true-life account that they'd happened upon or been given. Many readers assumed that Daniel Defoe's *Robinson Crusoe*, published in 1719, was an autobiography written by the plucky castaway; some probably wondered how Crusoe's man Friday was adapting to life in England, following the story's happy ending. Defoe drew on a real-life incident, but he mixed fact and fiction as he saw fit.

Embellished accounts of the careers of notorious criminals, climaxing with poignant last words as the executioner stood by, were perennial best sellers in eighteenth-century England. Both Fielding and Defoe wrote "biographies" of the notorious bandit Jonathan Wild, hanged at Tyburn in 1725. In Fielding's rollicking account, the scoundrel picks the pocket of the clergyman praying for him just before he's sent swinging. In his own version of Wild's life story, Defoe wrote with more solemnity, if not accuracy. In his book's preface, Defoe chided his many rival chroniclers for incorporating "so much falsehood and fable as to smother and drown that little truth which is at the bottom of it." Defoe's "history," as he called his largely fictional account, avoided mockery and ridicule, even if that displeased some readers. "They that had rather have a falsehood to laugh at than a true account of things to inform them, had best buy the fiction, and leave the history to those who know how to distinguish good from evil."

This self-professed historian, in other words, wasn't concerned with what really happened. He was concerned with what should have happened. To Defoe, the truth, so often confusing and inconclusive, mattered less than a good moral fable. Years later, William-Henry Ireland would view his very different task in much the same light. Even if we could know the real Shakespeare, perhaps we wouldn't want to. Better to fashion a Shakespeare we can all cherish and admire.

Books like *Robinson Crusoe* and *Jonathan Wild* weren't forgeries, of course, but they illustrated the reading public's tolerance for falsified history. Crusoe and Friday never made public appearances to buttress their story, and Wild was obviously unavailable, but a man named George Psalmanazar invented a whole persona to go with his remarkable life story.

Psalmanazar had arrived in England as a young man in 1703, supposedly a cannibal from the pagan island of Formosa, present-day Taiwan. Few people were bothered that he didn't look at all Asian—he was, in truth, a Frenchman from Avignon. The following year, he published an illustrated book about his imaginary homeland, where people routinely lived past 100 and his own grandfather was vigorous until his death at 117, thanks to his habit of sucking blood from a viper each morning. At an annual festival on Formosa, 18,000 boys under the age of 9 were sacrificed and their hearts burned on a pyre. To counter objections that this would in time depopulate the island, Psalmanazar explained that each family's oldest son was exempt from being sacrificed and was allowed a harem of wives to help him reproduce.

The book was a sensation and sold out immediately. Psalmanazar, or whatever his name was, briefly became a society darling. At dinner with Sir Hans Sloane, he impressed the learned collector by eating raw meat, supposedly a native custom. He enthralled scholars by speaking snatches of a language he called Formosan, for which he had devised a system of grammar and a unique right-to-left alphabet. To communicate with Englishmen, however, Psalmanazar spoke remarkably fluent Latin.

As it happened, a firsthand account of life and culture in Formosa was readily available at the time. A Dutch missionary had published a book earlier about his life on Formosa, where cannibalism was unheard of and the diet was mostly rice, fruit, and (cooked) fish. Psalmanazar's description was much preferred, however: It was more horrifying and exciting than the missionary's account—which Psalmanazar dismissed as a hoax. Indeed, the impostor's fanciful descriptions of tame rhinoceroses and camels, of copious gold and silver mines, seemed to mollify potential doubters. His stories were exactly what England wanted to read.

Eventually, the burden of keeping up his elaborate hoax proved to be more than he could handle, and critics succeeded in debunking it. Psalmanazar lived out his life in London as an opium-addicted hack who wrote anonymous pamphlets for booksellers. He confessed his imposture in his memoirs, published after his death in 1763 at age eighty-three.

Historians would later brand the eighteenth century the Age of Enlightenment, but the label was never a perfect fit. This was a time, after all, when people still believed in alchemy, palmistry, geomancy, wizardry, and magical nostrums. In London, hordes of people flocked at night to haunted houses, where they crowded into rooms by candlelight, thrilling to every unidentified noise. Joseph Addison and even level-headed Samuel Johnson judged that witchcraft was real.

Furthermore, a well-calculated hoax could have far more impact than in centuries past, thanks to England's growing class of scholar-experts. These men offered their opinions freely on matters of public interest, whatever their expertise. If a bizarre claim withstood the experts' fallible scrutiny, it came to be seen as accepted wisdom. The news, for example, that a young Surrey woman, Mary Tofts, had given birth to a litter of rabbits—an event accepted as fact by a string of prominent physicians—so riveted England in 1726 that much of the nation swore off rabbit stew for months.

A boom in document forgery, the creation of manuscripts that seemed old but weren't, was one of the salient features of the age. Oddly enough, the boom was fueled not only by widespread gullibility but also by what, in some ways, was its opposite: a growing interest in reliable historical texts. With nostalgia for Old England on the rise, people eager to understand the past were no longer satisfied with Herodotus's approach to history, which drew on hearsay and old tales. For the first time, primary sources were prized over secondary ones. This new interest in antique writings was an open invitation to forgers of all kinds.

Perhaps the most successful of these was James Macpherson, a Gaelic-speaking Scot who managed to be buried in Westminster Abbey in early 1796, just as William-Henry Ireland's shorter and more dizzying career was reaching its crescendo. In 1760, when he was twenty-three, Macpherson published *Fragments of Ancient Poetry Collected in the Highlands of Scotland*, a short anthology of heroic narrative poetry. He claimed to have gathered the poems in remote areas of Scotland and then translated them from Gaelic into English.

The following year, Macpherson announced the discovery of an epic in the same vein by a blind third-century Celtic bard named Ossian. It was a prose poem filled with imagery of storms, wild nature, mysterious supernatural forces, and a pervading air of heroic doom—the essence of late-eighteenth-century Romantic poetry, in fact (which it was, as young Macpherson had just written it). Here Fingal, the barbarian warrior king, confronts the enemy: "He came like a cloud of rain in the days of the sun, when slow it rolls on the hill, and fields expect the shower. . . . Dark he leaned on his spear, rolling his red eyes around. Silent and tall he seemed, as an oak on the banks of Lubar which had its branches blasted of old by the lightning of heaven. It bends over the stream, and the gray moss whistles in the wind: so stood the king."

Macpherson's timing was perfect. People bored with the witty, fussily constructed poetry of Pope and his ilk welcomed these rude sagas of courage, death, and bereavement. Boswell, unsurprisingly, was completely taken in, recommending the mysterious Celtic bard to a friend: "Take my word for it, he will make you feel you have a soul." From America, Thomas Jefferson wrote Macpherson in 1773 to say that Ossian's works were "the source of daily and exalted pleasure" for him, and might he see a copy of the Gaelic originals? Alas, that wasn't possible, Macpherson replied.

By the end of the century, Ossian's poetry was outselling everything in England but Shakespeare and the Bible. Few critics openly challenged Macpherson's story. An exception was the redoubtable Samuel Johnson. In his *Journey to the Western Islands of Scotland* in 1775, Johnson wrote of Ossian's poems: "I believe they never existed in any other form than that which we have seen." He noted with particular scorn Macpherson's refusal to show anyone the original Gaelic manuscripts. "Stubborn audacity is the last refuge of guilt," Johnson observed.

Furious, the forger demanded a public apology. He even suggested the wording he'd like to see. If Johnson refused to disavow his charge, Macpherson implied, he might have to challenge the sixty-five-year-old critic to a duel.

Johnson's immediate response was twofold: he bought a six-foot oak cudgel, which he kept within reach at all times, and he wrote Macpherson a letter that began, "I received your foolish and impudent note," and continued, "You want me to retract. What shall I retract? I thought your book an imposture from the beginning, I think it upon yet surer reasons an imposture still." A week later, someone leaked the letter to the *Morning Post*, which was happy to publish excerpts.

Macpherson's reputation didn't suffer appreciably from the dustup. Using the fictional Ossian as his entrée into society, he went on to a long and lucrative career as a writer of popular histories, a paid government hack, and a member of Parliament. In a bizarre twist, his final resting place in Poet's Corner was almost next to Samuel Johnson's.

REALIZATION THAT THE Ossian poems were fake didn't become widespread until well into the nineteenth century. Many of the ancient bard's admirers didn't care. Sir Walter Scott wrote perceptively in 1830 about the forging of old poems and ballads, a popular pastime since before Macpherson's day: "If a young author wishes to circulate a beautiful poem under the guise of antiquity, the public is surely more enriched by the contribution than injured by the deception."

As with Chatterton and his monkish alter ego, Thomas Rowley, Macpherson would never have won acclaim for his writings if he hadn't been a gifted poet. Without the gloss of antiquity, however, neither Chatterton's nor Macpherson's poetry would have attracted as much attention as it did; imagining a cloistered monk or a barefoot Celt chanting the lines centuries ago was a large part of what made reading them so pleasurable. As a literary strategy, their pretenses were morally questionable. Macpherson's made-up Highland dramas, in particular, confused the documentary record of old Scottish poetry for generations. But the deceptions of Chatterton and Macpherson—and Defoe and Fielding, for that matter—were relatively harmless. Conscientious scholars like the dogged ballad-collector Joseph Ritson were the exception, not the rule, in the eighteenth century. Most readers were, like Thomas Jefferson, happy for the "daily and exalted pleasure" that reading such compositions gave them, regardless of their provenance.

What William-Henry Ireland was attempting was not so innocuous. He was impersonating a known literary figure—and not just any literary figure. To pen old-fashioned ballads was to listen to one's muse. To produce carefully doctored, artificially aged manuscripts in Shakespeare's handwriting would be, in the eyes of literary society, to perpetrate a most grievous fraud. It would be an assault on English literature. It would be unforgivable.

CHAPTER EIGHT

DELUSIONS OF GRANDEUR

H IS SUPPLY OF custom-made ink restocked, William-Henry slaved through the spring on his various Shakespearean fabrications. The pressure from his father was unrelenting. Between his other productions, the boy continued to compose *Vortigern and Rowena* at his empty quarters at New Inn. He delivered finished pages to his father one or two at a time. This meant he could neither change nor even reread earlier scenes as he wrote each new one, a handicap for any playwright. The requirement of making every page, every line, worthy of the immortal Bard was a punishing burden for a novice poet. Could any poet, he wondered, take joy in writing under such pressure?

Some days he defied his father—"the voice of reproof," in the boy's mind—by turning over no new material "because I was not in the humor to compose it," he recalled in 1805. "As my muse was not so very prolific as to 'spin and weave' poetry as fast as it was required, I really began to loathe the very idea of the manuscripts."

In this same workspace six months earlier, William-Henry had been idling in a desk job that was uncongenial but not unpleasant. On sunny days, he'd look out his window at the neat rows of shade trees in the court-yard and mark the slow passage of time on the large clock above the entrance to New Inn's central hall. Now his office window was no more than a light source that aided him in his manufacture of forgeries.

Sometimes, in his haste, he scorched a page by holding it too close to a candle while darkening the ink. Someone familiar with a forger's tricks ought to have found the marks incriminating, but no one did. All the same, people were puzzled by the burned spots—until someone recalled the story of the late John Warburton, a well-known collector of sixteenth- and seventeenth-century theater manuscripts who had died in 1759. Warburton ill-advisedly stored his rare papers in the kitchen of his London home but neglected to tell his cook of their value. The soon-to-be-infamous cook, one Betsy Baker, used more than fifty of the manuscripts variously to line pie tins and to light fires before Warburton realized what was happening.

Three of these dramas, according to the distraught collector's inventory, had been unpublished works of Shakespeare. Unpublished they remained. Some of the papers—those used for baking—were thought to have escaped incineration, although their whereabouts were unknown. Until now, that is: Visitors to Norfolk Street deduced that the scorch marks could be traced to Warburton's cook. The marks were as good as a notarized pedigree. William-Henry was amazed. Once again, details that he'd overlooked or mishandled were taken as signs that the Shakespeare papers were genuine. How the papers ended up in Mr. H.'s trunk was left unexamined.

On another occasion, visitors became preoccupied with a set of hand-written marks on the *Lear* manuscript's final page. These were actually doo-dles that William-Henry had forgotten to clean up. Francis Webb of the College of Heralds determined the mysterious markings to be a shorthand of Shakespeare's devising, though he wasn't sure how to decipher it.

In hindsight, it's astonishing that some of William-Henry's careless habits didn't give him away. He bought not only his ink but also his paper and parchment in shops in his own neighborhood. He was a well-known cus-tomer at the bookstores of the Smith brothers, Benjamin and John, on Fleet Street, and of William Otridge on the Strand near Drury Lane. From both these establishments he carted away piles of old volumes dating from Shakespeare's day—this shortly before the same titles turned up on Norfolk Street as remnants of Shakespeare's personal library. More than careless, closer to bizarre, was his habit of disguising his customary script by occasionally forging with his uncoordinated left hand. The messy handwriting that resulted looked barely literate, though graceful penmanship was one of the most important subjects taught in English schools. This simple-minded ruse would later come within a hair of exposing his entire hoax.

Several times, William-Henry tried his hand at forging artwork, although his efforts looked childish—he hadn't inherited his sisters' artistic ability. Early on, he'd handed his father a wobbly line drawing on parchment of a balding man with a huge lace collar. Surrounding the man on all sides as though he were a jack on a playing card were four spears and two Shakespeare signatures. The man was pointing to himself comically with one finger. William-Henry told his father it must be a self-portrait by the Bard himself. In his mind's eye, the boy could already picture this historical curiosity reproduced in future editions of Shakespeare's works.

Samuel was unimpressed. Worse than that, he was disdainful. The drawing was a silly trifle, and it was ludicrous to trace it to the pen of the immortal Bard. William-Henry was taken aback. Until now, each of his forgeries, large and small, had been welcomed as a genuine artifact from Shakespeare's life. His father wasn't accusing the boy of having made the drawing himself; he simply didn't care *who* had drawn it.

At New Inn the next morning, William-Henry turned to a stratagem that would serve him well in evading future problems: He made a new forgery to corroborate the last one. In this case, he scribbled a quick note from Shakespeare to an actor friend, Richard Cowley, saying he was enclosing a self-portrait, nothing serious, just a "whymsycalle conceyte" he'd dashed off as a token of friendship.

Context was everything. Samuel, reading the note, immediately decided the sketch was Shakespeare's self-portrait after all. As such, it was unique in the annals of Shakespeareana, and the collector was thrilled to add it to his collection. Thus Samuel Ireland—a self-described connoisseur and man of the arts who second-guessed the attributions of fine paintings, who could look at a building and guess its architect (and spot his mistakes)—was taken in by an embarrassing doodle. The man had suspended his critical judgment and surrendered himself to his son's hoax.

Later, encouraged by this artistic triumph, William-Henry went a step further. He bought an old drawing he'd noticed hanging in full view on Butcher's Row, a narrow, shop-lined alley just east of New Inn. On one side was a crude sketch of a gray-bearded Dutchman in pantaloons. On the reverse was an equally crude drawing of a young Englishman with a sword from the time of James I. Carrying the picture to New Inn, William-Henry quickly made alterations. To the left of the old Dutchman, he drew a set of scales; on the right, a large butcher's knife. This, he hoped, would pass for Shakespeare in the role of Shylock, preparing to exact his pound of flesh from Antonio in *The Merchant of Venice*. To the drawing of the Englishman on the back, he sketched in a mustache and goatee, hoping to bring to mind the familiar image of the Bard in the Droeshout engraving. For good measure, he painted a huge "W. S." next to the figure, along with a few play titles. This, William-Henry intended, would pass for Shakespeare as a dashing young actor, perhaps in the role of Bassanio. It wasn't subtle, and it certainly wasn't pretty, but he presented it to his father that night anyway.

Samuel and his fellow enthusiasts immediately accepted the clumsy double-sided artwork as an authentic memento of Shakespeare's stage career—likely it had hung in the green room of the Globe Theater, they decided—though Shylock's Dutch pantaloons caused some head-scratching. An expert on old handwriting, John Hewlett, stopped in at Norfolk Street to inspect the piece under a magnifying glass. In one corner he thought he detected a faint signature—yes, it was that of John Hoskins, a well-known English miniaturist of the early 1600s.

"I must candidly confess, although my eyes are not of the weakest," William-Henry later noted, "that even with the aid of magnifiers I could never perceive anything like a resemblance to the name in question." He suspected the "signature" was ink that had spread unevenly along veins in the paper, but he was happy to defer to the expert.

In mid-April 1795, William-Henry handed his father the final pages of *Vortigern*. He'd managed to tie up the play's complicated plot with a minimum of bloodshed. Aurelius, the Hamletlike son of the murdered king, outduels the villainous usurper Vortigern. The latter is spared from death after a plea from his estranged daughter Flavia, the new king's beloved. The curtain falls, and the Fool steps forward to deliver a closing soliloquy:

Chance, you will ask if this be tragedy;
We kill, indeed, but still 'tis comedy:
For none save bad do fall, which draws no tear,
Nor lets compassion sway your tender ear.

Samuel was relieved to have the entire transcript intact and under his roof at last. Even if he had to wait a bit longer for Mr. H. to relinquish the play's original manuscript, so be it. While the collector never stopped pressuring his son for new papers, his attention was increasingly focused on the expensive edition of the papers that he was planning and on making sure each document from Shakespeare's hand, however trivial, was properly engraved for reproduction.

The visitors who converged on Norfolk Street during the thrice-weekly visiting hours accepted the *Vortigern* text as the words of Shakespeare—at least, those who spoke up publicly did. William-Henry sensed that doubts about the papers were dwindling. In the *Oracle* at the end of April, James Boaden wrote with his customary self-assurance that "the Shaksperiana which have been so luckily discovered are now considered as genuine by all but those who illiberally refuse to be convinced by inspection." The documents spoke for themselves. They were obviously Shakespeare's.

"The Manuscript Play of *King Lear*," observed the *True Briton*, ". . . is in a variety of passages so different from the printed work, and so much more beautiful, that it will doubtless by adopted at the Theatres." More exciting to the theater world than a mint quality *Lear*, however, was the newfound history play. The rival owners of London's two theatres royal were already vying for a chance to stage it. Sheridan at Drury Lane and Thomas Harris at Covent Garden both anticipated that *Vortigern* would draw crowds. Neither had actually read the play; Harris hadn't even looked at the manuscript. But this was immaterial. What mattered to both men was that London hadn't witnessed the premiere of a new play by Shakespeare since James I was king. It would likely never see another.

"IT WAS EXTRAORDINARY to observe," William-Henry later wrote, "how willingly persons will blind themselves on any point interesting to their feelings." It was absurd. His practical joke was poised to become an unprecedented literary and theatrical triumph.

Yet bit by bit, William-Henry was deluding himself, too. In his mind, the forgeries were becoming real. He had set out to write *Vortigern and Rowena* despite having written no more than a few poems. His play was nonetheless being praised as a masterwork. His stunning success as a forger was making him feel that he—a lightly educated lad with a pointless job, a dullard and a failure in the eyes of the world—was the Sweet Swan of Avon's true literary heir.

The boy's initial anxiety about having his forgeries published for the world was dissolving. Instead, he was now taken with the possibility— indeed, the probability—that *Vortigern* would appear in new and expanded editions of Shakespeare's complete works. A more immediate thrill was the prospect of seeing his raw material transformed into full-blooded Shakespearean drama by the London actors and actresses he had idolized all his life.

Years later, people were bewildered that William-Henry had not pulled back after his early successes but instead had forged ever more elaborate and implausible documents in Shakespeare's name, as though begging to be caught. But why should anyone have expected that this youth—an unpublished writer being showered with praise unheard by any living writer in history—would abandon what he was doing? It would have been far stranger if he'd stopped. The authenticity of ink and script was no longer a central issue for many of the Bardolaters who crowded around the papers on Norfolk Street. The authenticity of the words themselves were what mattered, and the words, they decided, were Shakespeare's. Having decided this was so, they were enraptured.

William-Henry was in a quandary. For the world to recognize his rare talent, he would *have* to reveal his authorship, as Chatterton should have. But he now realized that to come forward and confess to being a make-believe Shakespeare of nineteen would subject his admirers to ridicule. Worse, even if he managed somehow to convince his father of his achievement, a confession would make the man a public laughingstock.

As for his own fate, he believed that his writing was good enough to stand on its own. Webb and Boaden had already said as much. Like readers of *The Castle of Otranto* who were pleased to learn the author was a living Englishman, not a fifteenth-century Neapolitan, admirers of *Vortigern and Rowena* would be heartened by the news that its author was alive and planning new works of even greater scope and beauty. Or so William-Henry told himself, though he wasn't entirely convinced. And he wasn't ready to risk finding out if he was wrong.

It continued to gnaw at him that he couldn't reveal his achievement to his father. Until now, none of his highly praised forgeries had diverted any literary praise to *him*. He began turning the correspondence between Samuel and the imaginary Mr. H. to his advantage. Writing to his father in the guise of his secretive gentleman friend, William-Henry was able to plead his own case—indeed, to trumpet his achievements—in ways he would never have dared in person.

The tone of Mr. H.'s increasingly chatty letters made clear he was fond of the boy. "He tells me," Mr. H. confided to Samuel, "he is in general look'd upon as a young man that scarce knows how to write a good letter." The gentleman couldn't understand how William-Henry's talent as a writer had gone unrecognized. "I have now before me part of a Play written by your son which for style and greatness of thought is equal to any one of Shakspears. Let me intreat you Dear Sir not to smile for on my honour it is most true."

Included in the letter was a passage from the play in question, a saga in verse about William the Conqueror, so that Samuel could judge for himself. In the excerpt, Earl Edwyn, the Saxon lord plotting against the Norman invaders, muses outside old Westminster Abbey:

> . . . *As this Christal Arch this bright heaven*
> *Doth shine upon the Emerald tipt wave*
> *And paints upon the deep each passing cloud*
> *E'ene so the smallest & most gentle Plant*
> *That Waves fore the breath of thee sweet heaven*
> *To Man gives food for contemplation*
> *And shows how soon this blazing flame of youth*
> *Must sink on Age's chilling Icy Bed*
> *And dwindle down to second nothingness.*

Writing to the boy's father, Mr. H. seemed in awe at having such a precocious lad as a friend. "I often talk with him and never before found one even of triple his age that knew so much of human nature," he wrote. The two were evidently spending a great deal of time together. "He never comes in to me but instantly notes down everything that has struck him in his walk. I have asked frequently where he can get such thoughts. All the answer he makes is this: 'I borrow them from nature.' I also enquired why he wishes to be secret to which he says 'I desire to be thought to know but little.'"

As for the voluminous writing the boy was doing, which for now only his gentleman friend was allowed to see, Mr. H. declared: "*No man* but your *son* ever wrote like *Shakspeare*. This is bold I confess but it is true. . . . The more I see of him [the] more I am amaz'd. If your son is not a second Shakspeare I am not a man." William-Henry apparently thought this wasn't commendation enough. In a postscript, he had Mr. H. add: "Your son is brother in genius to Shakspeare and is the only man that ever walked with him hand in hand."

Samuel was astonished. He was having trouble reconciling the boy he knew with the litterateur being described. Of the excerpt from his son's work in progress, he confessed to Mr. H.: "It is the first specimen of my son's poetical talent I have ever yet seen." The collector then returned to his usual preoccupation—his desire for a face-to-face meeting: "If it is your wish to remain unknown to the Public, may I without intrusion on your friendship request to have an interview on the most private ground imaginable. You think [my son] can keep a secret, and I think he can; but my experience in life will, I flatter myself, certainly enable me to be equally secret if required." Samuel confided that he was embarrassed that his son was widely known as an intimate friend of Mr. H. while he, the boy's father, didn't even know his name. William-Henry, replying in the guise of Mr. H., once again ignored Samuel's plea and redirected his attention to his precocious son. "O Mr. I.," he implored, "you should be happy in having a son *who if he lives* must make futurity amaz'd." William-Henry's emphasis suggests that he was already styling himself as a tubercular Romantic poet.

The young man's bizarre correspondence with his bamboozled father must have been oddly satisfying, even if his father never joined in the effusive praise of his son's heretofore hidden talents. William-Henry was not just courting his father's attention. For once, he was commanding it.

For all his success as Shakespeare's secret double, however, William-Henry remained frustrated. He yearned not only to win his father's approval—something the man was incapable of bestowing—but more than that, to make his mark on the world as a man of letters. In his own mind, he was already one of England's most gifted writers. Now he desperately wanted the world to notice his genius.

William-Henry devised a strategy to accomplish this. This time there would be nothing furtive about it. He told his father, via the mythical Mr. H., exactly what he was up to. The boy was setting to work on a series of plays that, coupled with Shakespeare's histories, would form a complete history of the kings of England. Shakespeare's history plays featured seven English monarchs: four Henrys, two Richards, and a John. William-Henry's original plays would fill in the gaps in the Bard's chronology, from William the Conqueror to Queen Elizabeth. He was young. There was no literary feat that felt beyond his reach. He pictured himself enjoying a long and illustrious career as Shakespeare's worthy successor.

Writing under his own name would be a departure. His play about William the Conqueror would be the first work that he took credit for, although he planned it to be "imitative of Shakspeare's style." Stylistic backdating was a well-known device among eighteenth-century dramatists: New plays were sometimes written and staged in Elizabethan language. Some were intended as sequels to well-loved but overfamiliar Shakespearean dramas. They were a kind of homage as well as a way to ride Shakespeare's coattails. But the other playwrights bringing out pseudo-Elizabethan dramas were not known for having found, by chance in an old trunk, original works purporting to be Shakespeare's. The boy was clearly tempting fate.

A NEW WORRY, one that had nothing to do with being found out, arose in late spring 1795. It spurred William-Henry to produce a forgery more brazen than anything he'd done before. He was probing the limits of the Believers' credulity, as though daring them to see him for what he was: a fraud.

In some quarters, the discovery of a natural descendant of the Bard was a prospect as exciting as the discovery of his personal papers. To the regret of his admirers, Shakespeare's bloodline had come to an end during the Restoration. His only son, Hamnet, had died in childhood. His daughter Judith had married a local vintner, Thomas Quiney, by whom she had three children, but by the time she died in 1662 she had outlived them all. Shakespeare's other daughter, Susanna, had married a Stratford physician, John Hall. Their only child, Elizabeth, the Bard's granddaughter, had married, been widowed, and married again, but she died childless in 1670 at age sixty-one. Elizabeth Hall was Shakespeare's last known descendant. But might there be others? Susanna, Shakespeare's first child, had been conceived when he was unmarried, after all, and the poet had led an extremely active life in London—far from his wife—for more than twenty years.

William-Henry had not paid attention to any of this until a visitor to Norfolk Street one afternoon commented "that if a descendant of Shakspeare could be found, he might lay claim to all the papers which I had

Forger and would-be Romantic poet William-Henry Ireland in his early twenties. Stipple engraving, 1798.

A portrait miniature of the workaday writer at about age fifty, living in England once again after self-imposed exile in France.

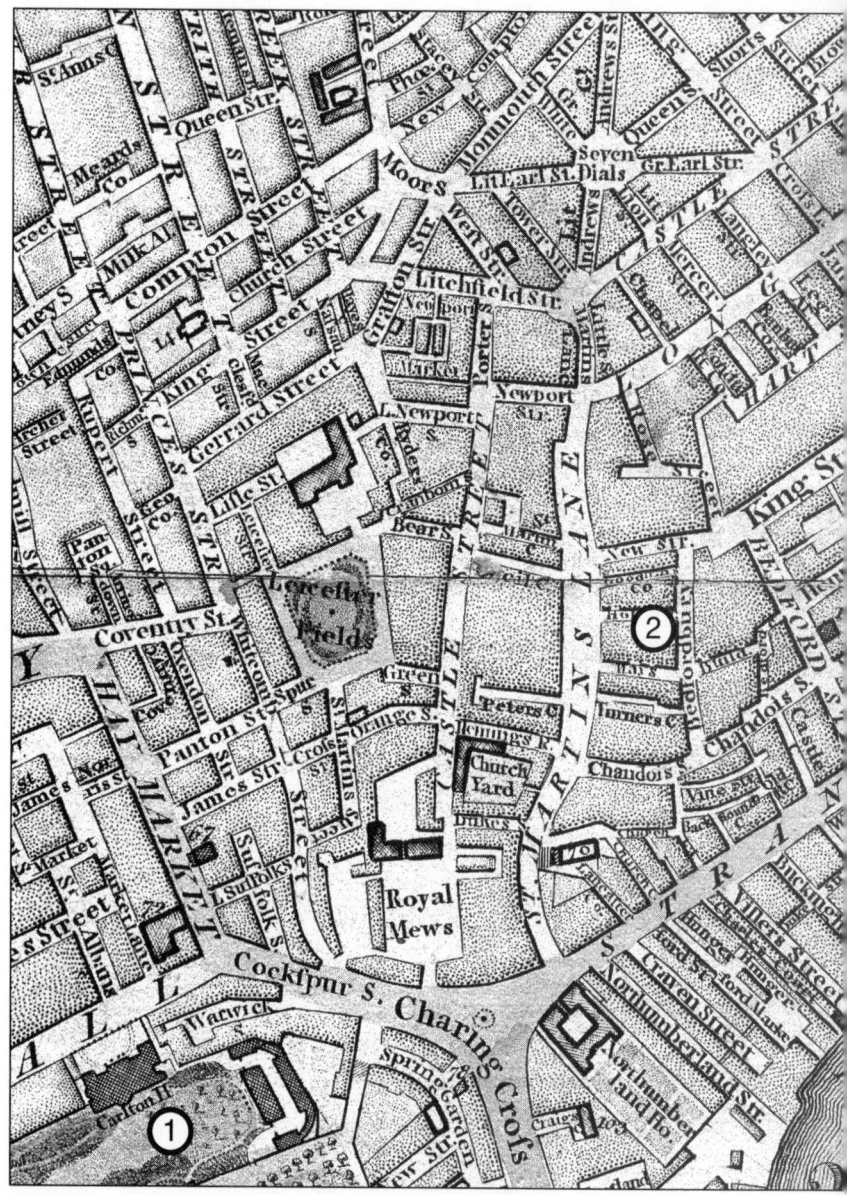

The West End and the Strand in 1795, from "Cary's New and Accurate Plan of London and Westminster." From lower left: (1) Carlton House, residence of the Prince of Wales; (2) Great May's Building, where William-Henry tore flyleaves from 200-year-old books; the two popular theatres royal, (3) Covent Garden and (4) Drury Lane; (5) Somerset House, where the Society of Antiquaries met; (6) New Inn, where William-Henry worked in secret; (7) the Irelands' home on Norfolk Street; (8) their earlier address on nearby Arundel Street; (9) the Church of St. Clement Danes.

The forger's father, ex-weaver and Bardolater Samuel Ireland, in 1776, shortly after William-Henry was born.

Gloomy, shuttered Clopton House in 1793, a few weeks after original Shakespearean papers were supposedly burned in one of the mansion's many fireplaces. Etching by Samuel Ireland from his *Picturesque Views on the Upper, or Warwickshire Avon.*

The Antiquarians.

Zealous collectors examine a broken chamber pot in a caricature mocking the antiquarian fad. Collectors who vied to possess such relics, observed one writer, "love all things (as Dutchmen doe Cheese) the better for being mouldy and worm-eaten."

New Inn, William-Henry's monastic hideaway. The campuslike enclave was a five minutes' walk from the Irelands' home on Norfolk Street. In a lawyer's office here, the young legal apprentice spent his workdays alone and unsupervised, surrounded by ancient documents.

Façades on Wych Street dating from Shakespeare's lifetime, as seen from New Inn's entrance in 1880, not long before the quarter was razed. The spire of St. Clement Danes rises in the background. William-Henry scoured shops in the neighborhood for old books and curios he could alter.

Richard Brinsley Sheridan, playwright, impresario, gambler, debtor. The forged play's premiere was his enormous theater's first sellout.

An aging, gullible James Boswell in the early 1790s. After kissing the *Vortigern* manuscript, he announced he could die contented.

Engraving from *Miscellaneous Papers*, 1795

The forged love letter from a young Will Shakespeare to his betrothed, Anne Hathaway, complete with a lock of its author's hair. In the letter and the love poem that accompanied it, one prominent critic in 1795 detected "the utmost delicacy of passion and poetical spirit."

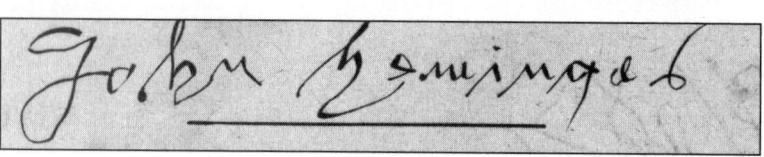

Top: A receipt from "short" John Heminge, written and signed with the forger's left hand. *Bottom:* Heminge's actual signature, tidy and fluent. The discrepancy almost toppled William-Henry's increasingly intricate hoax.

From Edmond Malone, *An Inquiry into the Authenticity of Certain Miscellaneous Papers and Legal Instruments*, 1796

John Philip Kemble, Drury Lane Theatre manager and ponderous leading man; he played King Vortigern against his better judgment.

Dorothea Jordan as the warrior queen Hypolita in 1791; her performance as Flavia in *Vortigern* won applause.

Fierce, meticulous, dogged Edmond Malone, the "generalissimo of the nonbelievers," after a painting by Sir Joshua Reynolds in 1778, when Malone was in his late thirties.

Malone's unscrupulous ex-mentor and rival George Steevens, a sometime forger in his own right, in a 1793 drawing.

Thomas Rowlandson, "An Audience Watching a Play at Drury Lane Theatre," ca. 1785. Also talking, flirting, gawking, lounging.

From Rudolph Ackermann's *Microcosm of London,* ca. 1808

Lit by candles, a full house takes in the action at the expanded Drury Lane Theater in 1806. Note the boxes directly on stage.

Forgery as a family affair. This 1796 caricature, "The Oaken Chest, or the Gold Mines of Ireland, a Farce," captured the popular view of the Irelands, post-*Vortigern*: Samuel Ireland, center, is the operation's mastermind; William-Henry, at left, idly enjoys the result.

The frontispiece and title page of William-Henry Ireland's 1805 *Confessions*. Below Shakespeare's forged signature is his supposed personal seal: a quintain at which a horseman would "shake" his "spear." The title page's promise of "the whole truth, and nothing but the truth" wasn't quite true.

produced." The forgeries could be poached! This dire possibility had never occurred to him. The boy hadn't worked to exhaustion and risked disgrace so that someone else could enjoy Shakespeare's inheritance. He had forged every scrap for the glory of his father and himself.

With his usual blend of ingenuity and naïveté, William-Henry devised a way to forestall a rival claim to the papers. He set about creating a packet of documents that would go beyond the playwright's wishes as stated in his last will and testament. These new forgeries spelled out, for the first time, what Will Shakespeare had done with his manuscripts.

The brashest of the forgeries was a formal document on parchment that he would come to regret within a year. It was a long-winded deed of gift signed by Shakespeare in 1604. In it, the playwright, being "of sounde Mynde ande enjoyinge healthe of bodye," made a generous bequest to "mye goode freynde Masterre William Henrye Irelande"—the obscure London haberdasher who rented part of the gatehouse in Blackfriars that Shakespeare would buy nine years later. The middle name was William-Henry's unwise embellishment of the historical record.

The carefully lettered parchment deed went into elaborate detail on what the Bard's future tenant had done to deserve the largess. On a summer's day in 1604, it seems, Shakespeare and a boisterous group of friends, among them William-Henry's seventeenth-century namesake, had gone boating on the Thames. Several of the party, "beynge muche toe merry throughe Lyquorre," caused the boat to capsize. Everyone splashed ashore except Shakespeare. The poet knew how to tread water, apparently, but not how to swim. "Masterre William henrye Irelande notte seeynge me dydd aske for mee butte oune of the companye dydd answerre thatte I was drownynge"— this last speaker went unnamed and unrewarded—"onn the whyche he pulledd off hys jerrekynne and jumpedd inn afterre mee." The valiant haber-dasher dragged his friend to safety, "I beynge then nearelye deade and soe he dydd save mye life."

In gratitude, the parchment deed continued, Shakespeare bequeathed his loyal friend—effective immediately—ownership rights to five of his plays and, for good measure, a gift of ten pounds. At the beneficiary's death, the theatrical rights were to go to Ireland's son, also named William-Henry, and later descendants "and soe onn for everre."

If true, this meant that as of 1604 this humble, possibly illiterate haberdasher was to collect all the playwright's earnings from *King Lear*, *King John*, *Henry IV*, *Henry V*, and an unpublished history play. It only remained for the young forger to expand the list of plays bequeathed and to conjure up a clear line of descent from the Ireland of Blackfriars to the Irelands of Norfolk Street. At that point, he and his family could plausibly claim that the Shakespeare papers were theirs by right.

Many years after his manic literary exploits, a calmer and wiser William-Henry wrote in the margin of a published facsimile of the deed: "I am absolutely astonished that even credulity itself should have been duped by this flagrant document." The deed was riddled with mistakes. At the time he forged it, he had been unaware that Shakespeare never held the rights to any of his three dozen plays; his theater companies did. Nor was he aware that in 1604 *King Lear* had yet to be written. For the time being, however, these were matters for theatrical scholars to quibble over. More potentially damaging was the whole saved-from-drowning scenario.

Up to this point, the boy had produced more or less believable documents. Some, like the theater receipts and IOUs, were so dull that they *had* to be believed. Others had flaws that should have raised suspicions: the love letter to Anne Hathaway, the thank-you letter to his patron, the earl. Still, they were at least plausible. But having an Ireland—a William Henry Ireland no less—pluck a deliriously grateful Bard from certain death was beyond far-fetched. It was preposterous. The story's absurdity should have been enough to doom the whole enterprise.

It should have been, but it wasn't. Samuel was delighted with the story, and so were other visitors who studied the deed, whose physical details William-Henry had lavished attention on. The coincidences were piling up—after Shakespeare's feeble self-portrait had appeared, hadn't a two-hundred-year-old corroborating note surfaced the following day?—but if anything, Samuel and the others were learning to expect them. Indeed, they welcomed them. Taken together, William-Henry's forgeries were fleshing out a story that England wanted to hear.

Samuel in this case was hardly a disinterested observer, and not just because the parchment was the latest jewel in his expanding cabinet of curiosities. He'd always told his children that the Blackfriars haberdasher was their ancestor. Now that "Masterre Irelande" was a hero who had single-handedly preserved the greatest living treasure of the English Renaissance, Samuel and his family stood to bask in their namesake's newfound prestige.

Along with the deed, William-Henry had forged a letter from Shakespeare to this "mouste worthye and excellaunte freynde" on which he drew in pen and ink the Shakespeare family's coat of arms alongside the Ireland family's, the two designs linked by a chain. In the letter, the poet gushes about his brave friend: "Norre verse norre sygh norre teare canne paynte mye soule norre saye bye halfe howe muche I love thee."

Rather than snorting at this touching fairy tale, Sir Isaac Heard, Garter king of arms and an authority on heraldic symbols, judged it authentic. Heard decided that in his official view, given the Bard's fond sentiments, it would now be permissible for the Irelands to add elements of Shakespeare's arms to their own family insignia.

Others suggested that this Ireland ancestor might be none other than the mysterious "W. H." to whom the Bard had dedicated his sonnets in 1609. The identity of this individual had been a literary guessing game for much of the century. As usual, the Believers were racing ahead of the forger to fill in gaps in Shakespeare's story and make a pleasing narrative.

Many people who heard the story of the Bard's savior knew immediately it was too good to be true. Perhaps until now they'd paid little attention to the Shakespeare papers' discovery. Some had likely suspected chicanery from the first. Edmond Malone's only public comment, after hearing of Shakespeare's generosity to a seventeenth-century William Henry Ireland, was to ask mildly how many Englishmen in 1604 had a middle name. Sir Horace Walpole, who had doubted both Macpherson and Chatterton, later confided in a letter to a friend that he expected Samuel Ireland would soon make public a document revealing him to be the Bard's grandson.

For now, the doubters were confining their suspicions to private letters and coffeehouse gossip, not pamphlets and newspapers. The exception was the *Morning Herald*'s irreverent Henry Bate Dudley, who belittled the story of the drowning Bard. "The *swimming* reasons given in a paper of yesterday in favor of the authenticity of certain *musty manuscripts*," he wrote, "shew to what Dangers we may expose ourselves by *wading* too far in pursuit of an *object*."

William-Henry was too deeply committed to his role as Shakespeare's alter ego to let Sir Henry's latest gibe bother him. Unlikely discoveries continued. In June, he presented his father with one more miraculous document from Mr. H.'s trunk. It was intended to tie up some of the loose ends that had nagged at his father—even as it left new ones. Samuel had continued to fret to the boy about the dicey position he was in. Samuel was not only proclaiming the papers to be Shakespeare's but also presenting himself as their rightful owner. The collector's claim to the papers rested on letters from a man he had never met and couldn't identify. All he knew was that the man's name began with an H. As for how the stranger had come to possess such an incalculably valuable archive, Samuel had no idea.

William-Henry's latest forgery was, in essence, a new version of Shakespeare's last will and testament. It was dated February 11, 1611, two years before the Bard had retired to Stratford and five years before he'd signed his only known will, which had been found in London in 1747. The new forgery was an elaborate deed of gift to John Heminge, Shakespeare's "trusty and tried friende." It made Heminge executor of the Bard's estate, as the poet distrusted lawyers, having "founde muche wickedness amongste those of the lawe and not liking to leave matterrs at theyre wills."

William-Henry's newest concoction was both clever and daring. It improved on Shakespeare's authentic will, notably by treating Anne Hathaway more charitably. The poet directed that "mye deare Wife" receive a sum of 180 pounds (roughly $30,000 today) along with a gray velvet suit edged with silver, three rings, and a silver case containing a small portrait for her to remember him by. Not least, he left her a packet of seven love letters he had written during their courtship—"these I doe beg herr toe keepe safe if everr she dydd love me." Samuel and others who saw this last request from the grave were too moved by its sentiment to wonder why Shakespeare needed to give his wife the love letters a second time.

There was more—the deed was packed with tantalizing information. It suggested the origins of Mr. H.'s paper-filled trunk and why the good gentleman insisted on staying anonymous. Upon the Bard's death, Heminge was directed to retrieve a stack of play manuscripts from "the oakenn cheste att oure Globe Theatre" and distribute them among various friends. Then William-Henry added an inspired touch.

"I further orderr hym to brynge up that chylde of whom wee have spokenn butt who muste nott be named here." This mystery child was clearly dear to the Bard's heart. He, or she, was due a generous sum of cash plus the proceeds from the sale of "mye three howses." And more: "I allsoe give toe said chylde the eyghte playes thatt bee stylle inne said cheste." One of these was a play "neverr yett impryntedd called Kyng Vorrtygerne." This was handy: a 1611 mention of the play William-Henry had just written.

Legally, the deed's implications were shocking. Heminge must have failed to carry out his dear friend's wishes and instead had kept many of his possessions for himself. There was no record of a Bardic love child—or anyone else—receiving this princely inheritance, including revenue from a real estate bonanza. As for William-Henry's friend Mr. H.: Might the H stand for Heminge? Was the gentleman lying low because his ancestor was a thief? Was he now relinquishing the trunk's contents because he knew they weren't his to keep?

And what became of this poor, cheated mystery child? The deed bequeathed the playwright's "deare daughterre" (William-Henry forgot he had two) only twenty pounds, seven shillings, along with some clothes and a ring; the child "who muste notte be named" must have been Shakespeare's favorite. Could it be that John Heminge had indeed raised the Bard's bastard child as his own? Might the elusive Mr. H., inheritor of the old oaken chest, then be Shakespeare's secret descendant? From these strands of quasihistorical odds and ends, William-Henry was weaving an overheated romance novel. That he never wrote in any of his later recollections of forging a love child for the Bard suggests he realized he'd been carrying things too far and didn't want to draw attention to this dubious plot complication.

In June 1795, though, anything seemed possible. Soon after producing the deed of gift to Heminge, William-Henry told his father that while Mr. H. had been rummaging in an old chest at his country estate, the gentleman had come across an illuminated manuscript dating from the early 1400s. The parchment showed a knight on his knees being awarded an armorial banner by King Henry V himself. For his father's benefit, the boy had copied down the inscription next to this drawing, which read: "Ireland, thou hast deserved well for thy valor, and shalt have a part of our Arms of England for thy bravery." Also inscribed on the parchment, he told his father, were dated signatures from a succession of Irelands who'd inherited it, from Sir Arthur Ireland, Henry's loyal companion at Agincourt, to William Henry Ireland, the strong-swimming London haberdasher.

There was more to come, the boy hinted to his father. Mr. H. had documents "to prove that I was the direct descendant of the William Henry Ireland to whom the bequest was made in the deed of gift"—surely Samuel had seen this coming—"and that consequently he no longer regarded my possession of the manuscripts as a favor but looked upon them as my own right by descent."

For Samuel Ireland, this was wonderful news, even if Mr. H. still couldn't bring himself to deliver it in person. As for William-Henry, these latest forgeries were doubly satisfying. He was not just solidifying his family's claim to the papers. He was reinventing himself. He had long had doubts about who his real father was—doubts that both Samuel and Mrs. Freeman had encouraged. The man's often callous treatment of him seemed to William-Henry evidence of a lack of any paternal bond. As for his mother, he wasn't sure who she was. If he suspected it was the distant Mrs. Freeman, he must have looked for reasons not to believe it. All his life, William-Henry clung to the suspicion that he was a bastard. It was a psychic wound that would figure in his later novels and poetry.

But being of unknown parentage could be a blessing, too. The neglected, illegitimate commoner who, by story's end, is revealed as an aristocrat's heir was a popular conceit of eighteenth-century novels, from Henry Fielding's *Tom Jones* to Fanny Burney's *Evelina*. For William-Henry, fashioning himself an indirect heir to Shakespeare was a variation on this fantasy.

The boy never got around to producing the illuminated manuscript or the genealogical records. He failed to find a copy of Henry V's signature that he could copy, and he was leery of guessing how it should look. A bigger stumbling block was piecing together a post-1604 Ireland family tree that would include him yet withstand the scrutiny of skeptics.

In his memoirs, William-Henry made clear that he understood why a career in forgery could turn disastrous so quickly. As soon as one of his documents was revealed to be a fabrication, all of the papers would be exposed as fakes. He had to be careful, he told himself.

But another, conflicting impulse dared him to outdo himself with each new deception. For the young forger, the acceptance of these latest tall tales confirmed once again that the more fantastic a discovery, the more joyously Shakespeare's worshippers welcomed it. Like a pied piper of antiquarians, William-Henry was leading his father and the other Believers on a winding path further and further away from reality. By now, he could lead them anywhere his imagination took him. It was a godlike power, and indulging it was exhilarating.

CHAPTER NINE

NONBELIEVERS

R ICHARD BRINSLEY SHERIDAN needed a hit.

A flamboyant, free-spending gambler and member of Parliament, Sheridan had been the impresario and part owner of the Drury Lane Theatre since 1776, when David Garrick had retired. The cramped old playhouse had grown seedy over the years, and in 1791 it had been condemned. Sheridan had staked his reputation and financial well-being on a complete overhaul of the theater, most of which he paid for himself. The theater's finances and his own were hopelessly entangled.

The expansion had cost £160,000 (£5 million pounds or $8 million dollars), double the estimate. This, along with gambling losses, had driven Sheridan dangerously into debt. With more than 3,600 seats, the new Drury Lane was by far the largest theater in England and one of the largest in Europe. Filling the mammoth space was a never-ending headache for Sheridan. Since its reopening in March 1794, he'd yet to see a full house.

Theaters had changed drastically since Garrick's day. Audiences in the 1790s demanded spectacle: huge stages, elaborate sets, opulent costumes, orchestral interludes, and tiers of private boxes for the gentry. The cost of running a theater had soared. In Garrick's time, most of Drury Lane's running costs went to paying the actors. Now two-thirds of that expense went into scenery.

Even before Drury Lane's makeover, its stage had captivated audiences in a way the spartan stage of Shakespeare's Globe had never tried to. In 1773, a London physician named John Knyveton attended Garrick's production of *A Christmas Tale*. Knyveton recorded in his diary that the clever set designer, Philip Loutherbourg, "astonished and amazed the audience by turning a summer landscape into an autumn one so softly and so naturally, I could scarce believe my eyes; a magical piece of hocus pocus effected by careful lighting in the wings and filtering bright candlelight, reflected from tin shield, through silken screens of various colours. Mr. Loutherbourg is indeed a genius, and I begin to understand something of the subtle miasma of the stage."

By the mid-1790s, the theatrical trappings of Drury Lane had come to include a stage eighty feet wide and ninety feet deep, five balconies, and water tanks in the attic. The latter were installed for fire safety, but in a 1794 pantomime Sheridan put them to use to feed a cascading rocky stream on stage that flowed into a small lake, complete with bobbing rowboat.

Sheridan's creditors were now hounding him for repayment. He spent most of each workday in bed, surrounded by unread scripts and unopened mail, where neither creditors nor importuning playwrights could find him. Sheridan desperately needed to recoup his losses. He needed attention-getting fare that would draw playgoers away from Covent Garden and the city's many smaller venues and help him avert ruin. Shakespeare was the most reliable of all theatrical draws. A *new* Shakespeare would be an unbeatable event.

Sheridan's rival at Covent Garden, Thomas Harris, had sent word to Samuel Ireland that he could name his terms; the theater was eager to have *Vortigern*, whatever it cost. Sheridan could hardly outbid a blank check, but he had the advantage of familiarity. He'd been acquainted with Ireland for many years, thanks to Ireland's friendship with Thomas Linley, the dramatist's father-in-law and partner at Drury Lane. And "the Lane," the most

storied theater in England, was the more attractive venue to a socially ambitious man like Samuel Ireland. Not long after the first pages of *Vortigern*
went on display at Norfolk Street, Sheridan and Ireland reached an informal
agreement: Drury Lane, not Covent Garden, would stage the new play.

Sheridan was taking a huge risk—he wasn't convinced that Shakespeare
had written the play—but he was a compulsive risk taker. At twenty, he'd
risked the displeasure of both his father and his future father-in-law when
he'd eloped to France with the lovely soprano Eliza Linley; he was supposed
to have been escorting the seventeen-year-old to a convent in Lille, which
she was entering to escape the harassment of suitors. He'd fought two
duels to defend her honor and in one had been seriously wounded. As a
member of Parliament, he risked the crown's displeasure by giving fiery
speeches on the superiority of American and French democracy to English
monarchism—this at a time when Pitt's government was arresting like-
minded ideologues for treason. And he risked hundreds of pounds he didn't
have on cockamamy wagers: whether the French army would manage to
occupy Amsterdam, for example, or which route between two houses in
Piccadilly was the shortest.

During the spring, Sheridan made periodic visits to Norfolk Street. He,
like his host, awaited the completed transcript of *Vortigern*, which they believed William-Henry was copying from an original. Samuel on these oc-
casions would drone on about "the transcendent genius of our bard," his
son recalled. On one occasion, Sheridan interrupted his host to say that
"however high Shakspeare might stand in the estimation of the public in
general, he did not for his part regard him as a poet in that exalted light."
Perhaps it was professional jealousy. Sheridan was already widely considered
eighteenth-century England's most distinguished playwright. Moreover,
like more than a few playwrights of the day, he had mixed feelings about
Shakespeare monopolizing so many English stages two centuries after his
heyday. To Sheridan the businessman, this was a boon. To Sheridan the
playwright, it was unwelcome competition.

In April, Sheridan came by the Irelands' home to read the finished manuscript. William-Henry had outdone himself: The 2,800-line opus was

longer than most of Shakespeare's known plays. Sheridan joked that he would be getting two and a half plays for the price of one. Seated in the study, with Samuel in his accustomed chair and William-Henry watching from a quiet corner, Sheridan began reading. After a few pages, he came to a line that struck him as unpoetic—as downright clumsy, in fact.

"This is rather strange," he said, "for though you are acquainted with my opinion as to Shakespeare, yet, be it as it may, he certainly always wrote poetry." After a few more pages, Sheridan stopped again, put down the manuscript, and looked up at his host. "There are certainly some bold ideas, but they are crude and undigested. It is very odd: one would be led to think that Shakespeare must have been very young when he wrote the play."

William-Henry held still, trying to be as inconspicuous as possible. He didn't want either of the men to begin wondering what other young person might have had the means and the motive to have written the objectionable lines. He was relieved when Sheridan added that no one could doubt that the papers as a whole were Shakespeare's, because "who can possibly look at the papers and not believe them ancient?" Sheridan didn't think *Vortigern* was forged. He simply didn't think it was very good.

For all his devil-may-care extravagance, Sheridan was beginning to worry about what he had gotten himself into. In the coming months, his worries grew. He dodged meetings with Samuel Ireland, who was trying to pin him down as to terms, and ignored the collector's importuning letters. Only with the intervention of Albany Wallis, Samuel's Norfolk Street friend and Garrick's one-time attorney, did the men agree to a contract in September.

By the terms of the contract, the Theatre Royal at Drury Lane would stage "a certain ancient Manuscript play called or intitled Vortigern and signed as supposed to be written by William Shakspear." Sheridan promised to mount the play no later than mid-December. The timing was crucial, though neither Sheridan nor Samuel Ireland would have said so out loud. It meant that few people in the initial audiences would know much about the Shakespeare papers firsthand, as none of their texts would yet be published; playgoers could enter the theater with reasonably open minds. Officially, William-Henry was deemed the play's owner, with Samuel acting as trustee for his underage son. Though Samuel had wanted twice as much up front and a bigger share of the gate, Sheridan agreed to pay £250 (about £10,000 or more than $15,000 today) and a modest share of the nightly receipts. Samuel turned over to his son a bit less than one quarter of the initial fee.

Sheridan had decided the risk was worth it. From the start, his interest in *Vortigern* had been more a commercial calculation than a literary one. Even if the play didn't please the critics, even if some critics branded it a fake, he was counting on the controversy over its authorship to create a succès de scandale. The play's notoriety would pack his cavernous theater night after night, he hoped, even if not everyone on hand believed they were seeing Shakespeare. As for Samuel Ireland, he reminded himself that Sheridan's advance payment was a mere token of things to come. The theatrical run of the sensational new work by William Shakespeare, he was sure, would earn him and his son rather more than a paltry £250.

SAMUEL'S *Picturesque Views on the Upper, or Warwickshire Avon*, with its preface extolling his newly discovered relics, had now appeared and was selling briskly. He anticipated that this, along with the mid-December premiere of *Vortigern*, would boost sales of his folio edition of the Shakespeare papers at Christmastime. At four guineas a copy, the enormous book stood to earn him a richer stream of income than the Drury Lane box office would. And the book, not the play, would be what inscribed the name Samuel Ireland in the history books. The collector's self-importance was swelling by the week.

At about this time, Samuel learned of the death of old Thomas Hart, the butcher and great-nephew of Shakespeare who owned the Stratford birthplace. The ramshackle house was now for sale; an offer of £350, he was told, might secure it. Samuel smelled a business opportunity. He'd grown weary of opening his Norfolk Street house to gawking strangers. And he worried that souvenir seekers might snatch relics or tear out pages that caught their fancy. How much more convenient it would be—and lucrative—to convert the Bard's own birthplace into a ticket-selling gallery of memorabilia from the great man's life. Samuel, like his son, had a lively imagination. He corresponded with a Stratford go-between about a possible purchase, but the following year he dropped the idea. By then, he had too many other matters jostling for his attention.

Samuel's aggressive, heavy-handed style fed the doubts that many people had about the Shakespeare papers. An anonymous letter to the *Gentleman's Magazine* from "K. S." complained about Samuel's insistence that only those who paid four guineas for the forthcoming folio were entitled to inspect the curious papers firsthand to decide if they "are in reality what they pretend to be." Furthermore, the writer noted, neither of the two leading Shakespeare scholars, Edmond Malone and George Steevens, had weighed in with their opinions on the papers. Nor had Richard Farmer, Cambridge University's preeminent Shakespeare expert, now retired. Samuel fired off a dismissive reply, which the magazine published in the following issue. "Is all knowledge of Shakspeare and of old papers stored in the breast of this triumvirate?" he demanded.

Samuel's unctuous habit of asking visitors to sign his Certificate of Belief also didn't sit well with many of London's literary types. Some people signed merely to avoid the awkwardness of refusing. The classical scholar Richard Porson, when he came to inspect the papers, deflected his host with admirable tact. It was widely known that the freethinking Porson had lost a lifelong fellowship at Cambridge when he refused, for reasons of conscience, to take holy vows; for years afterward, he survived on the charity of friends. When Samuel asked if he would care to sign the Certificate of Belief, Porson replied wittily that he never signed "articles of faith."

Porson would never have signed in any case—he spotted the papers as fakes right away. A few weeks later, he published a mischievous letter in the *Morning Chronicle* announcing the discovery of the lost tragedies of Sophocles in the false bottom of an old trunk. In case readers didn't get the joke, he signed the letter "S. England." Included was a twelve-line excerpt from one of the 2,300-year-old manuscripts, in Greek. It was actually

Porson's translation of a nonsensical old nursery rhyme, a tad grim if not exactly tragic:

> *Three children sliding on the ice*
> *Upon a summer's day.*
> *As it fell out, they all fell in,*
> *The rest they ran away....*

In the fall, the *Morning Herald*'s puckish Henry Bate Dudley began publishing, as a public service, what he described as excerpts from Shakespeare's new play—although he hadn't seen a page of it. He later collected the excerpts in book form as *Passages Selected by Distinguished Personages, on the Great Literary Trail of Vortigern and Rowena; a Comi-Tragedy, 'Whether it be—or be not from the immortal pen of Shakspeare?'* With a characteristic lack of subtlety, Sir Henry included on his book's title page a phony quotation from the play: "'Open me a huge Wardrobe aboundinge in motlie habittes, and marke howe fantasticallie poore mortals will arraie themselves!'—VORT. & ROW." This was followed by a fictitious blurb from Drury Lane: "Mr. SHERIDAN says, 'It is the finest play that SHAKSPEARE ever wrote!'—not that he has had leisure yet to read it."

Amusing as such items were, the average citizen awaited the verdict of England's two reigning Shakespearean authorities, Malone and Steevens. Yet neither man had come to Norfolk Street to see the manuscripts in person. Both felt that publicly visiting Samuel Ireland to inspect the papers was a trap. If either of them failed to detect clear evidence of forgery, he'd be in an uncomfortable spot. If he denounced the papers as fraudulent without offering proof, he risked ridicule. If he made no comment, he would seem to be accepting them as genuine. Both men were certain the papers were forged. As two of England's foremost collectors of Elizabethan literature, Malone and Steevens knew too much about Shakespeare and history and manuscripts to be taken in. Both resolved to wait until December, when they could pore over the transcripts of the papers that Ireland was publishing.

Malone, a member of the late Samuel Johnson's circle, was a star amid London's cultural elite. Trained as a lawyer but drawn to poetry, he'd left Dublin for London in 1777, when he was thirty-five, for a life as a literary scholar. Malone was precociously self-confident from the start. To mentors like Johnson and Steevens, he was courteous but never deferential. He was one of the first critics to expose Chatterton's faux-medieval poems as forgeries, on purely stylistic grounds—though he actually praised Chatterton's brilliance, reserving his scorn for those who allowed themselves to be duped. He was the first scholar to deduce the likely order in which Shakespeare had written his plays. Like his friend Edward Gibbon, the historian, Malone insisted on using verifiable documents as sources for his writing. With his 1790 edition of Shakespeare's works, he was lionized.

Still, Malone had his detractors. To them, he was arrogant and self-righteous, a pedant who believed he knew Shakespeare's mind better than anyone. If he seldom made a blunder, he never admitted to one. It was Malone who insisted in 1793 that the memorial bust of Shakespeare in Stratford's Holy Trinity Church be "restored" to its original white color, not realizing that the statue, the earliest undisputed likeness of the Bard, had been colored from the first. A verse left in the visitor's book afterwards soon made the rounds in London:

> Stranger to whom this monument is shewn
> Invoke the Poet's curse upon Malone
> Whose meddling zeal his barbarous taste betrays
> And daubs his tombstone as he marr'd his plays.

For all his eminence in literary circles, Malone was, in private, a bitter and deeply unhappy man by 1795. Plagued by depression, poor eyesight, and writer's block, he'd been devastated when a woman he loved had spurned his offer of marriage at the beginning of the year. Then fifty-three, the lifelong bachelor had been similarly rejected twice before. Though he was a fearsome intellect in print, in person he was rather meek. "He has never been a favorite of the ladies," observed Boswell, a ladies' man. "He is too soft in his manners." With his latest rejection, Malone sank into despondency. He barely ate for weeks and by February was dangerously thin.

That month, the critic first learned of the Irelands' claims. In the Ireland-Shakespeare papers, Malone found a therapeutic outlet for his bitterness: He resolved to wage a literary crusade to prove beyond any doubt that they were forgeries. He would use his lawyer's training and his Shakespearean authority to destroy the Irelands' pretensions. Later, more than a few of his peers would be shocked at how fiercely he threw himself into the battle. There would be nothing soft in his treatment of the Irelands.

Malone was careful not to denounce the Shakespeare papers prematurely, without hard evidence. But privately he let his views be known. At a dinner party in early February, days after learning of the papers' discovery, Malone had shared his suspicions about Samuel Ireland and his papers. "The story he told," wrote one of the guests, the artist Joseph Farington, in his diary, "does not engage confidence when a man of Sam Ireland's character is to support it." Among the other dinner guests was Sheridan's imperious actor-manager, John Philip Kemble, who seems from that moment to have suspected the papers were false. Unfortunately for the Irelands, it was Kemble who would play the role of Vortigern at Drury Lane.

George Steevens, too, was happy to spread his misgivings about the Shakespeare papers. Steevens was the only active Shakespearean scholar of Malone's stature in England in 1795. He had collaborated with Samuel Johnson on a richly annotated edition of Shakespeare's complete works in 1773—for which Steevens had done most of the work. After years of inactivity, he roused himself to bring out a revised edition in 1793 largely to upstage Malone's 1790 edition. Behind a pretense of collegiality, he and Malone were rivals, not friends. Indeed, by Samuel Parr's count, Steevens had only three friends, Parr included.

Steevens was a meticulous and well-respected critic and editor, but he was also hotheaded, thin-skinned, vindictive, and sneaky. His scholarship was less stringent and more biased than Malone's. He dismissed the Chandos portrait—likely the only surviving portrait of Shakespeare painted from life—because the swarthy, earring-wearing man in the painting didn't look

"English" enough for him. "Our author exhibits the complexion of a Jew," he complained in 1793, "or rather that of a chimney-sweeper in the jaundice." His comments were a dig at Malone, who had used an engraving of the portrait as a frontispiece for his edition of Shakespeare's plays.

Steevens was a master of the well-placed rumor and the anonymous attack. He was not above using forgery both to amuse himself and to settle scores. One of his victims was Richard Gough, director of the Society of Antiquaries, who had slighted him in some way. In 1789, Steevens had an old chimney slab incised with Anglo-Saxon lettering so that it appeared to be the tombstone of the medieval king Hardyknute, a favorite of eighteenth-century forgers. The improbable epitaph read: "Here Hardyknute drank a wine-horn dry, stared about him, and died." Steevens arranged for the carving, which he claimed had been dug up in south London, to be placed in the window of a curiosity shop that Gough frequented. The antiquary, an authority on the old king, saw the stone and pronounced it genuine. The prank was exposed just before the society went to press with an article on the discovery.

In the fall of 1795, Boydell's Shakspeare Gallery on Pall Mall became an informal meeting place for those skeptical of the Irelands' discoveries. Joseph Farington, then at work on a commission for the gallery, recorded in his diary that he encountered Steevens there one day in early November. "He is not at liberty to communicate what He knows on the subject"— Steevens's usual dodge before slandering someone—"but He is satisfied Sheridan has taken himself in, in the matter of Irelands pretended discovered play of Shakespeare."

That evening, Farington dined at the Royal Academy with another artist working on a Shakespearean tableau for the gallery, Richard Westall. This was the same Westall who, twelve years earlier, had painted William-Henry, his sisters, and the rest of the cast of *The Gentle Shepherd*, in which he'd played the lead. Westall, then nineteen, had been friendly enough with the Irelands to have been their house guest for several months. Westall had since come to view his one-time hosts with condescension. To Farington, he criticized Samuel's "curious maneuvers" to position the Shakespeare papers "as belonging to him by descent." Later, Malone would enlist Westall as an errand boy of sorts, sending him dashing from records office to church archive, tracing signatures and copying records, looking for flaws in the massive paper edifice that William-Henry had built from scratch at his desk at New Inn.

Even the *Oracle*'s James Boaden, the most passionate of the Irelands' early defenders, had a change of heart that fall. Boaden was close to George Steevens, and Steevens was relentless in tearing down the Irelands' claims. That both Steevens and Malone were preparing public denunciations of the papers was widely known. Steevens eventually dropped the idea of affixing his own name to an exposé. He preferred to lie low and let others do his bidding. He talked Boaden into publicly leaving the fold of the Believers and issuing a pamphlet attacking the papers once they were published at Christmastime. Boaden would be listed as the pamphlet's author, but the arguments and the evidence would come straight from Steevens.

THAT FALL, SAMUEL Ireland asked a dramatist and newspaperman named John Taylor to visit him at Norfolk Street. He was invited, along with an author and a barrister, to listen to the collector read *Vortigern* aloud, "that we might form some judgment as to its merits and authenticity," Taylor wrote in his memoirs. Taylor was impressed by Samuel's collection of curiosities and especially by his intricately carved Shakespeare armchair. Tea was served, and the reading was about to begin, he recalled, "when I requested to sit in Shakspeare's chair, as it might contain some inspiring power to enlighten my understanding, and enable me the better to judge. They laughed at my whim, but indulged me with the chair."

The visitors decided the drama had a number of passages "of great poetical merit" and originality, but other parts were strangely unliterary. One section struck the group as particularly muddled. Samuel asked his guests if they could suggest any "alteration or remoulding" of the passage. "At this question," Taylor recalled, "I affected to start, and said, 'God bless me, shall

I sit in Shakspeare's chair and presume to think I can improve any work from his unrivaled muse?'" His host calmly replied that he'd tackle the needed changes himself. Taylor left the reading suspecting that *Vortigern* must be a fabrication after all. Later, he decided that Samuel was too open about making changes to have been concealing a forgery.

Taylor was more innocent than most people in London's theater world. Despite the adulation that Englishmen at the close of the eighteenth century heaped on Shakespeare, they preferred drastically rewritten versions of what he originally wrote. Many of the lines David Garrick had recited in his acclaimed London debut as Richard III in 1741 were actually written by the comic actor and playwright Colley Cibber, not Shakespeare. Cibber had freely rewritten Shakespeare's tragedy, stealing bits from other plays and adding crowd-pleasing lines like "Off with his head—so much for Buckingham."* Shakespeare was sacrosanct only in theory; in practice, publishers and playhouses gave the public what it wanted. *Much Ado About Nothing* and *Measure for Measure* were blended into a single play. Romeo and Juliet were transported to ancient Rome. Henry V was followed to France by a cross-dressing mistress whom he'd rejected.

During the 1794 theatrical season, just before William-Henry began his forgeries, the Drury Lane Theatre had drawn crowds to its lavish production of *King Lear*. But this wasn't Shakespeare's *Lear*. It was Nahum Tate's. In rewriting the Bard for eighteenth-century audiences, Tate, a poet laureate early in the century, gave *Lear* a happy ending: Cordelia marries Edgar, and Lear, Gloucester, and Kent all survive to enjoy a peaceful dotage. Georgian England preferred its dramas that way.

---

* On stage, Cibber's *Richard III* eclipsed Shakespeare's until well into the nineteenth century. Even Sir Laurence Olivier's classic 1956 film version used Cibber's words.

IF SHAKESPEARE'S WORDS weren't tamperproof, then William-Henry's weren't either. The contract that Ireland and Sheridan signed in September for staging *Vortigern* at Drury Lane allowed for "such additions or alterations as they"—Sheridan, Linley, or anyone they chose—"shall think proper." The original forgery was half again longer than Sheridan thought an audience would sit through. Chopping seven or eight hundred lines didn't bother the collector unduly; he could do it himself. But Sheridan also wanted greater "measure in the poetry"—not just a smoother meter in places but more graceful language in general.

Samuel didn't agree, but he had no choice if he wanted to see the play performed. He began casting about for "some friendly hand" capable of making his Shakespeare more Shakespearean. Samuel preferred a low-level ghostwriter, not an established author. He didn't want someone who'd demand to share the editor's credit, which the former weaver was claiming for himself.

One of those who was given pages to rework was Thomas Caldecott, a lawyer and book collector who adored Shakespeare and had already signed up to buy the folio edition of the forthcoming papers. In a letter to a friend two years later, Caldecott claimed he had recognized the "loose disjointed, skimble skamble stuff" that Samuel handed him as un-Shakespearean from the start. He took it to be the work of a forger. Although William-Henry had confessed to the misdeed by the time Caldecott wrote his letter, the lawyer ridiculed the notion that Samuel Ireland, let alone his morose, evasive son, could possibly have written *Vortigern*. "Neither one or the other of them to my certain knowlege are capable of writing a sentence of English correctly, or know even the common parts of Speech." Caldecott's overstatement was absurd, but it reflected one reason William-Henry's caper succeeded so dramatically: Even people who suspected forgery dismissed him and his father as lacking the wit to have been responsible.

Sheridan was no longer feeling sanguine about *Vortigern*'s prospects. Despite his contractual agreement to stage it, his enthusiasm for the production had waned. Disorganized in the best of times, Sheridan now seemed to have little time for planning the premiere. The mid-December deadline was soon forgotten.

Samuel began to realize that fall how unreliable a partner Sheridan was. When Samuel and his son tried to arrange meetings at Drury Lane to see how work was proceeding, the playwright avoided them. Sheridan eventually told Kemble, his theater manager, to meet the pair instead. When the Irelands arrived at the theater for their appointment on November 17, they discovered the manager had slipped out early. Perhaps it was just as well. Kemble was even less enthusiastic about the play than Sheridan was, and he hadn't even read it. (When he finally did, the following month, he told friends it was "wretched stuff.")

Samuel cornered a carpenter backstage to ask about the set building. Sheridan had promised the Irelands that Drury Lane would stage *Vortigern* as a full-blown spectacular, with lavish new sets and costumes custom-made for each part. The carpenter looked perplexed. Sheridan had ordered him to stop work on *Vortigern* and turn his attention to building scenery for another play. Samuel was aghast. This was not at all what he expected. From here on, he began to regard Sheridan as an obstacle, not an ally. He resolved not to hand over the *Vortigern* script to Sheridan until there was evidence the theater was willing to do the play justice.

THOUGH BOSWELL WAS dead, Boaden disenchanted, and Sheridan undependable, the ranks of the Believers remained well-stocked with prominent names. The most prestigious of these was his royal highness the Duke of Clarence, second in line to the throne. The day after being snubbed by Kemble at Drury Lane, William-Henry and his father were invited to a private meeting at the duke's residence at St. James Palace. For this, the Irelands had Dora Jordan, the duke's live-in mistress, to thank. William-Henry had admired the unmarried actress for years. She'd been a favorite at Drury Lane with audiences, if not critics, since her debut ten years before. Curly-headed and vivacious, Mrs. Jordan specialized in playing spirited tomboys like Viola in *Twelfth Night* and Rosalind in *As You Like It*. It was undoubtedly she who arranged for the Irelands to be invited to the palace on Pall Mall for an interview.

The Irelands, father and son, had rubbed elbows with well-born Londoners for years, but being summoned to an audience with the Duke of Clarence, King George III's third son, was an extraordinary coup. Samuel brought along the *Vortigern* manuscript in Shakespeare's handwriting, which William-Henry had finally completed. Few people had seen the entire play, in any form. Even Sheridan, at that point, didn't have a copy.

The duke and his lady were a sympathetic audience. The future King William IV was a lifelong theater enthusiast. He was an excitable, free-spending, and dissolute but rather lonely man, despite his mistress and a fast-growing brood of young Fitzclarences. As a young navy midshipman, he'd acted in shipboard dramas, including Shakespeare's *Henry V*, in which he'd been typecast as the wayward Prince Hal.

By virtue of his social stature, the duke considered himself a keen judge of character and an authority on all matters of taste. Indeed, many people deferred to royal opinion. That his highness counted himself among the Believers was an important boost to the Irelands' cause. At St. James Palace, the duke peered at the yellowed *Vortigern* manuscript and pronounced it authentic, then signed up for seven copies of the bound Shakespeare papers. He also told Samuel he was wise to withhold the transcript of the play until Sheridan began work on the sets. The theater director, he exclaimed, was "one of the greatest vagabonds on the face of the earth." The duke's opinion was more political than dramatic. In the House of Commons, Sheridan was an opposition gadfly who enjoyed mocking the government in long speeches.

Mrs. Jordan took a liking to young William-Henry, whom she may have remembered from encounters backstage at Drury Lane. She was excited about *Vortigern*, especially since Sheridan had promised her a major role. William-Henry was grateful that she, too, was an ally. Her wholehearted support was more important, in his mind, than the scoffing of penny-a-line journalists. Having this famous beauty bring to life a character that he'd essentially patched together from other roles in other plays would give his forgery the gloss of legitimacy. William-Henry would remain devoted to the actress for years, longer even than the duke would. Clarence would abandon the mother of his ten children in 1811 and eventually marry a princess from Germany.

If William-Henry had another stalwart ally, it was his old law-clerk chum Montague Talbot, now part of a Dublin theater company. As an actor, Talbot loved the idea of expanding Shakespeare's body of work. Earlier, he'd begged his friend for a chance to write a scene or two of *Vortigern* himself. William-Henry agreed at first, but eventually changed his mind. Being able to write like Shakespeare was a rare, probably unique, skill, and he didn't think Talbot was up to it.

In November, Talbot came to London for a visit and made a point of seeing the Irelands. It wasn't a tranquil period on Norfolk Street, what with Sheridan's and Kemble's obstinacy, barbed insinuations in the press, and Samuel's ceaseless demands for information about Mr. H. Before Talbot arrived, William-Henry saw an opportunity to remedy this last problem, at least a bit. He told his father that Talbot, too, had met the unnamed gentleman. In fact, he went on, it was Talbot who'd introduced him to Mr. H. in the first place. William-Henry had many of the traits of a good hoaxer, but one he lacked was a habit of thinking through the consequences of the stories he made up.

Samuel insisted that the young man come to dinner at Norfolk Street his first evening in London. William-Henry intercepted Talbot at his lodging house and went over what he could and could not say that night. The dinner was an awkward one. Talbot had always been jovial and talkative at the Irelands' home, but this time he was strangely reticent. The lad seemed almost depressed. Samuel pressed him for details about Mr. H. and asked why Talbot couldn't grant *him* an introduction to the good gentleman. Talbot was evasive to the point of rudeness. The moment the cloth was cleared, he begged his leave and returned to his lodgings. A few minutes later, Talbot was told he had a caller. Samuel Ireland, red-faced and agitated, was downstairs. He simply had to hear what Talbot knew about Mr. H. His reputation, his livelihood, his very health depended on it. The collector was self-pitying and indignant at the same time.

Talbot had the unpleasant sensation of being mired in a web of someone else's lies, but he was unwilling to destroy his friend by telling the truth. He stalled for time. Drawing on his acting skills, he told the collector that he wasn't yet free to tell him all he knew—an oath of secrecy involving a man of Mr. H.'s stature was not something to be taken lightly. Once back in Dublin, Talbot promised, he would write a letter explaining everything. In the ensuing days, he and William-Henry worked out the details of their cover story, which Talbot would mail from Dublin. In the meantime, the pair agreed to destroy every scrap of their correspondence, even though it was mostly in code. With a man as unrelenting as Samuel Ireland, they were taking no chances.

Late in November, Talbot's letter arrived. It was detailed but unhelpful. Talbot recounted discovering old papers and other odds and ends at the home of Mr. H., "a friend of mine." When he discovered the papers had belonged to William Shakespeare, he arranged for William-Henry to come over and help him dig through the documents, with Mr. H's kind assent. The gentleman wanted no part of the business. He was a man "in the high walk of life," and he didn't want it known that "one of his ancestors was a contemporary of Shakspeare in the dramatic profession" who had been entrusted with most of the playwright's effects—from furniture to art—yet had allowed nearly everything to be lost or destroyed. After two centuries, the shame was still too great.

The letter left Samuel as much in the dark as ever. Though he thanked his good fortune that he now possessed the residue of Shakespeare's personal estate, still he chafed that he had no idea where it had come from. Uncertainty about provenance, he knew, was the downfall of many a collector. He tried not to think about it. Seeing that *Vortigern* was staged at Drury Lane took priority.

Until the play script was fixed, the Irelands both knew, Sheridan had no intention of following through on his promises. Eventually, a small army of variously skilled people would trim, augment, rewrite, and rearrange the drama that Shakespeare had supposedly judged his masterpiece. One moment the play was a priceless antiquarian relic; the next it was an overlong working script. To be sure, William-Henry's work needed heavy rewriting. One scene in particular, in which King Vortigern muses lustfully about his daughter, was deemed unfit for a Georgian playhouse—but then so was much of Shakespeare.

Mrs. Freeman and William-Henry's two sisters, Jane and the now-married Anna Maria, were all enlisted to copy out drafts of the play at various stages. Spelling was modernized, punctuation added, lines inserted and cut. Later, critics would unfairly conclude that the whole Ireland family had been busily forging Shakespeare.

Like so many novice writers before and since, William-Henry was incensed that his workmanship was being meddled with. Hadn't his words already been praised as the effusions of the mighty Bard? He ended up playing little role in the cutting and rewriting. He had more important work to do that fall. He'd embarked on his masterpiece.

EARLIER, DURING THE SUMMER—after the months of exhausting, solitary labor at Bingley's office—William-Henry had slackened the pace of his forgeries. His father already had more than enough Shakespeareana to publish even without *Vortigern*. Now a young man of twenty, William-Henry was aware that some people, at least, viewed him with suspicion. He made a point of socializing more, dining with friends, attending the theater, and generally being a man about town after hours. "My reason for appearing so much in public," he wrote in his initial confession the following year, "was to make the world think me a giddy thoughtless young man, incapable of producing the papers."

It was easy to miss how driven he was. Buoyed by his success, he was convinced that all his clandestine fabricating since the winter had made him a better writer. In September, he resumed his literary exploits with another original, full-length play. To pursue his plan to write history plays under his own name, he now realized, would be premature, not to mention foolhardy. Thus *Henry II*, like *Vortigern,* would be Shakespeare's.

The plot centered around the triangle of King Henry, his estranged queen, Eleanor, and his mistress, Rosamond, as well as his conflict with Thomas Becket, the stubborn archbishop assassinated in his cathedral by henchmen of the king. Beyond its obvious dramatic potential, the story proved a good choice: William-Henry didn't yet know it, but *Henry I* and *Henry II* were among the Shakespearean manuscripts that collector John Warburton had listed as missing and likely incinerated by his kitchen maid in 1730. Warburton's handwritten list, to Shakespeare cultists, was proof that *Henry II* had existed; that it had been destroyed was only a surmise.

As he set to work, William-Henry said nothing about the new play to his father. He wanted to be able to compose his text undisturbed this time. After writing the first three pages in old-fashioned script, William-Henry didn't bother with Elizabethan paper and faded ink. He wrote it in his own handwriting, intending to present it as his copy of an old manuscript that had just turned up at Mr. H.'s country estate.

And this time, he wanted more control over the editing as well as the writing. When he finished the script, in early December, ten weeks after he'd begun, he delivered it not to his father but to Thomas Harris at the Covent Garden Theatre. Samuel surely objected to his son's insubordination—the collector had come to view all Mr. H.'s papers as his own—though neither mentioned the matter in their writings. Covent Garden's manager, as William-Henry knew, was a less discerning critic than Sheridan and more apt to stage the new play without ham-fisted changes.

Indeed, Harris expressed delight with the new play. Covent Garden, it seemed, would have its own Shakespeare premiere after all. William-Henry put out of his mind the carping he'd heard about *Vortigern.* His new play was vastly better. He could already imagine the thunderous applause filling Covent Garden. And he had reason for optimism: Several literary men who saw the manuscript of *Henry II* praised a number of the speeches. In the opening scene, Henry refers to himself in the royal plural as he muses on the welcome death of his predecessor, King Stephen, England's last Norman ruler:

Why look then how this same death doth scoff us,
Cozening our minds with sweet, delusive thoughts,
Binding round our temples the glitt'ring crown,
Whilst we, short-witted fools, accept the task,
Dream but of smiles, look but for golden joys.
Now mark the chastisement of our conceits:
This regal gem becomes a galling thorn;
Treason and a whole catalogue of ills
That are attendant on a kingly state
Rush in upon our frail bark of nature,
Buffet us to and fro with the fell blast,
Which, like a meager, chatt'ring ague fit,
Turns our stern manhoods into peevish fear,
Sours the full tide of sweet with bitterness,
Till, lastly, tired with this dalliance,
The wick of life quite dwindled and bewasted,
We lay us down, beg only ground enough
To sink a grave, then groan, and welcome Death.

William-Henry paid only fitful attention to writing in iambic blank verse, but his words and sentiments were grandly Shakespearean. The scholars believed it to be a precocious work from the Bard's early career. They deduced this from William-Henry's sly reference to himself in the epilogue, which the forger later admitted was "incautious":

... Think how much the writer here hath toil'd
To please, and show in this our Harry's reign
The pride and glory of our English land,
The unstain'd thunder of our regal lion,
No brow so rough but sure will smooth at this;
No frown so black but will to sweetness turn,
And, bright as sun when bursting from the east,
Drive night away—Yet why entreat ye thus?

No more, no more: ye smile, and look so sweet,
I'll to our young and trembling author say,
Ye heard, ye smil'd, and did applaud his play.

In William-Henry's mind, the poignant, action-filled drama he'd written this time was as polished and compelling as anything from the Bard's own hand. He felt as though he were Shakespeare reincarnated. His latest achievement was so far superior to *Vortigern*, in fact, he wished he could have withdrawn it and made his theatrical debut with rugged King Harry instead. Had this been possible, the real-life drama about to consume him might have turned out differently.

CHAPTER TEN

FORGERIES FOR SALE

THE SHAKESPEARE PAPERS were published on Christmas Eve, 1795. They were gathered in an enormous leather-bound volume, the typeset text alternating with detailed, hand-tinted engravings of everything from young Will's lock of hair to the dangling wax seals on the parchment deeds. William-Henry's anxiety at having his forgeries exposed to public view was overcome by his writer's pride in seeing his work showcased in a tome worthy of a great library. A package this sumptuous was bound to make a powerful impression.

His father had grandly titled the collection *Miscellaneous Papers and Legal Instruments Under the Hand and Seal of William Shakspeare, Including the Tragedy of King Lear and a Small Fragment of Hamlet, from the Original MSS. in the Possession of Samuel Ireland of Norfolk Street.* Referring to himself in the third person, Samuel assured readers that "the editor" had carefully verified the papers' authenticity: "He has courted, he has even challenged, the critical judgment of those who are best skilled in the poetry and phraseology of the times in which Shakspeare lived; as well as those whose profession or course of study has made them conversant with ancient deeds, writings, seals and autographs." His conclusion: *"These papers can be no other than the production of Shakspeare himself."*

Samuel's preface described how his son came to discover the relics in the possession of "a gentleman of considerable property" who insisted he not be named. It noted that Shakespeare's original wording of *King Lear*, here revealed for the first time, showed that the printed versions known to the world are corruptions—"deviations from that spontaneous flow of soul and simple diction which so eminently distinguish this great Author, this Child of Nature." And it assured readers that the Bard's personal papers revealed him to be—as all England had hoped—a man of "acute and penetrating judgment, with a disposition amiable and gentle."

William-Henry must have had mixed feelings as he read his father's ill-advised slap at those foolish enough to have attempted forgery: "So superior and transcendent is the genius of Shakspeare that scarce any attempts to rival or imitate him, and those too contemptible to notice, have ever been made."

Then, six days after the *Miscellaneous Papers* were published, before most of the press and the critics had had a chance to weigh in on the matter, the moment William-Henry had been dreading arrived.

The Shakespeare papers were exposed as a forgery.

AN EXCITED ALBANY Wallis, the Irelands' antiquarian neighbor, called unexpectedly at 8 Norfolk Street shortly after midday on Wednesday, December 30, while William-Henry was at work. Wallis had just discovered yet another document from Shakespeare's lifetime, he told Samuel breathlessly. It was a second real estate contract related to the Blackfriars house; he'd found it in the same London records archive where he'd found the first, twenty-eight years earlier. Affixed to it, as before, was Shakespeare's signature—only the fifth that had ever been found, the other three being on the will that had turned up in 1747. Of more immediate importance was that the latest deed contained something else: the never-before-seen signature of his actor friend and business colleague John Heminge.

To Wallis's surprise, Heminge's handwriting looked nothing like the wobbly scribble that William-Henry had written with his left hand on the five-guinea receipt twelve months earlier. That signature looked like a tangled pile of string. The actor's actual penmanship was elegant and compact. Even the *i* in Heminge was dotted just so. The Shakespeare manuscripts, Wallis announced, must be fabrications after all. Wallis didn't suspect either of the Irelands of forgery. He had no doubt, however, that their papers had been forged by someone, perhaps by the shadowy Mr. H.

Samuel was devastated. A cover-up was out of the question—not that Wallis would ever have played along—for the forged signature was now reproduced in every copy of the *Miscellaneous Papers*. And if the revelation itself was dreadful, its timing was worse. Thanks to Mrs. Jordan, he'd just been summoned alone to an audience that afternoon with the heir to the throne, the Prince of Wales. Samuel was due at Carlton House, his art-filled garden palace on Pall Mall, in a few minutes. The prince's factotum was already on hand, warming himself by the fireplace; his carriage was waiting outside. The future king, less credulous than his younger brother, hadn't signed up for any copies of the *Miscellaneous Papers*, but he was eager to see the manuscripts for himself and especially the play script in Shakespeare's hand.

Before leaving, Samuel studied the two clashing signatures, then rode off to Carlton House with his cherished papers in hand. The prince received him alone and spent two hours examining the papers and peppering Samuel with surprisingly pointed questions about them. He reserved judgment on their authenticity but allowed that they appeared to be antique and even congratulated Samuel on his son's discovery. The collector should have been exultant about such a courtesy from the dashing heir to the throne. Instead, he had trouble concentrating. He was trying to imagine how John Heminge could have had two wildly dissimilar signatures. Something was very wrong. He needed to speak with his son.

Returning from Bingley's office that afternoon at three, William-Henry was shaken to learn of Wallis's discovery. He felt the familiar sensation of being trapped in his own tangle of invention, where each deception led to a new predicament, which required a new deception. This time, it seemed he'd made a fatal error. If the Heminge receipt was phony, then everything was.

William-Henry had worked too hard to abandon his hoax now. With barely any time to think, he resolved to try one more ruse. It was far-fetched, but his bluffing had never been timid. He raced the block to Wallis's Thames-side house at 21 Norfolk to see the conveyance for himself. With a pretence of casual curiosity, as Wallis watched him, William-Henry studied each letter in the authentic Heminge signature: the gracefully looping *h*'s, the lower-case *n*'s like stiff inverted *w*'s. Returning home, he told his father that he was off to Mr. H.'s mansion to tell him of the discovery.

Instead, he raced up Norfolk Street and charged through the late-afternoon traffic clogging the Strand, dodging horse-drawn carts and slow-moving pedestrians. He flew up narrow Wych Street and burst through the stone archway into the courtyard of New Inn. He needed to act quickly, before the well-connected attorney began showing off his latest find. In Bingley's empty office, he retrieved his papers and ink from under the window seat and began to write.

William-Henry had never before worked under pressure this acute. Never before had he felt so close to being a criminal. Perhaps Samuel Johnson was right: Knowing one is to be hanged does concentrate the mind wonderfully. In a few minutes' time, the lad had penned a new forgery—a receipt for some theatrical payments—and signed it with Heminge's name, "as similar to the original as my memory would enable me to give it," he later wrote. As he frantically darkened the paper and ink over a flame, he nearly set the receipt on fire by holding it too close. Finally, clutching the yellowed slip of paper, its ink barely dry, William-Henry hurtled back to Albany Wallis's townhouse. He was out of breath and sweating freely when he arrived, but he no longer felt doomed. He'd thought of a cover story.

Mr. H., William-Henry told the antiquary, had seemed amused rather than puzzled by news of the new signature. The anonymous gentleman had immediately walked over to a writing table and extracted from a drawer a small, discolored scrap of paper. Smiling at William-Henry's distress, the gentleman had said: "Take that to Mr. Wallis's and see if it does not correspond with the handwriting to his deed."

Wallis now peered at the smoothly written receipt that William-Henry handed him. Why, yes, this signature matched that on the newly discovered deed quite admirably. But what about Heminge's clumsy scrawl in the *Miscellaneous Papers*?

That was easily explained, Mr. H. had supposedly told William-Henry. There were *two* John Heminges in Elizabethan London. Both of them worked in the theater, and both did business with Shakespeare. The Globe Theater's Heminge was the *tall* John Heminge. The other, known as *short* John Heminge, was connected with the Curtain Theater in Shoreditch.

As an explanation, this was preposterous. That William-Henry could recite it with a straight face speaks to his growing fluency as a liar. The conjuring of dual Heminges, not to mention the miraculous convenience of Mr. H. having a receipt by the original John Heminge lying in the drawer of his writing table, was farcical. But the story worked. Albany Wallis accepted it without protest.

Actually, it was William-Henry, not Wallis, who was unsatisfied with the new signature. Having now had a chance to study Wallis's original a second time, he immediately raced back to New Inn to fashion a more convincing version. He burned his first attempt and returned home at last. Since his hectic odyssey had begun, just an hour and a quarter had elapsed. His father welcomed this latest document with relief.

The close call brought home to William-Henry how near he was to disaster at every moment. He'd been naïve to think he could settle into a comfortable career as a latter-day Shakespeare, like an author building a reputation. The more elaborate his interlocking fabrications became, the more vulnerable he was to exposure. He was one botched alibi away from infamy.

William-Henry's forgeries, like his explanations, had always been implausible. His convenient discoveries of new Shakespearean papers—just when they were needed—was about as credible as black magic. Yet for now, people were content to be entranced. William-Henry's thick-nibbed pens were his magic wands. He waved them, and people who should have known better swooned.

HAVING DODGED ONE threat, William-Henry now faced new ones—this time publicly. Having the forgeries collected in one place made it easy to see that Shakespeare's alleged handwriting varied wildly from document to document. Worse, with the texts published in crisp sixteen-point type, his bizarre spelling—inspired by Chatterton's own forgeries, not Elizabethan English—was impossible to overlook. There were altogether too many *e*'s and *y*'s, too many doubled consonants, too many weird constructions like "innetennecyonne" (intention) and "innefyrmytyes" (infirmities).

Several of London's high-spirited newspapers pounced on the papers with glee. On January 14, 1796, the *Telegraph* published a letter from the Bard to his friend and rival Ben Jonson: "Deeree Sirree, Wille you doee meee theee favvourree too dinnee wythee meee onn Friddaye nextte, attt twoo off theee clockee, too eattee sommee muttonne choppes andd somme poottaattoooeesse." For good measure, the letter was dated January 27, 1658, more than forty years after Shakespeare's death. The *Monthly Mirror*, less amused, denounced the would-be additions to Shakespeare's oeuvre in screaming capitals: "THE WHOLE IS A GROSS AND IMPUDENT IMPOSITION, AN INSULT TO THE CHARACTER OF OUR IMMORTAL BARD, AND A LIBEL ON THE TASTE AND UNDERSTANDING OF THE NATION!!"

Samuel's former ally James Boaden—the same James Boaden who had praised the juvenile love letter to Anne Hathaway for its "utmost delicacy of passion" and branded his disbelieving fellow editor Henry Bate Dudley an ignoramus—now publicly attacked the Shakespeare papers with all the fervor of a lapsed cultist. His seventy-two-page pamphlet took the form of an open letter to his friend and mentor George Steevens, though the stamp of Steevens's snide approach to criticism was evident throughout.

In a preamble, Boaden tried to explain away his outspoken support for the papers earlier: "To a mind filled with the most ardent love and the most eager zeal, disarmed of caution by the character too of the gentleman who displayed them, it will not be the subject of severe reproof"—or so he hoped—"that the wished impression was made." Boaden was not even pretending to have been an unbiased critic. Nor was he unbiased now, having switched sides.

The Shakespeare revealed in the Irelands' papers, Boaden sneered, was so inept at blank verse that he was unable "to number ten syllables upon his fingers." The supposedly original manuscript of *King Lear* he derided as "nonsensical, disjointed, inconclusive and mutilated." The profession of faith, "rationally pious and grandly expressed" nine months earlier, was now "exquisite nonsense" and "execrable jargon." Boaden wrote of the unknown impostor: "In his efforts after the lofty and sublime, he is frequently turgid and diffuse; his meaning is often buried under the pomp of his expression." Most of the pamphlet was along these lines. It was name calling, not analysis.

Boaden knew Samuel Ireland and his habits well enough to deem him innocent of forgery. Unlike other skeptics, however, he had suspicions about Ireland's son. In the *Lear* manuscript, he (or perhaps Steevens) noticed that the French word *hélas* appeared in place of Shakespeare's *alas*. "One might be tempted to believe that Shakspeare had received a French education," Boaden observed tartly.

William-Henry regarded Boaden as a dishonest hack who shifted his views to suit prevailing opinion, even if Boaden was right in judging the papers to be forged. Years later, William-Henry referred to some quasi-Shakespearean poetry that Boaden himself had published early in 1796. If context, not content, was so important, he observed, let Boaden have his own feeble attempts at poetry inscribed in Elizabethan handwriting on wire-wove paper. Only a "consummate blockhead," he wrote, would judge the verses improved as a result.

A few weeks after Boaden's tract appeared, a popular caricaturist named George Woodward entered the fray with an anonymous satire: *Familiar Verses from the Ghost of Willy Shakspeare to Sammy Ireland*. Woodward had the Bard's ghost confront Ireland, who is surrounded by

... auncient dirtie scrolls,
Long shreds of parchment, deeds, and mustie rolls. . . .
Samples of hair, love songs, and sonnets meete,
Together met by chaunce in Norfolk-street;
Where, fruitful as the vine, the tiny elves
Produce young manuscripts for Sammy's *shelves.*
Dramas in embrio leave their lurking holes,
And little Vortigerns *start forth in shoals.*

Shakespeare's ghost ends up allowing Ireland and his elves to continue their nefarious work. Theaters were already mutilating his plays beyond recognition—"I make oath and swear it on the spot/I know not what is mine, nor what is not"—so the Bard wasn't going to lose sleep about what the forgers were up to.

Characteristically, the *Analytical Review,* a sober counterweight to the larkier journals, held off judgment on the Ireland documents until they'd undergone "an impartial examination at the bar of an intelligent and candid public."

In the meantime, mockery of the *Miscellaneous Papers* in the press served only to fan public interest in the manuscripts. Most Londoners, whether they'd formed an opinion on the matter or not, regarded the Shakespeare papers controversy as an enjoyable diversion. They were accustomed to the intemperate nastiness of the press. Public figures in England could find themselves the butt of vitriolic attacks for nothing more than supporting the French Revolution—or being Roman Catholic, for that matter. Readers didn't necessarily agree. All the same, by the 1790s readership of London's assorted journals was soaring.

Many Englishmen were so addicted to their daily papers, in fact, that they'd arrive at coffeehouses to read them as soon as the papers were delivered, morning or evening. Often the ink was still wet; a group of avid readers at one popular coffeehouse was known as the Wet Paper Club. The coffeehouses' most vociferous habitués crowded into back rooms each week to hold forth in raucous debates on issues of the day. Among the questions debated in 1795: Should Pitt be impeached for obstinacy and wickedness? Which is harder to find, honesty among lawyers or piety among divines? In these circles, the Irelands and their documents were a reliable topic for loud and heated arguments.

On the central question of whether Shakespeare had written the mysterious manuscripts, however, neither Grub Street lampooning nor coffee-house bombast carried much weight with the average citizen. Forgeries, then as now, were notoriously hard to detect merely by judging the style and quality of the writing. If Shakespeare's genius was self-evident, there wouldn't be continuing uncertainty as to exactly which plays he'd written. Over the centuries, Shakespeare's canon would be added to (*Pericles*, *Henry VIII*) and subtracted from (*Edward III*, *The London Prodigal*) as scholars debated whether Shakespeare was working with a collaborator and, if so, who might have written what. The text alone didn't say.

In the 1790s, Samuel Ireland's claims were no more dubious than much of what then passed for literary scholarship. True, William-Henry's ersatz Elizabethan spelling was outlandish: Burregannedye was never a province of France, in any language. But Shakespeare and his contemporaries spelled words oddly, too. Noiz, themme, heereuppon, moovabl, wyndoz—all were acceptable words in the late 1500s. It took an expert to prove that words or handwriting was anachronistic, and few people, even antiquaries, were up to it.

Samuel Ireland, characteristically, was offended that his priceless manuscripts—and, by extension, the Bard himself—were being subjected to ridicule. He was too combative to tolerate the insolence of journalists and pamphleteers, so he mobilized a counterattack. He enlisted a young barrister at New Inn named Matthew Wyatt to publish *A Comparative Review of the Opinions of Mr. James Boaden*. Wyatt skewered the *Oracle*'s editor for his comically overheated condemnation of passages over which he'd trembled with joy a year before. Wyatt identified himself on the title page only as "A Friend to Consistency."

The lawyer's defense of the Irelands' papers was reasonable enough, if entirely wrong. "One deed or one letter may be forged, perhaps, with tolerable accuracy," Wyatt wrote, "but who can suppose that the same person should be equally skilled in forgeries of so many different kinds, and of so vast an extent?" The number and variety of documents make "the talk of imposture next to an impossibility."

Ireland also prevailed on his old friend Francis Webb, the heraldry expert who recognized Shakespeare's brilliance in *Vortigern* ("It either comes from his pen, or from Heaven"), to defend the papers publicly. Like a number of other Believers, Webb was not entirely comfortable being a front man in Samuel Ireland's campaign. He urged Ireland to ask the Reverend Parr instead, but Parr—the stalwart who'd composed the Certificate of Belief— now told Ireland he had questions about the papers' origins. Webb was a more malleable personality, and his pamphlet was as flattering as Ireland could have wished. Nonetheless, Webb, like Wyatt, chose to conceal his authorship. He signed his name as Philalethes, the pseudonym of a seventeenth-century alchemist, which wasn't the most reassuring of bylines.

In *Shakspeare's Manuscripts, in the Possession of Mr. Ireland*, Webb dismissed as ludicrous any suggestion that the manuscripts might be forgeries. The writing paper was indisputably from Shakespeare's time. Why would someone two hundred years ago have forged works of Shakespeare yet kept them hidden, never to profit from the scheme? The idea that a modern forger might have used old paper evidently didn't occur to him. In any case, to imitate a writer as uniquely talented as Shakespeare, on old paper or new, was "next to an impossibility," Webb declared. "Who could soar with his sublime genius? Who rove with his boundless imagination? Who could rival his pregnant wit?" Since the author of Ireland's manuscripts accomplished all these things, he could be none other than the Bard himself.

In hindsight, Webb, Wyatt, and the other Believers were misguided dupes. But in early 1796, it was easier to offer support for the Shakespeare papers than it was to take a public stand against them. To praise works that might later, perhaps many years later, be revealed as fabrications—if such a thing could ever be proven to everyone's satisfaction—would be embarrassing, certainly, but not especially injurious or noteworthy. To denounce as insipid the genuine works of the greatest writer in English literature, on the other hand, would be a catastrophe for any literary man's reputation. Worse, it would be blasphemous. Only a critic of great self-assurance would stake his reputation on publicly attacking the manuscripts.

Even Edmond Malone—whom William-Henry would label "the generalissimo of the nonbelievers"—refrained at first from branding the papers a forgery. All the same, as soon as the papers were published, he'd printed an announcement that he questioned their authorship and was preparing an investigation. The *True Briton* had chided Malone on December 29 for betraying bias unseemly in a scholar: "We wish, for his own sake, that he had not displayed so much eagerness to commence the attack." The same day, Malone was more forthright in a letter to one of the *Miscellaneous Paper*'s subscribers, the Earl of Charlemont, to whom he was dedicating his exposé. "The editor, a Mr. Ireland, a broken Spitalfields weaver, aided by his son, an attorney's clerk, are without doubt the inventors," Malone informed the earl, "though to avoid being pelted in the newspapers by such men, I shall leave that matter in uncertainty, and merely confine myself to prove the forgery."

Malone's first open denunciation of the papers came in mid-February, when he placed an announcement in the *Morning Chronicle* entitled "Spurious Shakespeare Manuscripts." He blamed the delay of his still-unfinished review on problems with the engravings. Even so, he wrote, he would have finished the task long ago if his only task had been to expose "the most inartificial and bungling forgery ever attempted." But the author had a larger responsibility: to protect from debasement "the reputation and character and history of his great master." His pamphlet would appear at the end of the month, he promised.

When by Leap Year Day it hadn't, the *Morning Herald* taunted him. "After having so long threatened to knock the Shaksperian trunk to atoms," the *Herald* reported, Malone had apparently realized "that all his tools are not ready for this curious operation." Mixing metaphors, the newspaper went on: "The Irelandites, piquing themselves on this declaration, challenge him to a drawing, and not only deny his power to knock out the *artificial bottom*, but even his ability to discompose a single hair of their favorite *old trunk*!"

In fact, Malone's indictment of the Shakespeare papers wouldn't be ready for another month. In March, he moved out of the house on Queen Anne Street where he lived alone, surrounded by two-hundred-year-old books and papers, and moved into his printer's quarters on the Strand near Black-friars Bridge. He wanted to be on hand around the clock to supervise the production of his opus. He brought with him piles of letters and manuscripts from his collection, using them as guides to period language and spelling. Day and night, he would interrupt the typesetters with voluminous new addenda and footnoted extracts for his ever-lengthening work in progress. England's most obsessive Shakespearean scholar was finding that a mere pamphlet couldn't contain all he had to say on the subject of Samuel Ireland's precious manuscripts.

CHAPTER ELEVEN

WARNINGS AND PORTENTS

WILLIAM-HENRY ALLOWED himself to imagine the worst was over. To his father's relief and his own quiet satisfaction, the *Miscellaneous Papers* sold well. None of the book's subscribers took Samuel up on his offer of a refund if they doubted the words were Shakespeare's. *Vortigern and Rowena* was to open at Drury Lane. William-Henry's second original play, *Henry II*, would likely appear at Covent Garden later in the year. The poet laureate, Henry Pye, had agreed to write the prologue to *Vortigern*. Pye had told Samuel tearfully that he wished he had the talent to have written the play himself.

At times, William-Henry felt buoyant. He'd shown up London's hidebound literary-theatrical establishment. And why not? He was young and full of ideas. He was in the vanguard of a new generation of dramatists that disdained the clichéd drawing-room farces and small-bore melodramas that had diminished the London stage of late. No wonder English audiences kept turning out for the Bard. Now William-Henry would be giving them a Shakespeare for the ages, an unseen masterwork.

Or so he imagined, when his spirits were high. At other times, after reading a sarcastic barb aimed at the Shakespeare papers, or hearing the malicious second- and thirdhand gossip swirling about them, William-Henry was uneasy. Taking stock of how his small private prank had ballooned into a heated public controversy, he had a growing sense that events were slipping out of his control.

At Drury Lane, preparations for *Vortigern* were resuming at last. Sheridan accepted the rewritten script and allowed set making to continue. By the end of January, the scenery for *Vortigern* was ready. In mid-February, the lord chamberlain, who approved all plays performed at London's public theaters, granted *Vortigern* a license for performance. First, however, he'd insisted that the murder of old King Constantius in Act 1 be moved offstage. Portrayals of regicide were a touchy subject so soon after Louis XVI's guillotining.

Rehearsals began. John Philip Kemble—the theater's manager and star, widely praised for his Hamlet—naturally assumed the title role. Robust and imposing, with a massive Roman nose and cupid's-bow lips, Kemble looked every inch the leading man, though he lacked David Garrick's mercurial stage presence and convincing naturalism. On stage, he was a stiff, dignified peacock of a man, an actor who strove for grandeur and was easily confused with the heroic roles he played. He was the closest thing that eighteenth-century England had to a living emperor.

At times, Kemble had trouble interacting gracefully with lesser mortals. At Drury Lane the previous winter, a young Parisian actress named Fanny de Camp had caught his eye. Kemble was already married. One evening backstage, unsure how to seduce such an insignificant girl, Kemble decided to force himself on her. Her hysterical screaming brought a crowd of rescuers, who pulled him away. In danger of being branded a sex fiend, Kemble placed a large advertisement in several newspapers apologizing to Miss de Camp for "the very improper and unjustifiable behavior I was lately guilty of towards her." She accepted the apology and later married Kemble's younger brother Charles.

Kemble was also guilty of overacting, according to some critics. Leigh Hunt wrote that Kemble could make "an eternal groan upon the interjection

Oh! as if he were determined to show that his misery had not affected his lungs." At other times, if a part didn't appeal to him or if he was simply having an off night, Kemble "dozed or walked through a part," according to his friend and biographer James Boaden. This tendency was exacerbated by the actor's habit of girding for battle—which performing before London's clamorous theater audiences resembled—with a nightly dose of opium.

Cast opposite Kemble, to William-Henry's immense satisfaction, was one of the most beautiful women in England—and certainly the most famous: Sarah Siddons. Mrs. Siddons, who was Kemble's sister, was a gifted tragedienne who had transfixed audiences as Ophelia, Desdemona, and, in her signature role, Lady Macbeth. The actress's bewitching good looks and regal bearing had been immortalized by both Gainsborough and Reynolds; engravings of her portraits graced many an English drawing room. Now she would put her stamp on Vortigern's woeful queen, Edmunda.

The sympathetic Dora Jordan, plucky favorite of the shilling-a-seat gallery gods, would play the monarchs' headstrong daughter, Flavia. A young ingénue of the company, a Miss Miller, was given the role of Rowena, the Saxon maiden who beguiles the king.

Among the leads, Kemble was the least enthusiastic about the new play. In fact, he was scornful of the whole enterprise. Sheridan, aloof from the day-to-day workings of his theater, tried to cajole his actor-manager into seeing the benefits of putting on the suspect drama. Crowds would be drawn to Drury Lane to decide for themselves whether Shakespeare was really its author, "for you know very well," he told Kemble, "that an Englishman considers himself as good a judge of Shakspeare as of his pint of porter." Kemble was dubious of this business strategy, as he was of so many of Sheridan's money-losing schemes. The actor's antipathy to *Vortigern* would prove to be an opening-night obstacle the Bard himself would have had trouble overcoming.

Having been convinced by Malone early on that the Shakespeare papers were a sham, Kemble mischievously set opening night for Friday, April 1. Samuel Ireland complained angrily to Sheridan about premiering on April Fool's Day, and the date was pushed back a day. Not to be outdone, Kemble chose as the afterpiece—a short comedy or pantomime added to placate late arrivals—a well-known musical farce called *My Grandmother*. Its plot revolved around an easily duped art collector. Samuel was outraged at this new insult, but his contract didn't extend to afterpieces.

There was more trouble. The Irelands had been counting on Henry Pye's prologue to put the opening-night crowd in a receptive frame of mind. However, instead of a gushing paean in rhyming couplets, the poet had written a noncommittal ode that invited the audience ("this tribunal") to judge for itself whether *Vortigern* was authentic: "No fraud your penetrating eye can cheat/None *here* can Shakspeare's writing counterfeit." Even if it *is* a forgery, Pye suggested, it's at least an *old* forgery. This wasn't even faint praise. It might as well have been written by Kemble. Indeed, Pye meekly told Samuel that he'd recently had a talk with the actor and had come away with doubts about the play—a play over which Pye had wept with joy a month before. Samuel was disgusted. William-Henry was more nervous than ever.

Drury Lane's spring season was already shaping up as a disaster. On March 12, three weeks before *Vortigern*'s opening night, the premiere of *The Iron Chest* was marred by hooting and jeers. Sheridan had paid the well-regarded playwright George Colman a princely commission of £1,000 for the work. The lead role was tailored for Kemble. The actor, who was ill, performed it with "soporific monotony," according to the furious playwright. Kemble "scarcely could have acted worse," Colman wrote in the preface to the play's second edition. "He groaned, he lagged, he coughed, he winced, he wheezed." At one point, Sheridan insisted that his opiated leading man step forward and apologize to the capacity crowd, which was growing ugly. The play—about a mysterious trunk, of all things—closed after four nights. Kemble later recorded in his journal that he thought the play "very bad indeed" and not worthy of extensive rehearsing. But it was good enough to become a long-running hit at the Haymarket Theatre and later in America. It was Kemble who was the problem.

Ultimately, the fate of any play was in the hands of its audience, which wielded its power freely. Although London's theaters were privately owned, every Englishman regarded them as public spaces. The six-shilling boxes, some of them directly onstage, were occupied by the nobility and other dignitaries. By contrast, anyone with sixpence could be admitted to Drury Lane's upper galleries after the third act. Plays were not only for dramaphiles. For Georgian men, a not inconsiderable part of any theater's appeal was the chance it afforded to ogle shapely women dressed in men's tights, now that actresses, not boys, played the cross-dressing roles in Shakespeare's plays.

On the backless benches of the pit, in the center of the hall behind the orchestra, sat the most avid and habitual theatergoers, many of whom came to be seen themselves. Drury Lane's massive candlelit chandeliers couldn't be dimmed during a performance, so the hall stayed illuminated throughout; audience members were part of a self-conscious crowd, not spectators in isolation. In the pit, wrote theater historian Benjamin Victor in 1761, "gay and wanton young men . . . hiss and laugh and talk loud and become by that means actors themselves." Many nights, there was an unstated competition between actors on each side of the footlights. Sometimes it was crossed, which is why both Covent Garden and Drury Lane had added sharp iron spikes along their proscenia.

Heckling, blowing catcalls, chatting with neighbors, eating, commenting loudly on the action, shouting lines before an actor could—all were considered the proper exercise of any Englishman's rights of citizenship. Some people brought along their dogs. Actors had to shout their lines to be heard. So popular was theatergoing that people viewed ticket prices as a form of taxation. Attempts to raise prices were routinely denounced as tyranny. At Drury Lane, furniture-smashing theater riots were a regular occurrence. Violence could erupt over price hikes, a program change, or simply the presence of French actors.

For any playwright and acting troupe with a new play, opening night was especially treacherous. Trouble could begin the moment the curtain went up—or before, during the prologue. At the opening of Sheridan's second play, *The Rivals*, at Drury Lane in 1775, the audience from the start was openly hostile, hooting and whistling. When one of the male leads was hit with an apple in the fifth act, the actor stepped forward to address the crowd: Is it me, he asked, or is it the play? Evidently, it was both. Sheridan withdrew the play for rewriting.

The audience attending *Vortigern*'s premiere on April 2, 1796, would be ready to judge its worthiness on the spot—probably well before the final lines were spoken. The Irelands knew that the play's public reception would mean more than any single critic's opinion, even Edmond Malone's. Although the public, unlike Malone, knew only bowdlerized versions of Shakespeare, Sheridan was right: Englishmen *thought* they knew Shakespeare as well as they knew their ale.

But an audience was fickle. Its verdict could be swayed. Some playwrights, Henry Fielding had noted approvingly, took the precaution of recruiting "a little army of friends" to sit up front—some carrying cudgels, the better to intimidate hecklers in the pit. In his pamphlet upbraiding Boaden, New Inn lawyer Matthew Wyatt had warned of agents provocateurs at the premiere: "It has been reported that a party is now forming to obstruct the just exercise of public judgment in its decision on the play of King Vortigern . . . by means of tumult and violence." If this happened, he declared, it would not be just the actors, the Irelands, and Shakespeare who would be in jeopardy. "It is the cause of English literature, the cause of genius and of truth, that is at stake!" Wyatt expressed confidence that such a vile obstruction of justice would be "repelled by a generous indignation" that would only disgrace the perpetrators.

In late March, barely a week before opening night, Mrs. Siddons announced she was withdrawing from the production. Her understudy, Jane Powell, would assume the role of the queen. This was a setback, as William-Henry well understood; having England's most distinguished Shakespearean actress perform in the new play would help give the work legitimacy. Mrs. Siddons cited illness as her excuse, which was likely true, but she'd also been listening week after week to the grumbling of her brother and costar. And she had her own doubts about the play. Having recited Shakespeare's lines onstage for two decades, she knew more intimately than most what his language sounded like. In a letter to a friend, she confided that "all sensible persons" were convinced the play was a forgery. If it wasn't, "I can only say that Shakspeare's writings are more unequal than those of any other man."

Samuel Ireland realized now that *Vortigern's* opening at Drury Lane might not be the glorious occasion he'd envisioned. To shore up support, he wrote an obsequious letter to the Prince of Wales, asking if his highness would grace with his presence the premiere of this "great literary treasure." The social prominence of those applauding a play from their velvet-trimmed box seats, he knew, was as important as the reputation of its cast. The prince sent word that, regrettably, he would be out of town that weekend.

At the last minute, Samuel drew up a new Certificate of Belief so that supporters could publicly restate their confidence in all the Shakespeare papers. He coaxed a total of fifteen supporters to sign it—fewer than before, and with less impressive credentials. Criticism and rumors about the papers were eroding the Believers' faith. Even Francis Webb suggested that perhaps Samuel should consider withdrawing the play until the papers had been examined more thoroughly.

Then, just two days before opening night, Edmond Malone attacked.

MALONE'S *AN INQUIRY into the Authenticity of Certain Miscellaneous Papers and Legal Instruments, Published Dec. 24, 1795, and Attributed to Shakspeare, Queen Elizabeth, and Henry, Earl of Southampton* went on sale on Thursday, March 31, 1796. The critic attributed his book's timing to printing delays. More likely, he'd decided to hold back his searing exposé until it would do the most damage. His intended pamphlet had metamorphosed into a 424-page, 256-footnote hardcover book. Even so, it found an eager readership. At two guineas apiece, the entire five-hundred-copy first printing was snapped up in forty-eight hours.

Malone's *Inquiry* was scornful, vitriolic, and relentless. He sought to prove not only that the papers were "a tissue of imposture" but also that whoever produced them was both ignorant and inept. He opened by quoting Alexander Pope: "Pens can forge, my friend, that cannot write." With his lawyer's training, he played the role of prosecuting attorney so zealously that he might not have surprised his readers if he'd ended by calling for the death penalty.

He didn't specify who was on trial. He seemed to believe William-Henry's "anonymous gentleman" was part of a forgery ring. He dismissed the idea that a single person had produced all the papers; someone adept at forgery was unlikely to be able to write poetry, and vice versa. He assumed both Samuel Ireland and his son, the dull-witted clerk, were incapable of doing either. In Malone's mind, the Irelands were dupes of Mr. H. and his accomplices.

As in his denunciation of Chatterton's forgeries fifteen years before, Malone reserved special contempt for the experts who'd vouched for the forgeries. He cited Samuel's claim in his preface to the *Miscellaneous Papers* that every scholar, antiquary, and man of taste who examined the manuscripts in person (as Malone had not) "unanimously testified in favor of their authenticity." Malone mocked Ireland's suggestion that the story of Mr. H. and his mysterious trunk amounted to "external evidence" that the writings were the Bard's. "These treasures were found in a nameless place, in the custody of a nameless person," Malone wrote. "If these profound Scholars, Antiquaries, and Heralds are satisfied with that account, I can only say that they are very easily satisfied."

Ireland and others had argued that the papers were surely legitimate because it was impossible so much could have been fabricated "without betraying itself." Here for once Malone agreed. "The fabrication of these manuscripts," he declared, "*has* accordingly betrayed itself almost in every line." This set the tone for Malone's entire investigation: Evidence of fraud shrieked for attention on page after page. "Life is not long enough to be wasted in the examination of such trash, when almost a single glance is sufficient to shew that it is a plain and palpable forgery," he wrote of the *Lear* manuscript. William-Henry would not be the only person who found grim humor in Malone's need to devote more than four hundred pages to proving what was obvious at a glance.

Malone based his detective work on spelling, phraseology, dates, and handwriting in the Irelands' published texts and facsimiles, which didn't include *Vortigern*. He avoided criticizing the writing itself, though at times he couldn't help himself. Of the short letter of thanks that Shakespeare supposedly composed for his haberdasher-savior in 1604 ("Norre verse norre sygh norre teare canne . . . saye bye halfe how muche I love thee"), the critic asked, "Is this the composition of Shakspeare, or of a young lady of fifteen, after reading the first novel that has fallen into her hands?"

Malone began his inquest with the letter to young Shakespeare from Queen Elizabeth, thanking him for his "prettye verses." The spelling here and elsewhere, he wrote, "is not only not the orthography of Elizabeth, or of her time, but is for the most part the orthography of no age whatsoever." He seconded Boaden in citing the impossibility of the Globe Theater existing during the Earl of Leicester's lifetime, as the letter would have it. And though Shakespeare's ordinary handwriting may have been unknown, authentic letters in the queen's neat script were well preserved—even if William-Henry had never seen any. To Malone, the fake Elizabeth's sloppily written letter was "spurious trash," an insult to the House of Tudor, "a manifest and bungling forgery." By the time he was through eviscerating this tract of fewer than fifty words, Malone had filled ninety-two angry pages.

Malone's most efficient attack needed no comment at all. He juxtaposed the shaky, illegible scrawl attributed to the Earl of Southampton—a product of William-Henry's left hand—alongside the actual earl's beautifully fluent script. The critic could have rested his case with this single page.

Malone found the timing of many of the discoveries highly suspicious. "The unknown gentleman," he observed, "fed the publick precisely in proportion to their credulity, issuing out his papers and deeds by *driblets*." Time and again, new documents surfaced to quell suspicions about earlier ones. It was all too convenient.

The critic also noted the curious fact that so many of the papers contained explanations and digressions that edified the 1790s public but would have been odd or unnecessary in the 1590s. Why would a legal deed include a long narrative of a man's near-drowning? What kind of lawyer would refer in another deed to a secret love child "who muste nott be named here"? These were, Malone wrote, much like soliloquies in which an actor pretends to be thinking aloud but is actually speaking for an audience's benefit. A "wild flutter of fiction" ran through the papers.

Finally, Malone noted the absurdity of all these items—Anne Hathaway's keepsakes, Heminge's deeds, contracts with actors, letters both to and from Shakespeare—ending up in the same magical trunk. "We are not furnished with even a plausible conjecture upon the subject."

Just as the Believers read too much into the papers' odd doodles and scorch marks and improbable narratives, so Malone—whose anger at the forgeries verged on paranoia—read too much into some of William-Henry's wordings. The reference to a king's crown as a "gilded bawble" in one of the forged letters sent Malone into a thirteen-page tirade. The Bard would *never* dismiss the English crown as a mere toy! Malone decided that the forger or forgers, whoever they were, were traitorous rabble, probably French sympathizers. This "contemptuous mention of kings," bearing the stamp of "the detestable doctrines of French Philosophy and the imaginary Rights of Man," he thundered, was an affront to all Englishmen.

Personal animosity toward the Irelands was surely behind much of the critic's hostility. Edmond Malone was a royalist and a conservative. He believed his role as critic was, among other things, to protect the British public from anarchy, incitement, treason, mass folly, and other dangers that the explosion in books and printing posed to eighteenth-century England. He also believed he had a sacred duty to keep the reputation of William Shakespeare, the British Empire's most hallowed cultural emblem, "pure and unpolluted." Samuel Ireland, his son, and most of the Believers in the Shakespeare papers, along with Sheridan, happened to be Whigs. Samuel, moreover, had written a book praising the French Revolution, and his son had been schooled in France. To Malone, the Irelands were under suspicion as unpatriotic, even if they weren't themselves the forgers.

For good measure, Malone found room in his diatribe for a two-page footnote disparaging France, "which every friend to the welfare of mankind, and the peace and true interest and happiness of England, must wish blotted from the map of the world." Clearly, this was not a work of unbiased scholarship. Malone was on a rampage.

The critic had promised his inquiry would contain "something of entertainment as well as instruction," but his sarcasm and disdain overwhelmed his labored attempts at wit. He ended his tract with an immodest fantasy of himself acting as "Counsel to Shakspeare" in a heavenly trial of the papers' authorship. Presiding over the trial is Apollo, the god of poetry, as the Bard and other poets idly play their lyres nearby. Apollo is won over by Malone's arguments and orders that all copies of the *Miscellaneous Papers* be burned on a pyre of "baleful and noxious weeds."

MALONE'S *INQUIRY* WAS a devastating blow to the Shakespeare papers' reputation. Those who worked their way through all 424 pages were unlikely to be well-disposed toward Samuel Ireland's claims. But it wasn't the fatal blow that Malone had intended. His arguments were too pedantic and unfocused to win over everyone, and his boastful, insulting tone and use of exaggeration didn't help. It was obvious that Malone believed himself to be a cleverer man than he was. At one point, he suggested that Queen Elizabeth would never have spelled the verb 'be' as 'bee.' Forty pages later, he reprinted a letter from the queen that began, "Bee well [a]ware. . . ." Longwindedness posed its own dangers.

Samuel Ireland felt he'd been personally violated, even if Malone wasn't accusing him of being an accomplice to forgery. Many of the other Believers were similarly outraged by Malone's condescending assault on what they knew to be glorious relics of the Bard. A friend of both antagonists, collector John Byng (the future Lord Torrington), wrote Samuel that Malone's "conduct, all must disapprove—as most malevolent, mean, and mischievous."

Samuel recognized that Malone, a rival collector, was in part settling old scores. The previous spring, the critic had tried to arrange a viewing of the papers on the neutral ground of Byng's home. Malone instructed Byng to say only that "a gentleman" wished to inspect them. When Byng told Ireland who the curious gentleman was, Ireland refused to cooperate, remarking that Edmond Malone was no gentleman. Byng reported the response to Malone, who then had to wait nearly a year to borrow a printed copy of the papers.

William-Henry's reaction was more complicated. He was startled and offended by Malone's insulting language, and he tallied a long list of errors, mostly minor, in Malone's indictment. He was astonished, even amused, that the great scholar had been brought to near-apoplexy by an adolescent's quest to write like Shakespeare. In his *Confessions*, William-Henry wrote that his antagonist reminded him of Angelo, the petty tyrant whom Isabella upbraids in *Measure for Measure*:

> . . . *Man, proud man,*
> *Drest in a little brief authority,*
> *Most ignorant of what he's most assured,*
> . . . *like an angry ape. . . .*

Malone, everyone knew, was supposed to be working on an authoritative, multivolume biography of the Bard of Stratford (which he would never write); he had amassed much of his massive literary collection as research material for it. William-Henry thought, not without cause, that Malone was mentally unhinged to have channeled so much time and energy instead to a crusade against a harmless literary adventure.

Still, William-Henry, unlike his father, couldn't deny the central truth of Malone's *Inquiry*. The scholar had seen the Shakespeare manuscripts for what they were. The papers were fakes from first to last. Although people in literary circles until now had mostly kept any doubts to themselves to avoid the embarrassment of being proved wrong, Malone's condemnation of the papers tipped the balance. Now it was safe to assail the bottomless Shakespeare trunk and the wondrous pages it had disgorged.

Malone's published verdict did nothing to cool public interest in the Shakespeare papers. If anything, the critic's furious denunciation brought the controversy to a rolling boil. By the time of *Vortigern*'s premiere on Saturday night, April 2, talk of the Irelands and their Shakespearean manuscripts was on everyone's lips. Malone was entitled to his opinion, but he was just one man. The thousands of citizens who would pack the boxes and benches of the Drury Lane Theatre that evening would be the final judges of whether the disputed words had come from a god or a scoundrel.

CHAPTER TWELVE

"WHEN THIS SOLEMN MOCKERY

IS ENDED..."

B Y LATE SATURDAY afternoon, the streets leading to the Drury Lane Theatre from every direction were impassable. All London, it seemed, was on hand to witness the first Shakespeare premiere in nearly two hundred years. Along with the usual pickpockets and street-walkers, men hired by Malone's allies circulated through the crowd wearing sandwich boards. In huge letters, the signs warned that the play was a fraud and that the public should stay away. Few people complied. The entrance doors on Brydge Street had to be barricaded from inside to keep the growing mob from forcing its way in.

Adding to the din was a squad of shouting boys who squeezed through the crowd passing out freshly printed handbills. This was Samuel Ireland's angry one-page rebuttal to Malone's "*malevolent* and *impotent* attack" on the Shakespeare manuscripts and a defense of the new play: "Mr. Ireland feels it impossible, within the short space of time that intervenes between the publishing and the representation, to produce an answer to the most illiberal and unfounded assertions in Mr. Malone's enquiry. He is therefore induced to request that the Play of *Vortigern* may be heard with that *Candour* that has ever distinguished a *British Audience*."

It was unlikely that a crowd this tumultuous could transform itself, once inside, into attentive, unbiased observers. Samuel's plea only inflamed the passions surrounding the event, which had the air of an incipient political riot. Many of those on hand came not to see the play so much as to take sides publicly and to have a jolly good time doing so. Both Samuel Ireland and Edmond Malone had encouraged their followers to attend. Samuel had given friends and allies forty complimentary tickets to the galleries. Malone's close friend Kemble, as theater manager, was well-placed to provide seats for nonbelievers. The theater that night granted free admittance to more than a thousand people.

To Samuel's distress, Sheridan had omitted Shakespeare's name from handbills for the performance and in his announcement in that morning's London *Times*. Everyone knew that the Bard of Avon was the purported author of the evening's entertainment—why else would a new play draw such a throng?—but Sheridan had decided at the last minute that he didn't want to affirm this in writing. In this he was influenced by Kemble, who'd threatened not to perform the title role if *Vortigern* was billed as Shakespeare's work. William-Henry was less disturbed by the omission. If, strictly speaking, the play's author was anonymous, then he couldn't be charged with deriving income from a forgery.

When the theater doors opened at 5:30, an hour before curtain time, there was a violent rush for seats. Shouting, jostling men clogged the pit entrance. Some got inside by paying for box seats, then hopped over the railings into the pit to claim seats on the benches there. The newly expanded theater seated 3,611. Still, huge numbers of playgoers were turned away. "In the annals of the theater, there never was such a crowd," the *Times* reported the following Monday. "There were people enough who flocked for admission to have filled the house twice over." Those who endured the unseemly press of bodies to find seats were overwhelmingly male. The mood was that of a sporting match, or perhaps a cockfight, more than that of an evening's entertainment. Had the audience's gender been more balanced, its behavior as the evening unfolded might have been less volatile.

WITH ALL THE dignity he could muster, Samuel Ireland forced his way through the crush of theatergoers to a large central box illuminated by a pair of chandeliers. There he took his seat, visible to everyone. He was joined by Mrs. Freeman and William-Henry's sister Jane. Their entrance had been applauded by their friends in the galleries, while a few jeers had arisen from the front of the pit. In a box nearby sat the Duke of Clarence, eager to show his support both to the Irelands and to his mistress on stage, Mrs. Jordan. Sitting quietly in another box, talking with friends, was Edmond Malone.

William-Henry joined his family shortly before the curtain, but "the box being so very conspicuous, I soon retired from observation behind the scenes." His optimism had vanished. For most of the evening, he hid in the theater's green room just off stage left. As actors came and went, he would chat nervously with Mrs. Jordan as she awaited her cues. From his outpost, he could hear—and feel, in his bones and his stomach—the muffled turbulence of the huge crowd. From time to time, he would steal out to the wings to watch snatches of his drama being enacted.

There was trouble from the start. Before the curtain rose, John Whitfield, the actor playing one of Vortigern's sons, stepped forward to recite the new prologue that Samuel had commissioned from a retired diplomat friend, Sir James Bland Burgess. Whitfield was a last-minute replacement for an actor who had thought better of his involvement and disappeared. Standing alone at the center of the spacious proscenium, the nervous young actor got out the opening lines, "No common cause your verdict now demands: / Before the court immortal Shakspeare stands," but then the catcalls began. Whitfield faltered and stopped. In his distress, he'd forgotten his lines—a cardinal sin on any English stage. The catcalls and whistling continued, but they were now mixed with encouraging shouts from the Believers. Whitfield finished his speech with the aid of the prompter:

From deep oblivion snatch'd our play appears:
It claims respect since Shakspeare's name it bears.
That name, the source of wonder and delight,
To a fair hearing has at least a right.
We ask no more. With you the judgment lies:
No forgeries escape your piercing eyes!
Unbias'd, then, pronounce your dread decree,
Alike from prejudice and favour free.
If, the fierce ordeal pass'd, you chance to find
Rich sterling ore, though rude and unrefin'd,
Stamp it your own, assert your poet's fame,
And add fresh wreaths to Shakspeare's honour'd name.

The first acts of the five-act play went well enough. There were no major interruptions, and several of William-Henry's speeches were applauded. The language certainly had the flavor of Shakespeare. After Vortigern dispatches two cutthroats to murder Constantius, king of Roman Britain, under cover of night, he awaits news of the assassination impatiently:

Come then, black night, and hood the world in darkness;
Seal close the hearts of those I have suborn'd
That neither pity nor remorse do sting them!

Vortigern's plot was fast-moving and action-filled, even if much of the action occurred offstage. The characters, however, were two-dimensional, if that. In pondering the decision to kill the old king, Vortigern grapples with his conscience for, at most, three lines. The two scenes with Prince Aurelius and Flavia, his betrothed, managed to avoid the subject of love. One could easily believe they'd been written by a very young playwright who was inexperienced with women.

A play is more than a script, of course, and several of the cast members played their roles with verve. Mrs. Jordan was lively and spontaneous, and both she and a Miss Leake, a member of the company, sang songs that won the crowd's approval. Mrs. Powell, in the biggest role of her life, filling in for Mrs. Siddons, brought some in the audience to tears as Vortigern's fragile, abandoned queen. The echoes of familiar Shakespeare plays were impossible to miss—it was *Macbeth* crossed with *Hamlet*, with touches of *Julius Caesar* and *Richard III*, featuring cameos by Viola, Prince Hal, and Ophelia. The very familiarity of the characters and situations, in fact, may have reassured many in the audience.

In the green room at the end of the second act, Mrs. Jordan congratulated William-Henry on the success of his foundling play. In his memoirs, the young forger recalled that up to this point "not a dissenting voice had been heard." This was an exaggeration. Parts of the huge audience had grown restless—*Vortigern* was obviously not a theatrical masterpiece, regardless of who'd written it. But there had been far fewer disturbances than three weeks earlier, for *The Iron Chest*. William-Henry thanked Mrs. Jordan for her encouragement but confessed to a premonition that this would be the play's first and last performance.

Unlike the actress, he knew the work was a fake. He sensed that the audience would conclude the same before the night was over. William-Henry was losing his nerve. As he'd moved from the cloistered world of New Inn and his father's study to the uproarious arena of the public stage, his fantasy of triumph as Shakespeare's master impersonator had come to seem less real. William-Henry hadn't anticipated seeing his handiwork put to this kind of trial by fire. It wasn't why he'd first put ink to parchment. He wished he were anywhere but Drury Lane.

The first hint of disaster came in the third act. Vortigern assembles a group of English barons to repel an invasion from Scotland led by Constantius's avenging sons. In what was intended to be a stirring call to arms, one of the barons, then another, orders trumpets to sound. The actor playing the second baron was Charles "Diggy" Dignum, a diminutive singer-comedian with a piercing tenor voice. His casting was a bit of sabotage on Kemble's part; as theater manager, he'd filled a number of *Vortigern*'s lesser roles with comic actors. When Dignum drew himself up and commanded in a shrill near-falsetto, "Let them bellow on!" the audience erupted in laughter. It wasn't so much that Dignum's line was comical as that it was a cue for the many nonbelievers in the crowd—Malonites, as they were called—to express their feelings. After nearly ten minutes of hooting and whistling, Kemble had to step forward and plead for calm.

There was worse to come. A few scenes later, a villainous Saxon warrior named Horsus is killed in a duel. Kemble had cast in the role a large-nosed buffoon named John Phillimore. The actor expired so far forward that the curtain ending Act 4 dropped onto his midsection, leaving his legs visible to the audience—a violation of theatrical decorum. This brought extended laughter and applause. Worse, the ungainly actor now struggled comically to free himself from the curtain's weighted bottom edge, groaning and squirming on his stomach "like a great boar rolling on earth, with his huge snout," wrote an eyewitness. Phillimore's antics brought the theater to the brink of pandemonium. An inebriated Believer seated in a box along the stage, a member of Parliament named Charles Sturt, tried repeatedly to grab the actor's costume as though to pull him into his box and thrash him.

Even if Phillimore hadn't been playing for laughs, the scene in which he died made little dramatic sense. As Horsus, he encounters a young stranger and his sister and immediately tries to buy her. The brother refuses, and the two men fight. Horsus dies, but not before complimenting his opponent, offering him his purse of gold coins, and warning him to beware the Saxon commander. It was a nonsensical patchwork, and many in the audience were losing patience with it. Moreover, after the outbreaks of unscripted slapstick, people were now waiting for things to laugh at.

From a nearby box, James Boaden had a full view of the Ireland family. "No earthly sum could compensate the agonies which I saw them endure that evening," he wrote. By the end of the fourth act, Samuel had abandoned his center box and moved to the front of the pit. There, according to another curious onlooker, diarist Joseph Farington, he "for a little time leant his head on his arm," as though exhausted. Samuel then left the hall. He chose to watch the rest of the play from backstage, away from the scrutiny of the audience.

An oddity of the script had become evident as the evening wore on. William-Henry had written *Vortigern's* scenes in order, turning the pages over to his father as soon he wrote them. As he worked, he'd grown more confident. He began indulging his own budding sense of himself as a Romantic poet. The language became more excessive. People longed with "aching heart" and "brimful sorrow" for the "eternal sleep" of death. Asked by his sister, Flavia, "What hour is it?" Pascentius replies:

> 'Tis now near five o' th' clock.
> Yon brilliant mass o' fire, the golden sun,
> Hath just saluted with a blushing kiss
> That partner of his bed, the vasty sea.

London newspapers in the 1790s were already publishing parodies of this kind of poetry. For John Philip Kemble, this was clearly not Shakespeare—nor was it verse he could take seriously. Even in plays where Kemble did his best, his strutting and overacting carried a whiff of parody. Now, given lines to declaim like "Gracious Gods! What lovely maid is this/Whose form doth raise the blush in Venus' cheek?" Kemble didn't have to exert himself to tip the mood of the piece toward farce.

In the climactic fifth act, King Vortigern has retreated to his castle's tower, besieged by enemy troops. In a long soliloquy, he recounts a vision of hell that has just gripped him:

> Full fifty breathless bodies struck my sight,
> And some with gaping mouths did seem to mock me,
> Whilst others, smiling in cold death itself,
> Scoffingly bade me look on that which soon
> Would wrench from off my brow this sacred crown
> And make me too a subject like themselves.

The passage was one of William-Henry's most effective, but Kemble recited it with a ghoulish intonation. After describing with horror Death's "rattling fingers" and "bony jaws," Kemble came to the words "And when this solemn mockery is ended. . . ." The actor drew out the line, William-Henry recalled, "in the most sepulchral tone of voice possible." Immediately, as if it were a prearranged signal to the Malonites—which William-Henry was convinced it was—"the most discordant howl echoed from the pit that ever assailed the organs of hearing." There was bedlam for at least ten minutes.

According to William-Henry's account, when the theater had finally calmed down, Kemble, "in order to amuse the audience still more," repeated the line in an even deeper and more emphatic voice. He left no doubt as to what mockery he was referring to. Again, the audience burst into prolonged whistling and sarcastic cheers. Kemble had to beg the crowd once more to allow the performance to continue.

At this point, *Vortigern* was doomed, even though the rest of the play was performed without disruption. At the final curtain, prolonged booing was mixed with enthusiastic applause. Mrs. Jordan, still in a boy's tights, delivered the epilogue with her customary good cheer. She was given an ovation for her efforts—a gauge more of her popularity than the play's. On Sheridan's instructions, the actor playing Aurelius, who used the stage name Barrymore, announced that *Vortigern* would next be performed on Monday evening. His words were quickly shouted down by catcalls and heckling from every part of the theater. Fighting broke out among Believers and non-believers. Charles Sturt, swaying drunkenly next to his box, gripped a stage-hand in a headlock and was pelted with oranges.

Fortunately, there was no swordplay in the pit, as there occasionally had been in Garrick's day, but the chaos lasted for nearly twenty minutes. Kemble restored calm at last by announcing a change in plans: The next show would be Sheridan's *The School for Scandal.* In his dressing room afterward, the actor was congratulated by a jubilant Joseph Ritson, the truculent ballad collector. "If the thing had been tolerated," Ritson said of the play, which he never doubted was a counterfeit, "it would be a canister tied to Shakespeare's tail for all succeeding ages."

William-Henry left the theater together with his family. Samuel was grim-faced and weary, William-Henry strangely impassive. They descended the house stairs from the green room and emerged from a side entrance onto Wooster Street, where they blended into the boisterous crowd heading toward Drury Lane and the Strand. When they arrived home at Norfolk Street, Samuel ranted and paced; fury had revived him. A small group of his friends joined him to commiserate. Samuel was furious at Kemble for undermining the production, furious at Sheridan for canceling the rest of the play's run, and furious that his opportunity to earn a small fortune had vanished in an evening. Now he was angry, too, that his son didn't share his sense of indignation.

William-Henry knew the postmortem would stretch into the early morning hours, and he wanted no part of it. Unlike his father, he'd never been obsessed with reaping a windfall from the play and the other Shakespeare papers. He was a young dreamer, and this dream hadn't come true. He was disappointed, but there were worse heartbreaks a young man could suffer. In fact, to his surprise, he was relieved by his play's demise. "I retired to bed," he wrote in 1805, "more easy in my mind than I had been for a great length of time, as the load was removed which had oppressed me."

IN YEARS TO come, it would be common wisdom that *Vortigern*'s premiere was a fiasco and that the performers were booed off the stage. That was an overstatement, made later by people who weren't in the audience and who knew for a certainty that the play was a fraud. In fact, as *Vortigern*'s audience dispersed on April 2, 1796, many in the crowd believed they'd been witness to an unseen Shakespearean drama. Indeed, much of the tumult at Drury Lane was the result of opposing factions seeking to drown each other out. The London theater audience may have prided itself on knowing Shakespeare when they heard it, but a raucous playhouse was an unreliable courtroom. *Vortigern* fared no worse than *The Iron Chest* on the same stage three weeks earlier. And Kemble was well practiced in the theatrical ritual of stepping forward on opening nights to plead for quiet. After worse nights than this one, he'd had angry mobs of theatergoers follow him home and jeer outside his windows.

On Sunday, the two Irelands marched back to the theater to collect their portion of Saturday night's takings. The treasurer handed Samuel a bit more than £100 (roughly £4,500 or $7,500 today). This was in addition to their £250 advance. The money was Samuel's, but he allowed his son to keep £90 of the total. It was the only income the young man was to earn from the forgeries he'd labored over for the past year and a half.

Sheridan, despite his waning enthusiasm for the play, had been expecting that Drury Lane would at least make money from it. Alas, Saturday night's receipts wouldn't even cover the cost of the scenery. That *Vortigern* had only deepened his and the theater's debts was disastrous. A few days later, Sheridan would reluctantly sell part of his ownership of the theater.

In the green room after the performance, Sheridan had upbraided Kemble for his treacherous performance in *Vortigern*. As the theater's manager and leading actor, Kemble had disgraced and injured the theater, Sheridan told him. Kemble was apologetic, but his conscience was clear. In his own mind, he would have been risking public shame had he acted his part as though he believed that Shakespeare had written it. Unlike Sheridan, Kemble adulated the Bard; Hamlet had made him the star that he was. Even so, as everyone knew, he could have expressed his objections more graciously by pleading illness, as his sister had, and letting an understudy take over.

It was now clear that Samuel's insistence on publishing the Shakespeare papers before *Vortigern* had been staged was a mistake. If he had waited, if he hadn't been so eager to start cashing in on the papers' notoriety, many of those thronging to Drury Lane wouldn't have been so quick to pass judgment on what they were seeing. There would have been fewer barbs and parodies in the newspapers beforehand. And Edmond Malone would not yet have launched his attack.

Many of the reviews that began appearing in the newspapers on the following Monday were scathing. Taking their cue from Malone's *Inquiry*, commentators denounced *Vortigern* and the Irelands' papers generally as fabricated nonsense. The *Times* said the play was no more than a weak imitation of *Macbeth*: "Let England and Scotland change places and the likeness is complete." The *Monthly Mirror* declared: "King Vortigern and the fabricator"—it didn't presume to say who that might be—"were dismissed to everlasting infamy and contempt."

A few of the responses were more temperate. The *Pocket Magazine* argued that the play's dismal reception at Drury Lane "does not prove the fact of imposition, and still less so against Mr. Ireland. It was the opinion of the late Dr. Johnson, as well as many other great men, that there are few of Shakspeare's plays which would not be damned if produced before a modern audience" for the first time.

Henry Pye, whose original prologue had pleased no one, made a similar observation. "How many persons were there in the theatre that night," he asked, "who, without being led, could distinguish between the merits of *King Lear* and *Tom Thumb*? Not twenty."

CHAPTER THIRTEEN

CONFESSING TO DEAF EARS

ALTHOUGH WILLIAM-HENRY felt a burden had been lifted after *Vortigern*'s calamitous end, his relief was short-lived. New pressures, public and private, would nearly crush him in the ensuing year. As a forger, he'd enjoying blurring the line separating what was real from what wasn't. In the aftermath of the Drury Lane uproar, he began to have trouble seeing the line at all.

His father was as resolute as ever in insisting the Shakespeare papers were genuine. He and other agitated Believers, rather than quietly withdrawing from the fray, now increased their pressure on William-Henry. A committee of Believers, including Wallis, Byng, Wyatt, and Burgess, convened at Norfolk Street. William-Henry was ordered to attend. It was essential, they told him, that his friend Mr. H. come forward. Only Mr. H. could prove that the papers were authentic. Only he could show that Malone was wrong.

Most important to Samuel Ireland, only Mr. H. could dispel the widespread suspicion that Ireland himself was the mastermind of a despicable hoax. The *Critical Review* in April belittled the collector's story that his nineteen-year-old son had happened on the Shakespeare papers by chance. "In a criminal court, he who has made use of a forged deed to his own advantage would be regarded as the author; and if he did not indicate how he came by it, he would be liable to every penalty of the law." The gallows, in other words. This was a bit harsh, since displaying or reproducing a forged deed for curiosity's sake wasn't the same as using it as a legal instrument.

William-Henry could see no way out. If he confessed, each of the bewigged gentlemen now facing him in his father's claustrophobic study would be a figure of public ridicule. And each would have him to blame. With confession unappealing, William-Henry chose the opposite tack. He decided to keep up his pretense. In fact, he would build on it. He gave the committee a list of *new* items from Shakespeare's long-lost estate, courtesy of Mr. H. Asterisks marked the items he'd seen; other things he'd only heard about.

Among the former were the original manuscripts of *Richard II* and *Henry V* and partial drafts of six other plays (all of which he planned to transcribe at New Inn from his father's printed texts). He also reported seeing handwritten poems that Shakespeare had dedicated to Sir Walter Raleigh and Sir Francis Drake. He hadn't yet seen Shakespeare's handwritten autobiography—a brilliant stroke, if only he'd thought of it sooner—or the full-length portrait in oil that he'd told his father about earlier. William-Henry apparently hoped he could allay the Believers' doubts by intoxicating them with new promises. Whenever his audacity was challenged, his natural response was more audacity.

Unfortunately, the list only whetted his father's greed. Disgusted with his son for evading his questions, Samuel wrote a long, self-pitying letter to his son's actor friend Montague Talbot in Dublin. The dispute about the Shakespeare papers' source, he wrote, was "the most painful and oppressive that I have ever been engaged in in the course of my life . . . and may perhaps terminate in my ruin." He refused to believe that his own son "would be so base as to involve me and his family in infamy" by becoming a party to forgery. Talbot, as the person now claiming to have discovered the papers, had "a duty that you owe to my injured family" to reveal the details surrounding Mr. H. and his chest.

In his reply, Talbot held firm, repeating that he had sworn to Mr. H. an oath of secrecy. Talbot remained loyal to William-Henry: "Whenever I may chance to meet him," he wrote, "I shall be proud to own him as a friend." Samuel's furious response gave Talbot a taste of what William-Henry was enduring: The collector threatened to use his connections to have Talbot fired from his Dublin theater.

By May, William-Henry saw that his subterfuge had to end. There was no way he could continue to fool the world with his forgeries. He was torn by conflicting emotions. He couldn't let go of the ego-inflating delusion that he was Shakespeare's, or at least Chatterton's, literary descendant. He was proud of what he'd done and more confident than ever of his literary gifts. At the same time, the knowledge that exposure of his forgeries would disgrace him—and humiliate his family—was seeping into his consciousness, much as he might deny it.

Walking with his sisters in the garden one day, he made a halting confession. Half contrite, half triumphant, he told them that Mr. H. didn't exist and that he, their brother, had written the Shakespeare manuscripts. Shocked, Jane and Anna Maria relayed the news to their father. To the sisters' distress and William-Henry's astonishment, Samuel refused to believe them. This was, he said, a lie resulting from the "arrogance and vanity" of his impudent son. The boy was taking advantage of Mr. H.'s reticence to steal glory he didn't deserve. You'll notice, he told his daughters, that the boy wasn't brazen enough to tell such an outlandish story to my face. It was true: He wasn't. And after what his sisters told him, he wasn't about to try.

A few days later, William-Henry tried to reveal his authorship to Mrs. Freeman, but she refused to listen. In her mind, what he was suggesting was ridiculous. How dare he compare himself to William Shakespeare! A failed playwright herself, she bridled at the idea that her untalented son was capable of writing for the theater at all. Later, in a bilious letter to his friend Talbot, she said of him: "Not any of his friends have ever discovered the least trait of *Literary Genius* in his character." The woman had always been distant and unsupportive, and her treatment of him now was plainly insulting.

FINALLY, IN MID-MAY, William-Henry announced that Mr. H. had agreed to divulge all his secrets, but with conditions. William-Henry, alone, would meet with attorney Albany Wallis at his house down the block. Mr. H. would join them there and explain everything.

Samuel, however, wasn't about to wait for Wallis to put together a lawyerly report afterward on what was said. He was still being pilloried in the newspapers for his supposed role in what were now widely taken to be forgeries, and he was desperate to turn the tables on his critics. Samuel had begun spying on his son. William-Henry spoke of visiting his anonymous friend almost daily, so Samuel would hurry out after his son and try to follow at a distance. Somehow he never tracked the boy to the elusive Mr. H.'s door.

The day of the meeting at Wallis's, Samuel arranged to call on a family he knew whose home faced Wallis's at the lower end of Norfolk Street. He was hoping he might recognize Mr. H. through the window. If not, he would at least be able to spot him in the future. Peeking out from behind a curtain, he saw his son arrive at the appointed time and be shown inside. Samuel waited, but there was no sign of Mr. H. An hour later, William-Henry emerged alone and began walking up Norfolk Street.

Samuel rushed across the street and confronted his son. What had happened? Why hadn't Mr. H. appeared? His son was unwilling to say. Furious, Samuel pounded on the door of number 21, demanding to talk to Wallis. The attorney, unruffled by his neighbor's tantrum, scolded him for interfering. The truth would come out in due time, he said, and without inviting Samuel to join him, calmly stepped back inside his house and shut the door.

What had actually happened, of course, was that William-Henry had made a full confession to Albany Wallis. The young man regarded the lawyer as a friend, despite the near catastrophe Wallis had caused when he'd called with John Heminge's original signature five months before. William-Henry needed an ally—someone reputable to help him escape the labyrinth of interlocking lies he'd constructed—and Wallis's even disposition and good humor made him the ideal person. That he was not a pompous Bardolater like Samuel Ireland was a point in his favor. And Wallis was a sympathetic listener. He had lost his only son, a fourteen-year-old, in a drowning incident in the Thames some years before. He may have transferred some of his paternal affection to William-Henry.

As the forger's bizarre confession came tumbling out—the intricate details of old parchments and rent rolls, specially brewed vials of ink, doctored drawings, reused wax seals—Wallis was stunned, then skeptical. After peppering his young neighbor with questions, and after watching him mimic Shakespeare's signature as if he were signing his own name, the attorney was satisfied that the Shakespeare papers were indeed a breathtaking and improbable hoax. Shortly afterward, William-Henry returned with corroborating evidence: scraps of uncompleted forgeries and what was left of his forger's ink.

Wallis advised his visitor to stay mum for the time being. It wasn't clear what had changed since late December, when Wallis had been ready to expose the papers as a hoax. Perhaps, now that he knew who the hoaxer was—a young friend and neighbor, not a cabal of clever, profit-minded criminals—he had a change of heart. It wasn't hard to see how the young man had gotten himself into a nightmarish bind by pursuing an essentially benign, if foolhardy, plot. And knowing Samuel Ireland as he did, Wallis could understand how the man's greed and ambition could have goaded his son into carrying out a fraud.

Staying tight-lipped was good legal advice, but it wouldn't help William-Henry live under the same roof as his father. He was in a quagmire. Nothing he could say or do could possibly persuade his father that he was the forger. He asked Mrs. Freeman to relay a question to his father: What if Mr. H. confessed that all the papers really *were* forgeries and that Mr. H. himself had masterminded them? The answer came back, via Mrs. Freeman: "Such a wretch surely does not exist." The housekeeper added that she had just carefully reinspected the documents herself. She assured him it was preposterous to suppose they were fake.

Somewhere in the back of Samuel's mind, he must have allowed the possibility that the papers were recent forgeries. He, more than most, knew that forgers abounded in England. But if Mr. H. was among them, he wasn't gaining materially from his subterfuge. To the contrary, he was giving the papers away. That, to Samuel, was the perplexing part. Why on earth would a stranger donate forged papers to his son, thereby ruining him, a respectable antiquarian, and incriminating the whole family? Such villainy Samuel couldn't conceive.

William-Henry was unraveling. By late May, he'd abandoned his clerkship at New Inn. In a letter to a friend, he wrote, "Pray excuse this scrawl but I have had another night without a moment's sleep and am more like a man drunk than in his senses."

His experience inventing an imaginary world of affectionate queens and brave haberdashers had now made deception seem second nature. He began concocting tall tales with reckless aplomb. He told his family in May that a sporty two-horse curricle that he'd begun using about town was a loan from Mr. H., though he was actually paying for it with borrowed money. His anonymous friend had also promised him, he said, the use of a luxurious manor with a well-stocked wine cellar and landscaped grounds near the sea. He told his sisters that Thomas Harris at Covent Garden had agreed to pay him seven hundred pounds a year to furnish the theater with two new plays annually. Sensing this wasn't enough, he disclosed to Mrs. Freeman the startling news that he was about to be married. His fiancée, he said, was a rich young woman who'd fallen in love with him at first sight at the opera.

This last claim Samuel felt compelled to investigate. The woman's last name was Shaw, and her family lived on Harley Street, a posh address near Cavendish Square. Finding no one of that name living on Harley Street, Samuel demanded his son explain himself. Oh, he had misunderstood Miss Shaw's name: She was actually a Miss *Shard*. Unbelievably, Samuel continued to take his son at his word. He succeeded in locating a Shard family on Harley Street—but there was no daughter.

Feeling frustrated and abused, Samuel and Mrs. Freeman left London at the end of May for rural Berkshire. From there, he wrote plaintively to his son that a week had passed "and not a word or a line from you!" He'd been hoping for a full disclosure of the papers' origins. "I do not recollect that any conduct of mine towards you has been other than that of a friend and companion." He resented being forced to search for the truth about the papers "when I ought to hear it voluntarily from yourself." Samuel's pleas always turned to threats before long. Now he threatened his son with disinheritance: "Reflect well what you do and what determination you make, for this is the moment that may in all probability render you comfortable in your future situation, or make you an alien to happiness for ever."

He ended his letter with an underlined request for the new documents that the imaginary Mr. H. had lately promised. Perhaps, in his befuddlement, Samuel regarded his son's claim to have written the papers as a trick to cheat him out of what was rightfully his. This was a man who would never believe that the enumerated treasures, as yet, didn't exist. His lust for Shakespeare's writings was too consuming to admit there were none. He was incorrigible.

William-Henry wasn't at home to receive the letter. He had already moved out. He told a maid he was going to stay with a wealthy gentleman, but he boarded the carriage he'd hired out of earshot of the servants so they wouldn't hear the directions he gave the coachman.

By this time, he'd confessed to several sympathetic friends of the family, in addition to Albany Wallis. A number of them, without telling his father, lent William-Henry small sums of money and found places for him to stay. None of them viewed the lad's sins as damning. Some openly admired his literary ability, especially after he imitated Shakespeare's writing as they watched.

"Your young man is a prodigy one way or other," wrote John Byng in a letter to Samuel that summer, "and to cover one deceit has told a thousand lies. But they have begat each other, and were not intended at starting." Byng invited Samuel and his daughter Jane to his house to see sample forgeries he'd seen William-Henry inscribe. Jane was impressed; not so her father. Maybe the boy had copied some printed text into old-fashioned script, Samuel grumbled, but he certainly didn't compose it himself.

As William-Henry had been unable to confess to his father in person, on June 14 he tried doing so in writing. He intended the letter as an apology—Albany Wallis helped him with the wording—but he couldn't hide his defiance. There was no return address.

If there remains "any particle of that love and affection for me which has always been proud to show itself, you will not, I am sure, destroy this before you have perused it," he began. He went on to claim sole authorship of the Shakespeare papers. "The Vortigern I wrote; if I copied anyone it was the Bard himself," he declared. "The Henry II was more mine than the Vortigern, as I scarce look'd into any one book while I wrote it." He promised Samuel, more boastfully than apologetically, that any profits from the plays' publication would be his to keep. This was a more assertive tone than William-Henry had ever used in person.

As the letter drew to a close, William-Henry's self-defense grew more heated. "If the writer of the papers . . . shows any spark of genius and deserves honour *I Sir your son am that person* and if I live but for a little I will prove it." Once again, the young man was hinting at a romantic early death—though if anything was threatening his sanity and well-being, it was his father's cold intransigence.

Samuel responded to his son's outpouring with disdain. "Let your talent be what it may—who do you think will ever sanction you or associate with you after showing an ability for such gross and deliberate impositions on the public, and through the medium of your own father?" He seemed at last to be accepting the idea that the papers were his son's doing. But a follow-up letter dismissed the boy's confession as foolish bragging that had to stop: "Your character, if you insist on this, will be blasted."

Possibly, if Samuel now realized the papers were fakes, he was warning his son to keep up the pretence that they were real. The scandal over the papers was beginning to undercut Samuel's livelihood, dampening sales of his books and casting doubt on his collectibles. Who now would buy an old print that Samuel Ireland swore was an authentic Hogarth? If Samuel was shifting from self-delusion to damage control, then his son's solitary fraud had become an unspoken conspiracy. But thereafter, Samuel gave no sign he'd changed his mind about his errant son, Mr. H., and the bountiful cache of relics. Despite his outward self-assurance, Samuel seemed, more than anything, to be confused.

William-Henry, in any case, didn't withdraw to Wales for a life of writerly solitude. He stayed in London and in early July, just shy of his twenty-first birthday, was secretly married. No one in his family knew the young woman, and he didn't volunteer to introduce her. Her name, they learned, was Alice Crudge. The daughter of one of Samuel's friends had encountered the young couple strolling at Kensington Gardens. Miss Crudge, she reported, was "a shortish woman who appeared to be a girl of the town and not very handsome." Marriage at this juncture in William-Henry's life seemed to be the impulsive act of a man losing his bearings. Or possibly he'd known the woman for some time; she might conceivably have been a party to the forgeries. Still, whether he'd acted rashly or not, it was an odd time to be thinking about matrimony.

Later that summer and into the fall, while his new wife stayed in London, William-Henry abandoned the city for the countryside, relying on borrowed funds and lodgings and traveling mostly on foot. He needed to escape the gossip and stares and tight-lipped greetings of the city. In Bristol, he visited the ancient strong room in the stone tower of St. Mary Redcliffe Church, where Chatterton said he'd found the Rowley parchments. He called on Chatterton's sister, Mrs. Mary Newton, who was still living next door. She spoke freely about the doomed poet's boyhood: his liveliness and precocity, his failures at school, his innate gift for poetry. But the Rowley poems weren't his invention, she insisted—he'd found them in a trunk. Her brother was no forger.

Her visitor knew better than to argue.

BACK IN LONDON in October 1796, William-Henry was dismayed to find that the Ireland-Shakespeare controversy hadn't died away. Forgeries, old trunks, and foolish antiquarians popped up in one satirical press account after another. On October 29, a new play by Frederick Reynolds, *Fortune's Fool*, opened at Covent Garden. It starred an obsessive collector named Sir Bamber Blackletter who was obviously based on Samuel Ireland. Sir Bamber brags that his library contains no book or manuscript less than one hundred years old, "except John Gilpin in four volumes." A conniving woman tries to lure him into marriage by offering him the manuscript of "Trickerinda, that ancient poem written by Dan Chaucer." As she prepares to open the trunk where the manuscript is hidden, Sir Bamber cries out, "I shall die— expire in all the agonies of an expecting lover!" Holding the poem in trembling hands ("Oh how the touch thrills me!"), the collector reads aloud a few lines:

> And lo! a monk all hallow'd from the cloyster
> Grey as the morn and white as any oyster.

That William-Henry had exposed his father as a fool was regrettable, but the ridicule aimed at Samuel was at least partly his own fault. Accusations that Samuel was a scoundrel, not a victim, were much harder for his son to bear. He, more than anyone, knew that his father was blameless. Though Albany Wallis had counseled him to keep quiet and allow the scandal to ebb, William-Henry now made plans to issue a public confession in the form of a tell-all pamphlet. He wanted to explain once and for all what he'd done and why, and he wanted to absolve his family of guilt—even if he underscored his father's credulity in the process. Also, with mounting debts and no income, he and his wife needed every shilling such a pamphlet would bring.

In the meantime, father and son hadn't seen each other in months. Wallis invited the two to meet at his house on December 12, hoping it would be a chance for them to settle their differences. Wallis was a savvy mediator who'd worked with his share of difficult personalities. The meeting, nonetheless, was a disaster.

Until now, William-Henry had been the obedient if sullen son, doing his father's bidding. Now, in Samuel's eyes, he seemed insolent. William-

Henry didn't tip his hat or defer to his father in anyway. "He met me in the room with much cold and indifference and said he was the author of the papers," Samuel wrote afterward. Offended, Samuel took a look at the planned confession. His opinion of his son's abilities was so low that he doubted he could have written even the pamphlet without help. When he asked point-blank who had written it for him, William-Henry was incensed. The meeting ended abruptly.

Both Irelands were proud, stubborn, and hot-tempered—they were more alike than either cared to admit. Now each was deeply resentful of the other. Samuel still seethed that his son refused to reveal where the Shakespeare cache was hidden. William-Henry was irate that his father viewed him as a failed clerk, not an accomplished writer. In the weeks after their contentious meeting at Wallis's, their relationship deteriorated into an exchange of bickering letters about which of William-Henry's household possessions he was allowed to retrieve and sell. In one letter, the boy went so far as to rub out his signature and sign his name instead as "W. H. Freeman" in bold, oversized script—a slap at his father's authority and an apparent acknowledgment that Mrs. Freeman was his mother.

An Authentic Account of the Shaksperian Manuscripts was published a few days after the meeting at Wallis's house. Its author expressed hope that his account "will meet with favor and forgiveness, when considered as the act of a boy." He protested that his father was unfairly accused of being behind the hoax when, in fact, his father continued to believe "*Shakspear* the author of the papers and me totally incapable of writing them." Thus, in a single sentence, his tone shifted from a defense of his father to a public complaint of ill-treatment.

He described the souvenir-hunting trip to Stratford with his father and their arrival at Clopton House too late to rescue papers that might have been Shakespeare's. He recounted procuring ink and paper for his first minor forgery, the purpose of which "was only to give my father pleasure." He recalled *Vortigern*'s unruly reception, which, he wrote, "did not lessen the satisfaction I felt in having at so early an age wrote a piece which was not only acted, but brought forth as the work of the greatest of men." This was hardly a confession. It was a claim to literary glory—he was the over-looked, underschooled misfit who'd been blessed by Shakespeare's muse.

At a shilling a copy, William-Henry's forty-three-page pamphlet sold out quickly. Within a year it was a collector's item selling for a guinea. Some readers were sympathetic; more than a few relished the story of the lad's mad caper. But many others, including Malone, took it to be fiction. The *Monthly Mirror* found his account "contemptible." The *Morning Herald* reported that "because of his pamphlet's gross ignorance and evident want of literary talents, there is not a man to be found so stupid as to give credit" to its claims. The *Morning Chronicle* cleverly noted that young Ireland's claim of authorship, "if *true*, proves him to be a *liar*."

This wasn't the reception William-Henry had expected. His father, showing wisdom for once, had advised him not to publish it. William-Henry had ended his confession with a request that, "should I attempt another play," the public would set aside any prejudices it might have toward him and judge his work with an open heart "which is the certain inmate of every Englishman's bosom." The plea was heartbreaking in its naïveté. From a disgrace this abject, there was no recovery.

CHAPTER FOURTEEN

"SHAKESPEARE" IRELAND

WILLIAM-HENRY, in his teens at the time of his forgeries, earned a modest living as a writer for the next forty years. With the near-manic industriousness he displayed in his forgeries, he poured out dozens of gothic novels, biographies, histories, collections of satirical verse, and even a play in the style of *Vortigern*, though it went unproduced. Understandably, for much if not most of his work, he used a pseudonym. His own name would remain indelibly stained by the Shakespeare forgeries.

William-Henry had thought, early on, that his forgeries would lead to a career as a celebrated author and playwright. By the age of twenty-one, he was sober enough to realize he wasn't a second Shakespeare. At best, he saw himself as a Chatterton who didn't die young. Scholars and critics had already praised his writing as superb; a change in byline shouldn't alter that perception.

It shouldn't, but it did. If William-Henry had been an older, distinguished man of the world, with a university education and, better yet, a title, he might have been forgiven by those he'd hoodwinked. That he was so young and inexperienced didn't excuse him, as he thought it should. Instead, his youth underlined their folly. "I was a boy—," he wrote in 1805, "consequently they were deceived by a boy." What could be more humiliating?

No one suffered more than Samuel Ireland. After the fraud was revealed, some of the embarrassed Believers talked of having the man arrested. His son's confession in 1796 did little to free him of blame. Early skeptic Joseph Ritson openly called for literary impostors to be hanged like felons. If the laws were so changed, William-Henry later observed bitterly, many of England's literary critics should "tremble for their own necks." The real frauds, he argued, were the many experts who claimed to know Shakespeare when they read him.

Samuel tried to clear his name by publishing in late 1796 an ill-advised self-defense, *Mr. Ireland's Vindication of His Conduct*, and a long-winded sequel the following year, *An Investigation of Mr. Malone's Claim to the Character of Scholar*. The collector insisted the papers were genuine and Malone a villain. He dusted off old testimonials from Believers and even enlisted "short Heminge" and "tall Heminge" as exhibits in his favor. He was pursuing a lost cause. Malone chose not to issue a response, deciding a man of Samuel Ireland's low character didn't merit one.

For several years, William-Henry and his wife struggled to get by without Samuel's help. Covent Garden was no longer interested in staging *Henry II*. Publishers and editors didn't want to talk to him. He tried and failed to find work as an actor like his friend Talbot. In a letter to his father, he described having to sell off his wife's furniture, dishes, and other possessions. He asked that his father keep his plight secret. Samuel, as if the son's straits were somehow a vindication of the father, made the letter public.

Later, William-Henry and his wife ran a small circulating library out of their home in Kensington. There they earned a steady trickle of income by selling patrons handwritten copies of the forgeries, which William-Henry produced to order. One customer commissioned him to copy the entire manuscript of his *Henry II* in his secretary hand—something he'd never gotten around to doing for his father. For several years, forgeries of his forgeries were the only writings he was able to sell. Eventually, collectors would own at least twenty "original" versions of young Will's love letter to Anne Hathaway.

At the start of 1797, William-Henry wrote Samuel an anguished letter begging for his trust and support. "If you are *really* my father I appeal to your feelings as a parent. If not I am the more indebted to you for your Care of my Youthful Education." Never before had he raised so directly his suspicions that he wasn't Samuel's offspring. His doubts helped feed his estrangement from his father. "I have said *If* you are my parent, being at a loss to account for the expression so often us'd [by] Mrs. Freeman . . . 'that you did not think me *your Son.*'" He noted that after the Shakespeare papers had made the family celebrities in the literary world, Mrs. Freeman would needle Samuel for now being "glad enough to own me for your son." He went on to plead for information about who his real mother and father were. William-Henry's disquiet about who he was had been simmering for some time. His uncertain identity may have made it easier for him to masquerade as someone he wasn't.

Samuel apparently never replied. If he wasn't William-Henry's father, possibly he didn't know who was. In the summer of 1797, the collector wrote an acquaintance about William-Henry's tiresome insistence that he'd written *Vortigern* and the rest, "no part of which declaration do I believe nor does the world. Till something further and more satisfactory does appear—we must be separated—and I fear that will be for ever." He suspected that the boy stole the Shakespeare papers from an unknown archive "and that he is afraid to declare the truth for fear of consequences." The break between the two was complete. During the three years leading up to Samuel's death in 1800, of complications from asthma and diabetes, they never crossed paths again.

In an unpublished, undated memoir years later, William-Henry described a touching reconciliation as his father lay dying: "A thousand times he declared with tears in his eyes that my presence constituted his sole happiness. . . . He died in my arms and thus have I to add one more hour of bitterness to those which this life has afforded me." There is no other testimony, even from the physician attending Samuel's death, that

Samuel Ireland ever saw his son in the last years of his life. William-Henry's account perfectly captures the tone of the popular romantic novels of the day, which he himself had begun writing. It wouldn't be surprising if, once again, he was using fiction to bring to life a more pleasing reality.

Samuel Ireland's obituary in the *Times* was unforgiving. Despite his denials that he was party to his son's forgeries, the newspaper wrote that his "complicity appears obvious." The following year, the auction of his huge collection of rare books and artifacts took eight days. Suspicions about his honesty dampened prices for some of the collectibles. No one bid on the mummy cloth, a piece of Charles I's cloak, or a bit of Wycliffe's vestment, so the auctioneer threw in someone's leather boots and sold the lot for a shilling. The purse of glass beads that Shakespeare had supposedly given his daughter Susanna sold for two shillings. A garter said to have been worn by James II to his coronation brought sixpence.

The prize of the collection needed no pedigree. The original Shakespeare forgeries, bound in russia calf and green morocco, complete with wax seals and lock of hair, sold for £130 (more than £4,000 or almost $7,000 today).* Curiously enough, Samuel's silver-edged goblet carved from Shakespeare's mulberry tree, or a tree much like it, fetched £6, a better price than artwork by Hogarth and Van Dyck. There were still plenty of monied collectors in London for whom an object's aura outweighed its questionable past.

AFTER MRS. FREEMAN died in 1802, Jane Ireland had the remaining leather-bound folios of the *Miscellaneous Papers* destroyed along with the copper-plate engravings of her brother's handiwork. William-Henry would have

---

* The volume was later donated to Birmingham's Shakespeare Memorial Library, where it was lost in a fire in 1879.

sold them to collectors if he'd had the opportunity, but his sisters wanted nothing more to do with the fiasco.

William-Henry's wife disappears from the record at this point. Most likely, she died. In 1804, the twenty-nine-year-old Ireland married the widow of an old friend. The marriage, which endured, produced two daughters. William-Henry must have forgiven whatever resentment he'd felt toward the unaffectionate Mrs. Freeman, whose real name he'd discovered by this time. He and his wife named their older daughter after her: Anna Maria de Burgh Ireland.

The year after he remarried, he published a greatly expanded edition of his 1796 mea culpa. He was motivated more by a need for cash than an urge to reconfess. Disturbing old ghosts was no deterrent—William-Henry remained unapologetic about his adventure in forgery, and he'd been careful to save all his press clippings. *The Confessions of William-Henry Ireland* was 317 pages of treasure hunting and document faking, furtive maneuvers and hairbreadth escapes, all broken up with long samples of his later writings. Woven into his disjointed narrative was invective aimed at Malone. Most of all, the book was an indictment of pretentious literary dupes like Webb, Warton, and Parr. William-Henry's replacement of the vowels in their names with asterisks did nothing to hide their identities.

To William-Henry's credit, he never reproached his father for treating him harshly, nor did he blame his father's greed for his own misdeeds. Nonetheless, the book was selective and sometimes dishonest in how it recalled events. The author claimed that he turned to forgery on a whim, not with careful planning, and then only to please his father. He said nothing about using his forgeries to puncture the pretensions of Shakespeare cultists and nothing at all about using forgery as a springboard for a literary career of his own. Rewriting scenes from Shakespeare's life had taught William-Henry how liberating it was to rewrite the past. In trying to present himself in the most positive light possible, he now put his age at the time he began his forgeries as seventeen, like Chatterton, not nineteen; his 1796 confession, in which he hadn't fudged his age, was now safely out of print.

He reasoned—wrongly, for the most part—that the public would more readily pardon misbehavior by someone that young.

William-Henry found that England was still unready to forgive him—or, in many cases, to believe him at all. His revised and expanded confession drew new scorn, though it sold well. To avoid unpleasantness, he and each of his wives spent long stretches of their lives in self-imposed exile in France. His fluency in French, his sympathy for postrevolutionary politics, and his relative anonymity all made him feel at home there. To help make ends meet, he wrote or translated a number of French histories and biographies for British publishers, including a three-volume biography of Napoleon in the 1820s.

As a Francophile, William-Henry never shared John Bull's horror of the French emperor. In 1815, during Napoleon's eventful Hundred Days reign between his escape from Elba and his defeat at Waterloo, the French ruler found time to grant the thirty-nine-year-old Englishman an audience at the Tuileries Palace. A lifelong admirer of Macpherson's rustic Ossian poems, Napoleon may have admired William-Henry for having humbled so much of the haughty English ruling class. He awarded his guest the small ten-pointed cross signifying membership in the Légion d'Honneur.

IN THE AFTERMATH of the Shakespeare affair, William-Henry as a writer was free of the strictures of imitating an Elizabethan. For better or worse, he could indulge his own taste. In the 1790s, shortly after his initial confession, friends had teased him about his purported literary ability. "I would lay any wager," he recalled one of them joking, "that some even think you cannot read." If he really was the author of the Shakespeare papers—a true impostor, not a fake impostor—why not demonstrate his talent by writing something of his own, like a novel?

This, according to William-Henry, was the genesis of his first self-professed work of fiction. The title page of *The Abbess: A Romance* identified

its author as "W. H. Ireland, the avowed author of the Shakspear papers."
The 1799 novel, and others to follow, showed the influence of Horace Walpole's eerie *Castle of Otranto*. *The Abbess* was an overwrought fantasy of love, torture, revenge, and redemption that well suited the tastes of the day. Writer John Feltham in 1802 identified the typical reader of the gothic novels then in vogue: "the female apprentice [who] longs for the hour of shutting shop, that she may . . . teach her sensitive heart to palpitate with terror at the mysterious horrors of romantic improbability." *The Abbess* found enough eager buyers that William-Henry's second novel, *Rimualdo, or the Castle of Badajos*, published the following year, described William-Henry only as "author of 'The Abbess.'"

Rimualdo, too, was a lurid, overwritten melodrama, but readers who knew of its author's upbringing would have noticed strands of fantasized autobiography in the book's opening paragraphs:

> With lingering step and a palpitating heart, the Conde Rimualdo, having bade adieu to his parents, was proceeding to quit the antique mansion of his progenitors. He was traversing the spacious hall which led to the grand portal, but suddenly paused; his resolution faltered, and the tender feelings of a son predominating, he retraced his steps, and was soon within the chamber, where sat weeping, in an agony of distress, his revered and much beloved mother.
>
> As he once more flew to receive the maternal embrace, his eye involuntarily fixed on the stern features of his father, who, contracting his brow, and averting his face toward the window, exclaimed, "Weak boy, shake off this folly, nor thus disgrace yourself."
>
> "Ah! my honored parent, call not the sorrows of my bosom a folly; it is the first separation I have experienced from the authors of my existence, and it may perhaps prove eternal."
>
> Tears flowed from his eyes, and the overcharged bosom of the Marquesa, his fond mother, vented its anguish in audible sobs.
>
> For the first time the countenance of his father relaxed; he approached, and folding Rimualdo in his arms, bade him an affectionate adieu. . . .

William-Henry's confused feelings about his parents and his own legitimacy persisted for years. His self-image as a man of unclear origin was both a torment and a release. One of the poems in a collection he published in 1803 was a manifesto called "The Bastard"—part of a trilogy, with "The Bastard's Complaint" and "Reply to the Bastard's Complaint." In it, he urged all those of uncertain parentage to revel in being free of the conformity and social expectations that shackle ordinary sons and daughters:

> *May bastards, tho' bereft of friend and name,*
> *Feel in their breasts eternal thirst of fame!*
> *May they with glorious emulation burn!*
> *And may the wreath in death adorn their urn!*

Thirty years later, William-Henry published a worshipful biography of his old Drury Lane friend Dora Jordan, who'd died in 1816. He included information about the ten Fitzclarences that her former lover, the Duke of Clarence, had sired. He evidently felt a kinship, so to speak, with Mrs. Jordan and her grown children, all of whom had been born out of wedlock. The title page identified the book's subject as "Late Mistress of H. R. H. the D. of Clarence, now King William IV." William-Henry was more modest about his own involvement—the book was written "by a Confidential Friend of the Departed." The crown interceded after a handful of copies were sold. The author was paid off and the rest of the books destroyed.

If William-Henry had been certain that he, too, was illegitimate, he'd have avoided much of the anguish his forgeries caused him. He never thought his hoax had hurt anyone—certainly not Shakespeare. But his father's persecution and decline in his last years surely nagged at William-Henry, bastard or not. Samuel Ireland was a fool, but he never deserved the abuse he suffered.

As an author, William-Henry never had the career that he'd hoped to have, but then he didn't have the talent that he thought he did. Indeed, his ornate writing style was one more way that he resembled his father more than he might have wished. As it was, he succeeded in being a prolific, versatile, and well-traveled author and poet and a successful husband and father. Perennial money troubles, including a short spell in the debtors' prison at York Castle in 1811, likely had more to do with overspending than a lack of income.

In the 1820s, when William-Henry was in his late forties, he encountered an aging James Boaden, the former supporter turned antagonist, in the London office of their mutual publisher, Robert Triphook. Leaving the office on New Bond Street at the same time, the two men walked across town together to the Strand. William-Henry had been speaking jauntily of his escapade of thirty years before when Boaden, then in his sixties, stopped him with an offended look.

"You must be aware, sir, of the enormous crime you committed against the divinity of Shakspeare," Boaden sputtered. "Why, the act, sir, was nothing short of sacrilege. It was precisely the same thing as taking the holy chalice from the altar and pissing therein!" William-Henry was both shocked and amused. The old newspaperman was still fuming about his youthful misadventure. If Shakespeare was a deity, it was curious that he was so vulnerable to the misbehavior of mortals.

William-Henry's prank had grown into a nerve-racking and painful ordeal, it was true. But it was also the dramatic high point of his life. How many living English boys had known the exhilaration of being likened to a god? In his preface to *The Abbess*, he admitted that simply hearing the word "papers" sent a thrilling sensation through his body.

When he died in 1835 at age fifty-nine, one of his unfinished projects was the full-length story of his life, in seven parts. He was going to call it *Shakespeare Ireland's Seven Ages*, a play on the "seven ages of man" speech in *As You Like It*. He didn't need to hide behind an anonymous pen name. He was at peace with the connotations his name evoked.

Admittedly, William-Henry often brooded over what had become of his life: the struggles for money, the snubs of the well-placed, the drawers stuffed with manuscripts and poems that no one would print. But he could console himself with knowing that once, for a glorious year and a half, he had been William Shakespeare.

A NOTE ON SOURCES

Delving into precisely what William-Henry Ireland did and didn't do is a tricky business. As the *Morning Chronicle* observed in 1796, his confession, "if *true*, proves him to be a *liar*."

Having been vilified for daring to impersonate the Bard, William-Henry used his three memoirs—published in 1796, 1805, and 1832—to present himself in the best possible light. He hid the elaborateness of his scheming and downplayed his dizzying brush with full-bore megalomania. Nonetheless, these accounts are essential starting places. The 317-page *Confessions of William-Henry Ireland*, in particular, though unreliable at times, is a fascinating, detailed, and emotionally fraught recollection of his adventure in forgery.

For years, given William-Henry's credibility problems, many people regarded these accounts as pure fiction. For most of the century after the hoax was revealed, his father was assumed to be the real forger—and worse, a man so depraved that he directed his son to take the blame. Samuel was "the general who devised and methodised the strategy, and executed the simulated handwriting," asserted Clement Mansfield Ingleby in *The*

Shakspeare Fabrications in 1859. "The house of the Irelands was in fact a manufactory of forgeries, done for the sole object of making money."

Only in the 1870s, with the donation to the British Museum of Samuel's diaries, letters, and other personal papers, did the collector's innocence become clear. Housed today in the Manuscripts Reading Room of the British Library, the papers offer visitors a vivid, unsettling picture of life in the Ireland household in the 1790s. To read the letters to and from Samuel, his son, and his son's imaginary friend, Mr. H., is to eavesdrop on what is perhaps the most bizarre three-way correspondence in the history of letter-writing.

A second rich archive of original papers relating to the Ireland forgeries is the Donald and Mary Hyde Collection at Harvard University's Houghton Library. The collection includes several large scrapbooks that William-Henry assembled early in the 1800s. Alongside engravings and cut-and-pasted pages from his printed books, the scrapbook margins are filled with William-Henry's handwritten comments and addenda about people he'd duped, others he admired, and slights that still stung.

As for later historical accounts, the Ireland forgeries have always been better known in England than in the United States. One of the best popular histories of the Ireland-Shakespeare affair remains one of the most concise: the 40-page section of the late Samuel Schoenbaum's masterpiece, *Shakespeare's Lives* (1970, revised 1994), which explores the forgeries in the context of the Cult of Shakespeare.

Other books that have brought the forgeries a degree of popular attention are John Mair's *The Fourth Forger* in 1938, Bernard Grebanier's more detailed *The Great Shakespeare Forgery* in 1965, and Patricia Pierce's lively *The Great Shakespeare Fraud* in 2004. Each of these authors appreciated the sometimes comic foolishness on all sides that helped William-Henry's secretive scribblings blow up into a public scandal.

Some recent commentators have taken a less charitable view of the boy's exploits. The young forger was characterized by Jeffrey Kahan of the University of La Verne in *Reforging Shakespeare* (1998) and by Jack Lynch of Rutgers University in *Becoming Shakespeare* (2007) as, respectively, "a master criminal" and "a compulsive and pathological liar." Professor Kahan argued that even the private letters between William-Henry and his father were deceptive, aimed at throwing historians off the scent of their joint conspiracy.

Despite his misgivings, Kahan in particular has worked tirelessly to make public the forger's post-*Vortigern* writings, editing his Romantic poetry and several of his gothic novels. For a modern edition of *Vortigern*, he sifted through the many extant manuscripts of the play to deduce which version was likely acted at the Drury Lane Theatre in April 1796. Kahan also had a hand in seeing that William-Henry's mock-Shakespeare opus was revived—if briefly—at London's Bridewell Theatre in 1997. Professor Lynch meanwhile is at work on the first full-scale biography of the forger.

Novelists have occasionally used the tragicomedy of the boy forger's doomed escapade as grist for fiction. In James Payn's Dickensian *The Talk of the Town* in 1885, young William Henry Erin exults at his newfound celebrity but later, on his deathbed, regrets the immoral path he chose. More recently, Peter Ackroyd in *The Lambs of London* (2004) added sex and violence to the mix. He merged the story of William-Henry Ireland with that of his troubled neighbor and contemporary Mary Lamb, who murdered her mother with a kitchen knife in London a few months after *Vortigern* was staged. Mary recovered sufficiently to write *Tales from Shakespeare* with her brother Charles a decade later.

As if by magic, many of the documents relating to the forgeries are, for now, freely available at one's desktop—or café table—with a few keystrokes. Google Books offers full-text facsimiles of several of Samuel and William-Henry Ireland's books, Herbert Croft's *Love and Madness*, and the 1799 first edition of *Vortigern*, as well as searchable complete texts of Boswell, Pepys, Fielding, Addison, and, of course, the incomparable William Shakespeare. Scrutiny of historical texts has never been so convenient.

INDEX